Beyond the Difference

M. Wynn Thomas

Beyond the Difference
Welsh Literature in Comparative Contexts

Essays for M. Wynn Thomas at Sixty

Edited by

Alyce von Rothkirch
and
Daniel Williams

UNIVERSITY OF WALES PRESS
CARDIFF

2004

© The Contributors, 2004

All rights reserved. No part of this book may be reproduced, stored in a retrieval system, or transmitted, in any form or by any means, electronic, mechanical, photocopying, recording or otherwise, without clearance from the University of Wales Press, 10 Columbus Walk, Brigantine Place, Cardiff, CF10 4UP.
www.wales.ac.uk/press

British Library Cataloguing-in-Publication Data
A catalogue record for this book is available from the British Library.

ISBN 0–7083–1886–X

The right of the Contributors to be identified separately as authors of this work has been asserted by them in accordance with sections 77 and 79 of the Copyright, Designs and Patents Act 1988.

Published with the financial support of the Welsh Books Council

Printed in Great Britain by Cambridge Printing, Cambridge

To think the difference will still continue to others, yet we lie
beyond the difference.

Walt Whitman, *Leaves of Grass*

Contents

Notes on Contributors   ix
Acknowledgements   xv

Introduction   1

Part I: Cymru and Wales
1. Emyr Humphreys, 'Manawydan'   6
2. Hywel Teifi Edwards, 'Y Pentre Gwyn' and 'Manteg': From Blessed Plot to Hotspot   8
3. Tony Brown, 'Stories from foreign countries': The Short Stories of Kate Roberts and Margiad Evans   21
4. Jasmine Donahaye, 'Gartref – bron': Adversity and Refuge in the Jewish Literature of Wales   38

Part II: Engendering Wales
5. Gillian Clarke, 'The Accompanist'   56
6. Kirsti Bohata, En-gendering a New Wales: Female Allegories, Home Rule and Imperialism 1890–1910   57
7. Alyce von Rothkirch, 'There's a change come over the valley': The Crisis of Masculinism in Early Twentieth-century Welsh Drama in English   71
8. Jane Aaron, Valleys' Women Writing   84

Part III: American Perspectives
9. Menna Elfyn, 'Perlïo Geiriau', translated by Joseph P. Clancy   98
10. Helen Vendler, Under Milk Wood: Lists, Made and Undone   100
11. Barbara Prys-Williams, Web of Connection: Denise Levertov's Construction of Origins   116
12. Daniel Williams, 'For Old Tom read Uncle Tom': Emlyn Williams and Ralph Ellison   132

Part IV: Translations
13 Tony Conran, 'Civilization in Waiting' 148
14 Dafydd Johnston, Early Translations of Dafydd
    ap Gwilym 158
15 Melinda Gray, Uncle Tom's Welsh Dress: Ethnicity,
    Authority and Translation 173
16 Michael Cronin, Global Questions and Local Visions:
    A Microcosmopolitan Perspective 186

Part V: Welsh Correspondences
17 Grahame Davies, 'Cyfannu' 204
18 Jeremy Hooker, Poetic Lands and Borderlands:
    Henry Vaughan to Robert Frost 206
19 James A. Davies, 'In a different place, / changed':
    Dannie Abse, Dylan Thomas, T. S. Eliot and Wales 223
20 Katie Gramich, 'Extravagant and wheeling stranger[s]':
    Dylan Thomas, Derek Walcott and the House of
    English Literature 237

Part VI: Epilogue
21 Seamus Heaney, 'Brothers' 254

Part VII: Bibliography
22 Rhian Reynolds, Bibliography of M. Wynn Thomas
    (1970–2003) 258

Index 271
List of Subscribers 283

Notes on Contributors

Jane Aaron
Jane Aaron is Professor of English at the University of Glamorgan where she teaches Welsh writing in English. Editor of the Honno Classics series of reprints of Welsh women's writing in English, she has prepared for that series an anthology of Welsh women's short stories, *A View Across the Valley: Short Stories from Women in Wales 1850–1950* (1999) and other volumes.

Kirsti Bohata
Kirsti Bohata is Research Associate at the Centre for Research into the English Literature and Language of Wales (CREW), and the author of *Postcolonialism Revisited: Writing Wales in English* (2004). Her current research focuses on the New Woman in Wales.

Tony Brown
Tony Brown is Reader in English at the University of Wales, Bangor, where he is also co-director of the R. S. Thomas Study Centre. He has published widely on Welsh writing in English, especially on the work of R. S. Thomas and Glyn Jones. He is the editor of *Welsh Writing in English: A Yearbook of Critical Essays*.

Joseph P. Clancy
Joseph P. Clancy is an American poet and translator who now lives in Wales. His recent books include a collection of poems, *Ordinary Time* (2001), *Other Words: Essays on Poetry and Translation* (1999) and the anthology *Medieval Welsh Poems* (2003).

Gillian Clarke
Gillian Clarke was born and brought up in Cardiff and now lives in Ceredigion. A poet, playwright and tutor on the M.Phil. in Creative Writing course at the University of Glamorgan, she is President of Tŷ Newydd, the writers' centre in Gwynedd which she co-founded

in 1990. Her latest full collection of poems – her sixth – *Making the Beds for the Dead*, was published by Carcanet in 2004.

Tony Conran
Tony Conran was born in Bengal in 1931 and educated at Colwyn Bay and the University College, Bangor, where he tutored until 1980. He has published over a dozen volumes of poetry, and is editor and translator of *The Penguin Book of Welsh Verse* (1967) and a selection of Waldo Williams's poems, *The Peacemakers* (1997). His most recent publication is a selection of his poems on Wales, *The Shape of My Country* (2004).

Michael Cronin
Michael Cronin is Director of the Translation Studies Centre at Dublin City University. He is a founder member and former president of the Irish Translators' Association. He is the author of *Translating Ireland: Translation, Languages, Cultures* (1996) and *Across the Lines: Travel, Language and Translation* (2000).

Grahame Davies
Grahame Davies is a poet, editor and literary critic. His volume *Cadwyni Rhyddid* won the 2001 Welsh Book of the Year award. He gained a doctorate from the University of Wales, Cardiff for a study on anti-modernism in European literature. This was published by the University of Wales Press in 1999 as *Sefyll yn y Bwlch*.

James A. Davies
James A. Davies is Honorary Research Fellow at CREW and a Fellow of the Welsh Academy. Along with Professor Wynn Thomas, he founded the MA in Welsh Writing in English at the University of Wales Swansea, and has published extensively on Victorian literature and Welsh writing in English.

Jasmine Donahaye
Jasmine Donahaye has a BA in Celtic Studies from UC Berkeley, and has just completed her doctoral dissertation on Jewish writing in Wales. Her publications include chapters in *From the East End to East Africa: 'The Jew' in Edwardian Culture*, edited by Nadia Valman (forthcoming) and *Jewish Women Writers and Twentieth Century British Culture*, edited by Claire Tylee (forthcoming).

Hywel Teifi Edwards
Hywel Teifi Edwards has now retired as Professor and Head of the Welsh Department at the University of Wales Swansea. He was born and bred a 'Cardi' at Llanddewi Aber-arth but has lived in Llangennech in Sir Gâr since 1965. His research interests have focused on the culture of Victorian Wales and he hopes to remain active in the field for some time to come.

Menna Elfyn
Menna Elfyn is an award-winning poet and playwright. She has published seven volumes of poetry as well as novels for teenagers and educational books for children. In 2002 she was made Children's Poet Laureate of Wales. She has held residencies in the US and, as librettist, worked with the New York Philharmonic Orchestra in 1999. She is a Fellow at the University of Wales, Aberystwyth.

Katie Gramich
Katie Gramich is from Ceredigion and she studied at the Universities of Wales, London and Alberta. She is currently Assistant Director of Lifelong Learning at the University of Bath. Her research interests are in Welsh and postcolonial studies, women's writing and comparative literature.

Melinda Gray
Melinda Gray has taught and served as a resident dean at Harvard College since completing her Ph.D. in Comparative Literature. She is working on a book about nineteenth-century Welsh-language translations of *Uncle Tom's Cabin* and also editing a book of essays on the international reception of the novel.

Seamus Heaney
Seamus Heaney was born in Northern Ireland and is the author of numerous collections of poetry including *Opened Ground* (1999), *The Spirit Level* (1996), *Selected Poems 1966–1987* (1990) and *Sweeney Astray* (1984). He is also an eminent translator and has written several volumes of criticism. In 1995 he received the Nobel Prize in Literature.

Jeremy Hooker
Jeremy Hooker has published ten collections of poetry (most

recently *Adamah*, 2002), and his critical books include *Imagining Wales: A View of Modern Welsh Writing in English* (2001). His *Welsh Journal* was published in 2002. He is Professor of English at the University of Glamorgan.

Emyr Humphreys
Emyr Humphreys is Wales's pre-eminent novelist. Over a long career he has published twenty novels, together with collections of stories, poems and essays. He has written, produced and directed for radio, television and film. His latest book is *Old People are a Problem* (2003).

Dafydd Johnston
Dafydd Johnston is Professor of Welsh at the University of Wales Swansea. He has published a number of editions and translations of medieval Welsh poetry, and is currently leading a research project to produce a new edition of the poems of Dafydd ap Gwilym.

Christine Kinsey
Christine Kinsey was co-founder of the Chapter Arts Centre in Cardiff and was its artistic director between 1968 and 1976. From 1976 she lived and worked on St Maarten in the Caribbean, returning in 1980 to west Wales, where she still lives and works. She has had national and international touring exhibitions and has exhibited and had work displayed in collections worldwide.

Barbara Prys-Williams
Barbara Prys-Williams returned to academic life after twenty years teaching in France, Madagascar and Britain. She gained her Ph.D. at CREW, University of Wales Swansea, in 2002. She is author of *Twentieth-century Autobiography* (2004) in the *Writing Wales in English* series.

Rhian Reynolds
Rhian Reynolds completed her Ph.D. at CREW and is editor of the *Bibliography of Welsh Literature in English Translation* (forthcoming). She worked for a Welsh media company, implemented ELWa's bilingual commissioning programme and worked as a senior resource development manager there. She is about to embark on a trip

to South America and will be teaching Welsh in Patagonia for a time.

Alyce von Rothkirch
Alyce von Rothkirch is Widening Participation Research Officer at the University of Wales, Newport. She has an MA in English Literature from the Johannes Gutenberg-University at Mainz (Germany) and recently completed a Ph.D. on Contemporary Welsh Drama in English at CREW, University of Wales Swansea.

Helen Vendler
Helen Vendler is the A. Kingsley Porter University Professor at Harvard University. She is the author of books on Yeats, Stevens, Keats, Herbert, Shakespeare and Heaney. Her new book, *Poets Thinking*, will be published by the Harvard University Press in 2004.

Daniel Williams
Daniel Williams is lecturer in English and Assistant Director of CREW at the University of Wales Swansea. His most recent publication is an edited collection of Raymond Williams's writings on Wales, *Who Speaks for Wales? Nation, Culture, Identity* (2003).

Acknowledgements

We would like to thank all the contributors for their enthusiasm for this project and their punctuality in getting the work to us. Jane Aaron and Tony Brown, in particular, offered their valuable advice and encouragement along the way. We should like to thank the team at the University of Wales Press for their helpfulness and characteristic thoroughness throughout a period of change, and were particularly grateful for the assistance of Duncan Campbell and Claire Powell at the project's early stages. Christine Kinsey's permission to use her striking cover painting 'Signs and Symbols VII' was greatly appreciated. Lowri, Sioned and Tejay cheered us on to the finish.

Diolch yn fawr iawn.

Introduction

ALYCE VON ROTHKIRCH AND DANIEL WILLIAMS

Having decided to collaborate on this project we faced a whole range of problems. A mere glance at the bibliography which concludes this book makes it quite clear that it would be impossible to represent the diversity of Professor M. Wynn Thomas's interests within a single volume. We chose to construct a collection of essays clustered around one of Wynn Thomas's prime and abiding interests – the literature of Wales in both its languages – whilst also encouraging comparative approaches from our contributors that not only paid homage to, but also developed and furthered, discussions initiated in Wynn's writings. The book begins with explorations of the interactions between Wales's two literary cultures, an approach that in Wynn Thomas's subtle hands allows for the tensions between competing visions of 'Wales' to be registered, whilst gesturing towards a critical approach that seeks to foster a common ground beyond the bitter divisions. The sections that follow broadly reflect the directions that Wynn's writing has taken in recent years, as manifested in *Corresponding Cultures* (1999) where the chapters range from gender to translation to Welsh connections with the United States. Whilst some readers will inevitably find this volume's contents somewhat diffuse, our frustration at having barely scratched the surface of Wynn's range of interests is alleviated by the belief that we have managed to assemble a collection with a broad internal coherence.

Deciding on a team of contributors posed a different set of problems. The range of contributors and subscribers to this volume are testament to the respect and affection in which Wynn Thomas is held in the various academic and cultural circles enriched by his presence, and we are profoundly aware that there are many writers who would have liked to contribute. Our attempt has been to foreground the international range of Wynn's academic connections, to register the major contribution of that innovative generation of Welsh critics to whom Wynn belongs, to reflect Wynn's close connections with the critical and creative writers of Welsh-language culture, and to include the work of a younger generation of literary critics which has drawn so much from Wynn's inspiration and example. At a time when education is increasingly forced to serve the needs of a corporate world, when faculties are rebranded as businesses and students as consumers, when the humanities become increasingly devalued, when bigoted attitudes towards the Welsh language are routinely clothed in the language of the market ('a hindrance to recruitment strategies' as one enlightened member of Swansea's academic community put it recently), the student of literature seeks recognition in the community of writers and fellow thinkers who, when at their best, defy the conventionalism, mediocrity and pettiness that seem inseparable from the ways in which we run our institutions. In this respect the new works from contemporary poets is particularly valuable. We deliberately invited contributions from poets who not only have connections with Wynn, but who, like him, have acted as cultural mediators, writing across, beneath, between and beyond Wales's two main linguistic cultures (and the charged cultural divisions of Ireland in the case of Seamus Heaney).

Our title, however, does not suggest an attempt at transcending the internal differences on the contested Welsh ground in order to rediscover an organic wholeness. Rather – in the spirit of the Whitman poem from which the phrase is taken and on which Wynn has written so illuminatingly – writing 'beyond the difference' entails a move out of any self-enclosed, exceptionalist, circles where identities are valorized only with reference to themselves. In seeking to break out of the national boundaries in which literary studies have traditionally taken place, several critics have recently advocated an 'Atlanticist' or 'Transatlantic' perspective. While several of the contributions to this volume may be seen to reflect this trend in cultural studies, there is a sense in which – as a critic of Whitman as well as of Welsh writers, of 'regional forecasts' as well as 'American Dreams' – Wynn Thomas has been writing from a Transatlantic perspective for some time. He belongs to a tradition of Welsh critics – from Emrys ap Iwan to Raymond Williams – who have related Wales to the world, and have consistently weighed the claims of a precarious 'Welshness' against other varieties of subjectivity and identification. This is a project pursued and developed in many of this volume's chapters.

Finally, if editing this *Festschrift* proved problematic enough, there was always the danger that this introduction would read more like an obituary than a tribute to a critic who remains at the height of his powers. This, we feel, is neither the time nor the place to offer an overview of the critic's life and work. In celebrating Wynn Thomas's sixtieth birthday we look forward, expectantly, for the work to come from a critic admired for his subtle intellect, respected for his selfless generosity and loved for his infectious enthusiasm. We hope that the writings collected in this volume prove to be a source of inspiration in the years ahead.

I
CYMRU AND WALES

1

EMYR HUMPHREYS

Manawydan
i
M. W. T.

All justice is poetic: between
Mice and men there needs to be
An understanding, a writ
Of habeas corpus.
In the world of sentences, refined
Or carried out, no justice
Is valid without love; no love
Even with melting eyes, without
Justice; therefore in this fiction
The throne and the gallows are one
Mysterious mound.

A prince must be his own
Hangman not so much to strangle
Rhetoric as twist a silken thread
Around a mouse's neck and not shrink
At looking ridiculous.

There will be challenges:
The pulse of fear in two bewitching
Eyes, contempt in Cigfa's voice,

Cheap student justice from Lloegr,
A portly bishop's threat of ex-
Communication.

Civilisation is a legend
In which deterrence holds back
Vengeance: the ordeal and affliction
Are kept in check when justice
Holds the balance:

Prisoners are set free, a mouse
Metamorphoses into a grateful lady:
Words and sentence released
From an underworld of weeds:
Mice and media restrained
From mincing up meaning or
Munching the seedcorn
While society starves.

Revenge and tribal tit for tat
Must submit to one transforming power.

Magicians with words transform
Acres of animosities into gentler
Courses: as one magic deserves
Another, an order of release restores
All internees to those ordained
To cherish and preserve them.

2

'Y Pentre Gwyn' and 'Manteg': From Blessed Plot to Hotspot

HYWEL TEIFI EDWARDS

During the war-wracked 1940s J. M. Edwards, a Cardiganshire-born poet-schoolteacher domiciled in Barry, wrote a poem, 'Pentrefi Cymru', saluting the villages of Wales as impregnable strongholds of simplicity standing on the shores of a turbulent sea. Facing the Nazi beast from within the security of their timeless defences, the memory of them acted both as balm and bidding for their children scattered far afield. At a time of devastation they embodied the hope at the heart of their children's longing ('Gobaith ein hiraeth ydych'). J. M. Edwards had already won the Crown at the Machynlleth National Eisteddfod in 1937 for his poem on 'Y Pentref', depicting the rural village as a showcase for craftsmen and communal goodness, and a reworking of this poem would be broadcast by the BBC in October 1951, as part of a series of radio *pryddestau*. Furthermore, his mid-century prominence as the poet of rural beneficence had been boosted in 1944 when tiny Llandybïe, a quintessential Carmarthenshire village, played host to a National Eisteddfod *rediviva* in which Edwards again took the Crown for a poem on 'Yr Aradr' ('The Plough') which, needless to say, also revelled in country life. As witness to the way the village was still in place, despite the horrors of war, to feature in Welsh literature as a synecdoche for national wholesomeness, we need look no further than J. M. Edwards. And lest we think that he points up a singularly Welsh naivety we need only look to England, where he would have found himself in good company.[1]

English literature from the Industrial Revolution and the onset of the Romantics would reinvigorate what was an old theme, celebrating country life and village communities, insisting on their curative worth for times increasingly at the mercy of mechanized living. Writers of all kinds, artists and musicians, would look past the poverty and back-breaking grind of working the land to create their pastoral visions of 'the good life' for the delectation of urban dwellers, many of whom had but recently fled the reality. Literature and art would endow country and village with life-enhancing properties, so 'real' that many thousands in urban England would march to fight in two World Wars singing the praises of a land that would endure as long as there were country lanes and cottages beside fields of grain. During the inter-war years, ramblers flocked to the country to discover 'England as it "really was", unspoilt and natural'. H. V. Morton recalled in his hugely popular *In Search of England* (1927) how, when sick in Palestine, he had a vision of the prototypical English village 'at dusk with a smell of wood smoke lying in the still air' which engulfed him with a longing so intense that he would 'never forget the pain in my heart'. For Morton, '[t]he village and the English countryside are the germs of all we are, and all we have become' and no sooner had the struggle against Nazism begun than C. H. Warren echoed Morton's conviction in *England is a Village* (1940). There is, in brief, running through English literature from the great Romantics down to the late twentieth century a strong strain of pastoralism, urging the belief that 'Englishness' reposed in the country and its rooted villages, just as in Welsh literature 'Welshness' was similarly enshrined.[2]

The context for the celebration of rural Wales with the village as its cynosure was essentially shaped by O. M. Edwards (1858–1920). Brought up in Llanuwchllyn on the shores of Llyn Tegid (Lake Bala), the stunningly beautiful setting of his childhood village and the Christian worth of its inhabitants would remain with him throughout his life as a perfect image of a pastoral Wales inviolate. Bolstered by a love of Welsh poetry, in particular that of Ceiriog (1832–87), captivated by the English Romantics and deeply appreciative of John Ruskin's writings, O. M. Edwards would not cease to wonder at the glories of nature in his homeland. His regenerated Wales would be a country of communities living in harmony with nature, at peace with God and man.

O. M. Edwards dedicated himself 'i godi'r hen wlad yn ei hôl'; that is, to resurrect the old country after its denigration in the Blue Books of 1847 – that government-sponsored report that both enraged and terrified Nonconformist Wales, forcing its leaders to construct a national image to boost Welsh morale and disarm, so they hoped, future detractors. They came up with 'Cymru lân, Cymru lonydd' ('Pure Wales, docile Wales') and no one was to serve that image with greater belief and industry than O. M. Edwards. His literary programme for a Welsh recovery would project an idealized country and *gwerin* ('folk') calculated to engender self-esteem. Central to his labours as Welsh historian, author, editor, social reformer, Methodist zealot and HMI was a determination to get his countrymen to think better of themselves, walking abroad in a land bathed in the light of a past characterized more by romance and heroic endeavour than by mean actuality and subservience.[3]

In turn Romantic idealist and salvationist, Edwards's view of the 'true' Wales was a palpably selective one – a Welsh-speaking Wales, sustained by the values of a God-fearing Nonconformist *gwerin* wedded to a land and a culture whose beauty was imprinted on their spirit and imagination. Time and again he rejoiced in a Wales where a symbiotic relationship between nature and human goodness appeared to have been preordained. Welsh geography and topography, Welsh history, language and literature, religion, music, architecture, arts and crafts, Welsh folklore, customs and traditions – all was grist to his mill. Imbued with the Keatsian certainty that 'a thing of beauty is a joy forever', O. M. Edwards in his books and periodicals fought a war of survival that could be won only in the Welsh mind, and he went armed with a vision of Wales so seductive that to see it, as he saw it, would be to will its realization.

Like Iolo's 'Morganwg', Edwards's Wales was an idealized conception and, as such, easily disparaged by commentators who championed a 'real' Wales, seen as deracinated, urban, industrialized, Anglicized and, of course, cosmopolitan. Their Wales, sometimes characterized as 'American Wales', also owes not a little to an imagination in the service of selectivity. In respect of O. M. Edwards, however, there is no gainsaying his great influence as a visionary, whose writings enthused generations of his countrymen and stirred in them a desire to live for Wales as patriots. To this day his readers find themselves yielding their hearts awhile to the depiction of the country he had fixed in his mind's eye. From the time Edwards started writing in the 1880s, with the intention of fixing his Wales as firmly in the reader's eye, he was to prove an irresistible advocate for a legion of admirers.

Throughout almost thirty years of editing his splendid periodical, *Cymru* (1891–1920), he featured an ongoing series depicting 'Ardaloedd Cymru' ('The Districts of Wales') which was to include hundreds of villages, the vast majority of them rural, from all parts of the country. Scores of writers contributed essays similar in intent to Edwards's commendation of Llanuwchllyn, more often than not adopting the formula which allied scenic delights with a fair communal life rooted in a traditional culture. Viewed in retrospect with a nostalgic eye they can still come shimmering off the page in a haze of idyllicism.

One of the contributors to the *Cymru* series of village portraits was the Revd Robert David Rowland (1853–1944) who, in his mid-fifties, and when long since known to the public as Anthropos, published in 1909 *Y Pentre Gwyn* ('The Blessed Village'), which he subtitled 'Ystori Bore Bywyd' ('A Story of Childhood'). A writer whose literary style O. M. Edwards thought exemplary – they were students together at the Methodist College in Bala in the late 1870s, when Edwards thought him 'a charming conversationalist' – Anthropos wanted above all to recreate his boyhood village as representative of so many unsung places scattered across the land that bred 'natural' and 'valuable' characters, the influence of some of whom had permeated the mind and life of Wales.[4]

The middle-aged Anthropos would see and think again as a boy, all bitter experiences expunged from memory, the better, as he put it, to present to his young readers a picture of his village suffused in the light of dreams, a picture focused on the recall of 'y dyddiau braf, claerwynion' ('the fine, shining days'). *Y Pentre Gwyn* was a literary undertaking fit for the imprimatur of O. M. Edwards, who had dedicated himself to winning the hearts, minds and imaginations of the children of Wales by delighting and instructing them in books, and by enticing them with their very own periodical, *Cymru'r Plant* ('The Children's Wales', 1892–1920). Anthropos was to edit the Methodist *Trysorfa'r Plant* ('The Children's Treasury') for many years and contribute much to the growth of children's literature in Welsh, but nothing he wrote before or after the publication of *Y Pentre Gwyn* better illustrates his response to the stimulus provided by O. M. Edwards for so many writers, particularly in *Clych Atgof* ('The Bells of Memory', 1906), that beguiling collection of essays that Anthropos was still enthusing about in 1927.

Less perceptible than O. M. Edwards, there is another energizing presence hovering over *Y Pentre Gwyn*, none other than J. M. Barrie, the author of *Auld Licht Idylls* (1888), *A Window in Thrums* (1889), *The Little Minister* (1891), *Margaret Ogilvy* (1896), and the conjuror of *Peter Pan* (1904) – that deathless fantasy in which the children of Mr and Mrs Arthur Llewelyn Davies, in the guise of the Darlings' children, were to find themselves in that 'Neverland' for which the boy in Barrie quested all his life. Born in Kirriemuir in 1860, Barrie's plays were popular in Wales during the first half of the twentieth century and there is little doubt that Anthropos was drawn to *A Window in Thrums* and *Peter Pan*. *Y Pentre Gwyn* is infused with a Barrie-like longing for a 'land of lost content' and, as with O. M. Edwards, Anthropos responded to Barrie's rhapsodic use of memories, seizing upon his happy dictum that 'Memory has been given us that we may have roses in December'.[5]

The twentieth century saw the flowering of a pastoral of childhood, written and read by adults seeking meaning and solace in a world of incessant turmoil. Pre-dating the Great War, *Y Pentre Gwyn* is the first significant Welsh example of the genre, written by a 56-year-old Methodist minister who had grown up during the Victorian high summer to witness the inexorable transformation of Wales.[6] Like *Aelwyd Angharad*, a stage version of a traditional *noson lawen* written in 1908, *Y Pentre Gwyn* was responding to O. M. Edwards's call to arms in a war of survival for 'their kind of Wales'. For Anthropos, its winning required that the spirit of *Y Pentre Gwyn* should somehow be transposed in a land where material change would be ongoing.

In fusing a pastoral of childhood with Edwards's idealized rural village, Anthropos hit upon a powerful conception that was to resonate long in Welsh Wales. The very name, 'Y Pentre Gwyn', gave to the village he conjured up a claim on universality. It was his 'Neverland'. He chose to disguise its true identity but we know it was Tŷ'n-y-cefn, if anything more of a hamlet than a village, near Corwen in Merionethshire. The Revd John Baker went there as a minister as the Second World War began and stayed for some years, quickly succumbing to the reality of the place as much as to its depiction by Anthropos. But John Baker's Tŷ'n-y-cefn is not *Y Pentre Gwyn*. In calendar terms, the Tŷ'n-y-cefn of Anthropos was almost a century removed, but his 'Pentre Gwyn', in the language of recall, was on a far horizon. Tŷ'n-y-cefn was a tiny, exact spot on a map; *Y Pentre Gwyn* is a place only accessible to yearning. That is why Anthropos does not give it its proper name. It isn't so much a place as a passion; hence its universality.[7]

The village Anthropos recalled was unclouded by want or injustice. Children went happily to the 'Britis Scŵl' in Corwen where their mother tongue was silenced; poverty had its own nobility; wealth in the person of Colonel Wood was beneficent and deference seemly. The *Slendai* (Almshouses) bring to mind Helen Allingham's watercolours, 'where the banks of hollyhocks and the cottages tumbling under the weight of rambler roses threaten to suffocate the inhabitants', and their inmates, such as Miss Green, Tomos Olfyr, the old Waterloo soldier and his wife, Catrin, naturally exude goodness.[8] Indeed, Tomos Olfyr is 'saved' by the village children visiting regularly to read him the Bible and sing hymns, and nothing better illustrates the godliness of *Y Pentre Gwyn* than Tomos's funeral. Anthropos built an idyll on a Christian charitableness that readily embraced an alcoholic ballad-singer like Eos Mawddwy and rogue pedlars like Martin and Uncle Sam, and it is fitting, given the correspondence in beauty between nature and human nature that pervades *Y Pentre Gwyn*, that the last sound the author would have us hear is the children's choir (they are tonic sol-fa children) gathered around 'Ffynnon y Ddôl' ('The Meadow Spring') singing 'Cawn ni gwrdd tu draw i'r afon' (a Welsh equivalent of 'In the sweet bye and bye') as the sun sets over 'Coed y Barcud' ('The Kite's Woods'). It is fitting because *Y Pentre Gwyn* has to be somewhere 'on the other side' and, as such, its hold on our assent cannot be broken by any critical demonstration of its unreality.

Sometime after the Great War, probably in the early 1920s, Anthropos published *Pentre'r Plant. Atgofion Bore Bywyd* ('The Children's Village. Childhood Memories') which he dedicated to the children of 'the new age' – the children of post-1914–18 disillusionment. More novel than autobiography – it brings to mind Barrie's *A Window in Thrums*, particularly in the character of Nansi Owen y Llofft, who has something of Barrie's mother, Margaret Ogilvy, about her, in her observational role in the story –

its popularity did not match that of *Y Pentre Gwyn*. Drawing again on childhood memories, the narrative viewpoint is no longer that of a child but that of an adult, intent on showing the triumph of goodness in a traditional Welsh village. Sadrach Jones, lame cobbler and custodian of the moral and spiritual wellbeing of 'Llanaber', uses his friendship with the old squire of Hendre Lwyd and its new owner, the progressive Bleddyn Rees, to build a hall and reading room for the village youth in which they can prepare themselves to confront the new age. It is a community project brought to fruition by a simple craftsman, whose view of the rightness of things had been shaped by the village culture into which he was inducted as a child. *Pentre'r Plant*, written shortly after O. M. Edwards's death in 1920, shows how much Anthropos shared his belief that the national life of Wales would require the vitamin intake of places such as 'Llanaber' if it was to retain its vitality, and he lived to see J. M. Edwards crowned in 1937 for a poem that said very much the same, if in a somewhat different style.[9]

Six years after the appearance of *Y Pentre Gwyn*, Caradoc Evans trampled it into the muck of 'Manteg' in *My People* (1915) – 'Manteg', which translates equally well for satirical purposes as 'a fair place' or 'a hotspot', caused an almighty row, which is too well chronicled to need recounting now. But it cannot be said too often that there is no understanding the furore caused by *My People* unless it is seen in the context of 'Cymru lân, Cymru lonydd' – that compensatory national image promoted after 1847 which was to become for O. M. Edwards almost a reason for living. His Llanuwchllyn, as already said, together with most of the villages celebrated in *Cymru*, could be located only within 'Cymru lân, Cymru lonydd', and Caradoc Evans's monstrous affront was to unearth in their midst a place so degenerate as to negate the very concept of pure docility.[10]

O. M. Edwards did try to replicate the 'Cymru lân, Cymru lonydd' image for an English-speaking readership in his periodical, *Wales* (1894–7). In the January 1896 number, alongside a photograph of four old people, captioned 'In a Merionethshire Village', he appealed to his readers: 'I am collecting photographs illustrating Welsh life of the last century, and would be very grateful for photographs or pictures of village corners, old farmhouses, spinning wheels, old furniture, and of everything relating to the good old times.' A year later, for want of support, he gave up on

Wales, seeing in its failure further proof of the impoverished culture of an Anglicized peasantry compared with that of the Welsh *gwerin*. He had hoped to see *Wales* become 'a power in the development of our people in the direction of happiness and purity' but the world-soiled English language appeared to work against the grain of his hope. And that was before Caradoc Evans put it to his use.[11]

Before *My People* erupted, attempts to idyllicize Wales in English included Alfred Thomas's *In the Land of the Harp and Feathers* (1896), first published in *Wales* (1894–5) as 'A Series of Welsh Village Idylls', and H. Elwyn Thomas's *Where Eden's Tongue is Spoken Still* (n.d.), but they hardly bear comparison with the remarkably popular series of novels written by Allen Raine between 1897 and her death in 1908 – novels which, while not blind to the failings of the *gwerin* in the coastal villages of Tre-saith, Llan-grannog and the surrounding countryside in south Cardiganshire, invariably have much of the rural idyll about them. She, too, appreciated Ceiriog's poetry, translated his 'Alun Mabon' for Edwards's *Wales* and was rewarded by his urging the children who received *Cymru'r Plant* to read Raine's *A Welsh Witch* because it was a story about the 1904–5 religious revival![12]

Caradoc Evans was unmoved. Prompted by a visceral hatred, rooted in a conviction that his parents and he, too, as their son, were the victims of a society rotten with religiosity, duplicity, cupidity, ignorance and beastly lust, Caradoc fixed his baleful eye on Rhydlewis and redrew it as 'Manteg', a Cardiganshire village wherein a debased peasantry, the very perversion of O. M. Edwards's *gwerin*, moved like creatures of the dark. It served his purpose to believe that his mother had been denied her lot by a grasping brother and subsequently stigmatized by her chapel on account of her poverty. The fact that his father, who died when Caradoc was an infant, was despised for his part as an auctioneer, when a Tory landlord post-1868 was evicting a Liberal-voting tenant, and was 'known' as an adulterer, who had suffered public humiliation astride the 'ceffyl pren', is also supposed to have festered long in Caradoc's mind, intensifying his need to be revenged.[13]

David Jenkins, a social anthropologist steeped in knowledge about Caradoc's background, argued long ago that the facts as known to him could not justify his malevolence, but when all is said and done all that matters is that Caradoc Evans felt in his marrow that he had been wronged. Anthropos, who knew himself to have been born illegitimate at a time when an abhorrence of bastardy counted for more than the fear of God in post-1847 Wales, could claim to have as much cause to lash out at a punitive, hypocritical society, but his literary temperament was of a different cast from Caradoc's. *My People* is not so much a work of social correction by a socialist reformer manqué as a powerfully contrived assault by an enraged inadequate, projecting his self-loathing on to the community he held responsible for what he was. No one becomes 'Manteg' – that hotspot which is the very perversion of 'a fair place' – as much as the disturbed author himself.[14]

Keeping in mind that the promoters of 'Cymru lân, Cymru lonydd' had been beaming a *gwerin*-dominated image of Wales at the nation for over fifty years, that they were neurotically concerned to avoid English derision, especially of their language, and discouraged the writing of satire in their *eisteddfodau* as something unworthy, it is little wonder that *My People* caused near apoplexy. The National Eisteddfodau of 1911 and 1913 had seen Crwys (the Revd Crwys Williams) and Sarnicol (Thomas Jacob Thomas, a Cardiganshire-loving schoolmaster) crowned and chaired respectively for poems on 'Gwerin Cymru' (1911) and 'Aelwyd y Cymro' ('The Welshman's Hearth', 1913), perpetuating the myth of O. M. Edwards's redemptive *gwerin*. Their sentiments were all the more reassuring at a time when the publication of Arthur Tyssilio Johnson's *The Perfidious Welshman* (1910), and T. W. H. Crosland's *Taffy was a Welshman* (1912), and the performance in 1913 at the Strand Theatre in London of Laurence Cowen's comedy *The Joneses*, in which the rustics of 'Llynwllanwllyn'(!) are easily duped by an Englishman calling himself Plantagenet Jones, had started the pot of Welsh anxieties bubbling again. Even (Sir) Ifor Williams was moved to urge his countrymen to attend performances of *Aelwyd Angharad* as an antidote to what he saw as Cowen's mockery.[15]

And then came *My People*. It was as if Caradoc Evans had gone to a Thanksgiving service to let loose a reverberating fart and, on being confronted by an outraged congregation, followed it up with a volley to prove that the opening salvo had been no accident. There is no denying the explosive impact of the stories in *My People*. It was, of course, all a matter of style. The ills that Caradoc seized

upon were not suddenly exposed to view; the sins he harvested were
by no means secret in Wales. Preachers had condemned them from
pulpits throughout the land; denominational literature as much as
the popular press frequently drew attention to the revelations of
court cases. Daniel Owen in his novels had exposed the corrosive
social effects of a status-serving religiosity in a far more insightful
manner than that of *My People*. But of course he wrote in Welsh.
What Caradoc Evans did was hit upon a way of telling 'his truth'
about Welsh failings that temporarily stopped a nation in its tracks.
He contrived a combative form of disjointed English, at the expense
of Welsh syntax, and used it to expose, to ridicule and to disgust
the moral turpitude of an out-and-out *gwerin* way of life which he
concentrated, in all its hideousness, in the kind of rural village long
imagined in Welsh literature as the place where 'true' Welshness
flourished.

'Manteg' as much as 'Y Pentre Gwyn' was meant to serve an
artistic purpose. To ask if it really existed is fatuous. In respect of
literary effect the village as idyll and as hell-hole can be equally
arresting, depending on the imaginative reach of the author and the
writing skills at his command. But neither image can bear too much
exposure. The Welsh village as 'Y Pentre Gwyn' was bound to run
foul of 'Manteg' sometime. It was asking for it. But so was Caradoc
Evans if he thought he could repeat the success of *My People*
simply by carrying on farting. One thinks of the pub bore who,
having scored once with a floorer of a dirty joke, told with relish,
insists on repeating it, with ever-diminishing returns. Caradoc
Evans was a limited writer because he lacked the gift of renewal and
because he was emotionally better equipped to demonstrate the
workings of Welsh humanoids than engage with Welsh humanity.

Professor M. Wynn Thomas has remarked how much more
fruitful the relationship between the two literatures of Wales could
have been from the outset had J. O. Francis, not Caradoc Evans,
been seen as the standard-bearer of modern Anglo-Welsh writing –
as it was once known. My regret is that the success of *My People*,
particularly its reception in England as confirmation that Wales
was a disgustingly backward little country where a language little
better than gibberish prevailed, aggravated old anxieties, thereby
ensuring that Welsh literature would be on the defensive for longer
than was good for it in the twentieth century. O. M. Edwards in
Cymru did not so much as mention Caradoc Evans; neither, to my

knowledge, did Anthropos, who continued to write until the 1940s, concern himself with him.

The Welsh-speaking literary promoters of Wales continued to write as if nothing had happened, and it was not until Caradog Prichard published *Un Nos Ola Leuad* ('One Moonlit Night') in 1961 that the village as 'Y Pentre Gwyn' took a tumble in the Welsh imagination from which it would never recover its primacy.[16] Not that it disappeared. A spate of memoirs and autobiographies by ageing *gwerinwyr* after the Second World War would kiss it into life time and again down to the end of the twentieth century, as in England Roger Scruton noted that 'the rural theme' continued to occupy 'a seemingly immovable place in the national culture, feeding illusions, soothing troubled hearts, and – let it be said – often preventing people from perceiving that the England of their dreams was no longer a reality'.[17] In the year 2000 Lisa Pennant, a native of Bwlch-y-groes in south Cardiganshire, published *Tai Mas a Thai Bach* ('Outhouses and Closets') which purports to show 'the Cardi at his worst'. The picture that emerges hardly casts the Cardi down and has nothing of Caradoc about it. Indeed, Lisa Pennant notes in passing that 'old Doctor Powell', maligned by Caradoc as the avaricious brother who did his mother down, was loved by the *gwerin* for his caring nature and generosity to the poor.[18]

There is, however, no denying the change wrought in the image of the Welsh village by *Un Nos Ola Leuad*. In this powerful autobiographical novel, the slate-quarrying village of Bethesda is seen through the disturbed memories of a middle-aged murderer, intent on suicide by drowning in 'Y Llyn Du' ('the Black Lake') – the antithesis of O. M. Edwards's Llyn Tegid – as he traces his boyhood steps through the village of his birth. The picture that unfolds in the opening chapter would have appalled Anthropos and gratified Caradoc Evans. There is no doubt that T. Rowland Hughes, who unfailingly championed the quarrymen's culture, particularly in *Chwalfa* ('Disintegration'), his 1946 novel about the Penrhyn quarry strike, would also have recoiled from Caradog Prichard's village scene.

But Prichard was no Bethesda-basher, for all the stigma he feared attached to his family on account of his father being a *bradwr* (traitor) during the shattering Penrhyn strike of 1900–3 and his mother being committed to Denbigh Asylum, worn down by poverty and unhinged by religious mania. The grotesqueness of the village in *Un Nos Ola Leuad* is in the eye of the narrator; it is he who is out of joint, not the community. Anthropos's 'Pentre Gwyn' knew no ill; Caradoc's 'Manteg' knew nothing else. With them it was a case of 'see no evil' and 'hear no good'. But with Caradog Prichard it was a case of seeing all humans as flawed beings at the mercy of the stuff of life – sexual lust plays its part in *Un Nos Ola Leuad*, too, but not as mere bestiality, the better to encourage a sickened rejection in others. In respect of imaginative daring and empathy Caradog Prichard leaves both Anthropos and Caradoc Evans trailing in his wake, and it is thanks to his novel that the Welsh village finally escaped stereotype and caricature to come convincingly alive.[19]

Notes

[1] J. M. Edwards, *Y Casgliad Cyflawn* (Abertawe: C. Davies, 1980), pp. 73, 96–106, 132–47.

[2] Alun Howkins, 'The Discovery of Rural England', *Englishness: Politics and Culture 1880–1920*, eds Robert Colls and Philip Dodd (London: Croom Helm, 1986), pp. 62–88 (69); H. V. Morton, *In Search of England* (London: Methuen, 1927), pp. 1–2, 14.

[3] Hazel Davies, *O. M. Edwards*, Writers of Wales series (Cardiff: University of Wales Press, 1988).

[4] Anthropos, *Y Pentre Gwyn: Ystori Bore Bywyd* (Wrexham: Hughes a'i Fab, n.d. [1909?]); O. Llew Owain, *Anthropos* (Caernarfon: Llyfrfa'r Methodistiaid Calfinaidd, 1953).

[5] Anthropos, *Y Pentre Gwyn*, p. 110; idem, 'Clych Atgof', *Y Dinesydd Cymreig*, 2, 9 (Tachwedd 1927), 3.

[6] It had been preceded in 1908 by *Aelwyd Angharad*, a stage version of a traditional *noson lawen* confected by John Lloyd Williams and Llew Tegid for the students at Bangor University College, which showed how two young girls, on the road to frivolous Anglicization, were 'saved' by a triumphant demonstration of wholesome rural culture on old Angharad's hearth.

[7] John Baker (Batley), 'Un o Gymeriadau Pentre Gwyn', *Y Fflam* (Awst 1952), 20–3.

[8] Quoted in H. T. Edwards, 'O'r Pentre Gwyn i Llaregyb', in M. Wynn Thomas (ed.), *DiFfinio Dwy Lenyddiaeth Cymru* (Cardiff, 1995), 22.

[9] Anthropos, *Pentre'r Plant: Atgofion Bore Bywyd* (Caernarfon, n.d.).

[10] Caradoc Evans, *My People*, ed. and intr. by John Harris (Bridgend: Seren, 1987).

[11] *Wales*, 1 (1894), iii–iv; ibid., 3 (1896), 3.

[12] Sally Jones, *Allen Raine*, Writers of Wales series (Cardiff: University of Wales Press, 1979).

[13] Barbara Prys-Williams, 'Fury Never Left Him', *New Welsh Review*, 31, vol. 8/3 (Winter 1995–6), 60–2.

[14] David Jenkins, 'Dai Caradog', *Taliesin*, 20 (Gorffennaf, 1970), 79–86.

[15] I am indebted to Mr Stephen Lyons for sharing with me his knowledge about Laurence Cowen's *The Joneses*; Ifor Williams's protest appeared in *Y Brython* (20 November 1913), 2.

[16] Caradog Prichard, *Un Nos Ola Leuad* (Dinbych: Gwasg Gee, 1961). His novel was well translated by Philip Mitchell as *One Moonlit Night* (Edinburgh: Canongate, 1995).

[17] Roger Scruton, *England: An Elegy* (London: Pimlico, 2001), p. 235.

[18] Lisa Pennant, *Tai Mas a Thai Bach: Y Cardi ar ei Waethaf* (Aberystwyth: Cymdeithas Lyfrau Ceredigion, 2000), pp. 124–5.

[19] I wish to thank Menna Baines for letting me profit from reading excerpts from her forthcoming study of Caradog Prichard's writings.

3
'Stories from foreign countries': The Short Stories of Kate Roberts and Margiad Evans

TONY BROWN

On 12 November 1946, Kate Roberts wrote from her home in Denbigh to the novelist and short-story writer Margiad Evans:

> I want to thank you most sincerely for your review of 'A Summer Day' in 'Life and Letters'. Others have praised without understanding. It is always interesting to notice how Englishmen like H. E. Bates, who know nothing about Wales or the Welsh language, react to stories like mine. I have come to the conclusion . . . that one must know something about the country from which the stories come, especially if they are stories of a native author who writes in the language of that country. It makes me think how often stories from foreign countries have been misinterpreted by English critics.[1]

Only this one letter from Kate Roberts to Margiad Evans survives, along with six letters from Margiad Evans to Kate Roberts, though it is evident from these seven letters that the correspondence was in fact more extensive. The tone of the correspondence between the two women is an unexpectedly warm, even intimate one; it would seem that Roberts felt she could be open and trusting in her letters, perhaps because Evans was not part of the Welsh-language literary scene.[2] In this respect it is a matter for regret that more of Kate Roberts's side of the correspondence has not survived; the letters were presumably lost in the many changes of home that Evans and her husband undertook in the 1940s and 1950s. The surviving letters refer not only to personal matters, including the writers' health – by 1952 Margiad Evans was experiencing fits that were the symptom of the brain tumour that was to kill her in 1958 at the age of 49 – but also to their reading and views on various aspects of writing. This tantalizingly short correspondence leads one to compare the creative work of these two women, whose backgrounds and relations to Wales were so different. While the contact between the two writers has been noted previously, the present chapter seeks to consider those concerns, especially aspects of female experience, which Roberts and Evans share, while ultimately suggesting that it was Roberts's sense of communal tragedy, rooted in her background, that primarily distinguishes her short stories from the rural lyricism of Margiad Evans.[3]

A Summer Day, published in Cardiff by Gwyn Jones's Penmark Press, contains English translations of twelve stories by Kate Roberts, selected from her first three collections of stories: *O Gors y Bryniau* ('From the Marsh of the Hills'), 1925, *Rhigolau Bywyd* ('The Ruts of Life'), 1929, and *Ffair Gaeaf* ('Winter Fair'), 1937, with a thoughtful introduction by the novelist Storm Jameson.[4] Somewhat ironically, the review by H. E. Bates to which Kate Roberts refers had been commissioned by Gwyn Jones himself for the *Welsh Review*. One can see why Roberts was unimpressed: not only does Bates seem not to understand her natural desire to express herself in her native language ('She elects to express herself for reasons of her own, in a language that is more foreign to Englishmen [sic] than most languages of western Europe') but he insists on seeing 'her little ironies . . . gloved and oblique' as emanating from 'the flat dark calm of country backwaters'.[5]

Margiad Evans, on the other hand, did 'know something about the country from which the stories come'. She had stayed for some weeks in the summer of 1930 in the village of Pontllyfni, only a few miles from Rhosgadfan, the village in which Kate Roberts had been brought up, on the edge of the quarrying area of Dyffryn Nantlle, which is the setting of Roberts's earlier fiction. Evans refers to this stay both in her review and in her reply to Roberts's letter ('I know not one word of Welsh (now) and very little of Wales, but I have never forgotten the fact that thousands of men and women and little children speak nothing else').[6] At the time, however, not only had Evans learned a little Welsh – the family she stayed with was bilingual and many in the area were monoglot Welsh-speakers – but she had taken a interest in Welsh literary culture, especially the *Mabinogion*. She mentions in her first letter to Roberts, 'I know – or knew – Dr Ifor Williams. He helped me'.[7]

Margiad Evans's first novel, *Country Dance* (1932), draws on her experience of Wales, being set on either side of the Wales–England border.[8] But her relationship with Wales was a complex one. Born Peggy Whistler, in Uxbridge, she published this novel and her ensuing writing under the *nom de plume* she had constructed from the surname of her paternal grandmother, who may have been of Welsh extraction, and a Welsh version of her own name (Peggy/ Margaret). Clare Morgan has recently located Evans's attraction to Wales in the Neo-Romantic impulse, during the 1940s, to mythologize Wales as a place of rural, timeless continuities in a period of widespread cultural insecurity.[9] At the same time, Wales, and more specifically the countryside along the Welsh border in Herefordshire, seems to have answered to some deep personal need in Evans herself, from the time that she visited it as a child and spent, at the age of eleven, what she later looked back on as an idyllic year on her aunt's farm at Benhall, near Ross-on-Wye.[10] This rural area became emblematic for Evans of stability and rootedness, in a life which provided her with no permanent sense of home.

However, though she published under her constructed Welsh name, Margiad Evans seems never to have pretended to herself, or to others, that she *was* Welsh. She continued to be drawn psychologically and emotionally to Wales; she writes, for instance, to Gwyn Jones in January 1946 from her cottage at Llangarron, a village near Ross-on-Wye, only some three miles from the Welsh border:

> I'm glad of my drop of Welsh blood and I'd never want to move out of the range of the Welsh voice.
>
> A lot of my stories are English people and English scenery but if you listen you can hear that drop! And whether it's that or something even further back – but the sound of the harp makes my heart mad with happiness.[11]

However, another letter to Gwyn Jones makes clear her awareness that ultimately she does not belong to that cultural community:

> And I'm *not* Welsh: I never posed as Welsh and it rather annoys me when R[obert] H[erring] advertises me among the Welsh short stories

because *I am the border* – a very different thing. The English side of the border too: I don't speak fretfully: you know how I honour the Welsh writers and how hospitable they have been to me. [Evans's emphasis]¹²

She goes on to emphasize that the characters in her fiction are not Welsh, 'with the exception of *Country Dance*, of course' – but are 'stolid English, flavoured with Celtic ancestry'. In other words Margiad Evans is acutely aware of the liminality of her situation, not just in terms of where she lives but also of her creative imagination. The contrast with Kate Roberts, living and working not only in Wales but at the heart of the Welsh-language literary community, could, it would seem, hardly be starker. At the same time, however, by the point at which she was corresponding with Margiad Evans, Roberts was living alone in Denbigh, and the stories she produced when her writing career resumed, the later stories collected in *Hyn o Fyd* ('Such is the World'), 1964, *Prynu Dol* ('Buying a Doll'), 1969, and *Gobaith* ('Hope'), 1972, repeatedly centre on an older woman, often living alone, marginalized in a Wales which seems to have lost any sense of its traditions and values.¹³ But even in the early stories, including those collected in *A Summer Day*, set mainly in the quarry villages of Caernarfonshire, the community's bonds of attachment are under stress and, beyond it, the universe seems to yield the individual little comfort.

Margiad Evans, then, came to *A Summer Day* with a very different perspective from that of H. E. Bates. Her review makes no reference to 'regionalism' or 'little ironies'; instead, there is a strong sense of the 'otherness' of Wales and its language: 'The Welsh will understand me when I say that their great language is an island. Its difficulty makes it remote and few of us who are not born there have the patience and the daring to land on its fervent rocks.'¹⁴ Again we have Evans's sense of being an outsider, but Wales's 'remoteness' and its size are seen by her as a source of creative intensity – 'its enormous mental capacity at odds with its small actual heritage *in land*, must produce effects on the imagination of a writer such as happened in the case of great masterpieces conceived by people whose lives were narrow and vivid' (Evans's italics) – and she cites *Castle Rackrent*, *Grimm's Fairy Tales* and, perhaps most tellingly, *Wuthering Heights*.¹⁵ For Evans, the intensity which comes from a life lived within its own culture, however 'remote' from an English perspective, in fact gives Welsh 'a start over the Cosmopolitan tongues'.

However, the real insight which the review gives into Roberts's fiction comes when Evans moves on to regard the stories from a perspective which transcends matters of national identity:

> The human beings concerned in these stories are natives in no derogatory sense, but only in the sense of poor people, living and dying in the place, or very near the place, where they were born. Yet they appear not so much as natives of a country, as the human beings of a world, as, indeed one might speculate, they appear to God – the aborigines of a Star . . . The deaths, loves, debts, adversities, and pleasures of poor people: there *can* be no more universal theme for tragedy than this.

It was mainly this perspective on the stories, it seems, which caused Roberts to write to Evans:

> I am so glad you have spoken about the universal theme for tragedy in the stories . . . I cannot see why an author who can take any country for his background has anything more to say about life than an author who has stayed at home. To my mind the latter has all the advantages. I think that even richness of expression comes from the depth of one's knowledge of one small patch of this earth, it does not matter whether that be a pool of tadpoles or the Court of Louis XIV. The thing is to know it. I'll admit, of course, that history at times, and in some countries, provides soul stirring events for great works of art. I have never been at the heart of such events, but I believe my stories are the ripples of very great tragedies. It was the last war and the tragedy that it brought to my family in Caernarvonshire that made me want to write in the first place. I had to do it or die. It is this last war that has brought me the greatest tragedy of my life.[16]

That tragedy of course was the loss of her husband, Morris T. Williams, earlier the same year; Roberts's letter to Evans ends poignantly: 'If you are in these parts at any time, please look me up. I am very lonely.' Margiad Evans's reply reveals much about her own temperament: 'Of course you are lonely. My dear, it took no tragedy to make you that whatever has happened to you. But loneliness – don't *fear* it – everything durable, everything eternal, comes out of loneliness.'[17] One perhaps needs to make a distinction here between 'loneliness', the pain of being alone when one feels the need for other people, and 'aloneness', the state of being contentedly solitary. It is clearly the latter state to which Evans is referring, seeing it indeed as a fundamental human state. Much of the time she seems herself to have relished aloneness, especially when writing. 'I DO LIKE TO BE ALONE' she writes emphatically in a letter in 1946, exasperated at the visits of a neighbour 'all anecdote and interruptions'.[18] Evans had been living alone in the cottage at Llangarron through the war years while her husband, Michael Williams, was in the navy, and the stories which were largely the product of these years, collected in *The Old and the Young* (1948) are filled with characters who are alone.[19] In other words, this writer, who is so conscious of being an outsider, repeatedly explores the nature of separateness, the experiences of both aloneness and loneliness.[20] For instance, in 'Thomas Griffiths and Parson Cope', Griffiths, an old man who gardens for the local rector, feels, 'for a moment the doom and trouble of those who exist alone on their two hands' (*The Old and the Young*, 25); he is 'sensitive about living alone' (26), and fearful of becoming as eccentric as the elderly rector. He recalls a time when life was very different: 'We was ten to feed at once at 'ome, but now us be gone from 'ere. Us be gone . . . I do know what I be saying. Bain't 'olesome to live by yerself' (26).

More usually the lone figure in these stories is a woman. Old Mrs Ashstone in 'The Old Woman and the Wind' has lived in her isolated hillside cottage for twelve years; by now 'many voices inside her' speak to her, articulating her own fears: 'You've lived alone, and that makes a woman a witch' (39). But when she finally gets the opportunity to move down to the village, she turns it down: 'I've worked with people, not loved them, and now I be done with work I do want to be shut of 'em' (43). Life for many of these women involves domestic labour as strenuous and unrelenting as that of the quarrymen's wives in the stories of Kate Roberts: the elderly Mrs Owen, on whose door a young boy calls at night, afraid of being alone in the dark, whitens her step twice a day and is still scrubbing the floor at night ('The Boy Who Called For a Light', 64, 67), while Maria in 'Mrs Pike's Eldorado', when her husband falls ill, is forced to look after the cows, pigs and poultry, as well as carry on with the household chores: 'She felt as lonely as overworked people usually do' (181). Here perhaps we glimpse a less positive side of Evans's life at Llangarron: very short of money, she not only tended her own vegetable garden but often had to take labouring jobs on neighbouring farms 'beet-hoeing, pulling beet, lifting potatoes or apple-picking' – as well of course as doing her own cooking and cleaning.[21]

Few of these women are married and, when they are, marriage provides little relief from work or even from loneliness. In the remarkable story 'People of his Pasture', the protagonist, a boy of fifteen with 'bright young enticing eyes and hair' (53) visits an isolated farmhouse – 'the land was one great pasture, one loneliness so large, so lost as to stir a kind of abstract pity' (52); out walking he has seen a ewe in distress. The woman, 'bowed and fruited', who answers the door has a baby in her arms and another child grizzling at her skirts; she and her husband know there are sick ewes, though there is little that can be done: 'He's away now back up yonder after something for 'em. What with one thing and another the man's always from home . . . Always, always off' (56–7). She walks with the boy to show him a short cut; then, as they cross a narrow bridge, her arm presses around his neck: 'The woman was kissing him! She held him imprisoned and she seemed to be kissing the astonishment out of him, pouring her kisses in between his bones' (59). As the confused boy pulls away, she clasps her hands to her face: 'I wouldn't have hurt you . . . There are days when I could scream and scream and scream . . . days when I could go mad.' This is manifestly a woman on the edge; she embraces the youth not merely out of sexual desire but because he is *there*, he has come into her loneliness, and he is caring in the concern he shows for the sick ewe. However much she relished being alone, it would seem that, inevitably, Evans was familiar with the pain of loneliness, especially in the period when her husband was away. The loneliness of Jessy in 'The Ruin' seems to be over; her husband has just returned to her having been demobilized. After years in which contact could only be maintained by 'hundreds of hard letters which had taken so long even to scribble' (137),[22] she feels that they are now 'together perfectly', though the story – importantly – is narrated almost entirely from Jessy's point of view. She takes her husband to see a remote, half-ruined cottage which she hopes they 'might patch and prop together for a home' (141). As they walk, though, symptomatic differences of opinion occur, over trivial things like the species of a bird and the direction of the flow of a stream; Jessy begins to sense a disjunction between the husband who is with her and the 'Gabriel' she has constructed through their time apart. His reaction to the cottage which she has already imagined as their home is firmly practical: it is remote, exposed to the weather and would need a new roof and floors. Jessy stares at him 'as if he were some new, wide countryside which she had never seen before' (144–5). As they walk back, her plans abandoned, she confronts the difficult adjustments to living with the man who is her husband and she is close to panic: 'I wish I could get away. I wish I could get away and be alone again' (146). Her previous aloneness, with her imagined, accommodating version of her husband, feels preferable to the sense of isolation she now feels.

One of the finest of Margiad Evans's stories, 'The Lost Fisherman', also expresses a young woman's longing for creative space, for a sense of personal fulfilment. Emily, living in a small border town – based on Ross-on-Wye – in wartime, becomes aware of an enigmatic young man whom she regularly sees fishing along the nearby river; they converse only casually but she comes to associate him with a tranquillity that is missing both from the world around her and from her own life, living with her mother and then also her sister and her children, evacuees from the London Blitz: 'he's part of something that's being lost. And I want it to come back. It's life. At least it is to me' (*The Old and the Young*, 76). Increasingly, indeed, the man comes to represent a kind of alter ego:

> she felt as though each of them sent the same lights and shadows up to the surface . . . And in their perfect familiarity with each other there was incalculable individual solitude . . . [W]ith him or thinking of him she became again the real Emily . . . who was free.
>
> (82–3)

It is not a romantic attraction in any conventional sexual way – they never even kiss – but he comes to represent to her a kind of wholeness and self-fulfilment her life lacks. As the fisherman rows her, late one evening, to her aunt's riverside house, in a final scene of remarkable tranquillity, he tells her: 'I've got the habits of a tramp now . . . oh, not the visible ones, I hope – no – but I can't stand houses simply because it seems you can never be alone in them.' Emily replies – perhaps with an echo of Virginia Woolf – 'I don't expect *a whole house* . . . I like a *room* I can be alone in' (93, italics in the text).

Thus, while being alone can mean loneliness and frustration, Evans more usually associates female aloneness with freedom and self-fulfilment, with creative space. Indeed, that space, in a literal sense, is manifested in the natural world which her characters inhabit in almost every story in *The Old and the Young*: its smells, its colours, its shifts and changes through the seasons. At times it is experienced, as it is by Emily in 'The Lost Fisherman', as 'a sort of connection with something one doesn't know' (92) and this sense of nature as a wholeness, a place with which one can feel at one, at home, is even more central in Evans's *Autobiography* (1943). The volume is not an account of her life but a series of close observations of the natural world and meditations upon it, taken from the journals she kept at Llangarron; the book indeed becomes, as Ceridwen Lloyd-Morgan has suggested, a chronicle of Evans's 'spiritual progress'.[23] At the end of the first section, 'A Little Journal of Being Alone', Evans is lying at evening on the hillside, tired from her work, smelling the grass and the herbs, aware of a nearby horse and of the stars, '*Thou* Father knowest me ... God be between us all like the lovely air'.[24] In the final section of the book Evans expresses a sense of a natural oneness in which the separate existence of the individual is transcended, though this awareness is approached only through a state of meditative aloneness:

> Must I die apart? ... No, I believe. I believe all creation, all life whatever to be a oneness, and then once more thought and happiness sweep through all my sense as the sunlight sweeps through the tree ... now I am in Eternal Time, as a child, as the oak tree ... No sound and yet all the earth and the bits of sky – all, the senses humming unheard harmony ... call it God ... call it the music of the living world ... eternal animation.
>
> (*Autobiography*, 153–5)

Such a perception, essentially a form of nature mysticism, helps us make sense of her response to Kate Roberts's expression of loneliness, especially if one reads Evans's 'loneliness' as 'aloneness': 'I am not a scrap religious – entirely indifferent to creeds and Christians, but I think that loneliness trains one for death – for life too – and that when you are away from people you are with God.'

There is, however, no such sense of spiritual reassurance in the stories in *A Summer Day*. Kate Roberts was, of course, brought up in the potent Nonconformist traditions of Caernarfonshire at the turn of the century, but there is little or no sense of the chapel as a spiritual force in these stories. Indeed, such references to the life of the chapel as there are here are far from positive: in 'The Loss',

Annie is grateful for the chance to get her husband away from the Sunday School teachers' meeting for a rare day out, while in 'Folded Hands' the elderly Beti has been to chapel only 'now and then' and '[o]n her own testimony, she had never been to a Quarterly preaching meeting, an eisteddfod or a circus: she always named them in that order, and they all meant much the same to her' (*A Summer Day*, 118). Like Beti, most of the characters in these stories, in their struggle for economic survival in this world, do not find, or even seek, consolation in the spiritual.

Moreover, unlike the more generalized rural settings of Margiad Evans's stories, Kate Roberts's earlier short stories are, of course, firmly located in a particular Welsh community at a particular time. And the community is always there in the background of Roberts's stories; the central action takes place for the most part in the privacy of domestic interiors, but the sounds and rhythms of the community are present as noises off – the echo of the quarrymen's boots as they walk to work, the sound of the hooter from the quarry. News travels through that local community: for instance, in 'Two Storms' the men at the inn have already heard of Aels's marriage to the protagonist's rival (*A Summer Day*, 19) and in 'Old Age' the narrator more than once hears news of the deteriorating health of his friend who lives some miles away (56). The fact that the *details* of life in a north Wales quarry-village are not dwelt upon – we see nothing of the routines of the quarry itself, for example, as we do in the stories of Dic Tryfan – ultimately contributes to the 'universal' character of Roberts's stories, to which Evans refers. These are simply working people, in episodes of day-to-day life. Moreover, and crucially, it is this sense that the individuals we see in the stories are not extraordinary but part of a wider way of life that gives Kate Roberts her great theme: individuals and communities caught up in the grip of forces, economic and cultural, which they only partly understand and over which they have no control; it is a vision of human helplessness that is finally tragic.

At the same time, Storm Jameson is right when in her Foreword she detects 'a solitude' in Roberts's stories (*A Summer Day*, 11). But here that solitude has none of the positives that Evans associates with aloneness; despite the presence of the community outside the protagonists' houses, Roberts's stories are haunted by loneliness, both social and ultimately spiritual. *A Summer Day* opens with the story of a man who, when his sweetheart marries another man, takes himself away to live for the next thirty years in a 'lonely cottage' (23). But more usually, as in Evans's stories, it is the woman who is lonely. In 'The Wind' a young girl is effectively imprisoned by her father, alone with a senile grandmother who is herself trapped in her memory of the day, years before, when her fiancé failed to appear at their wedding. For the most part, the unfulfilled females are the wives of the quarry-villages and, like many of the women in *The Old and the Young*, these women's work, done mostly alone in their homes, never stops. Beti, for instance, in 'Folded Hands', has found 'little room in her life for anything but housework, milking, and butter-making' (*A Summer Day*, 118).

Again, while many more of Roberts's female characters are married than those in Evans's stories, marriage seems once more to bring little alleviation to their plight; indeed, for Roberts, in story after story, the pain of marital disappointment brings more loneliness.[25] In 'The Loss', Annie 'had expected married life to be an extension of courtship' but for her husband 'marriage was "a settling down" – slippers, a fire, tobacco, the newspaper, and his wife completing the picture by sitting on a chair opposite, knitting' (*A Summer Day*, 39).[26] When she married, Beti, in 'Folded Hands', had felt that her husband 'was one man in a thousand, but living with him had reduced him to something very much like the rest of the thousand' (120).

The disappointment that marriage brings in these stories is not of course simply a matter of individual culpability but also of social circumstances: relationships are inexorably ground down by the week-to-week struggle for economic survival. Moreover, husbands and wives inhabit totally separate domains; the elderly wife in 'Folded Hands' reflects that '[h]er house was her world . . . She had never been to the quarry, and had not the faintest idea of the conditions in which her husband worked' (118). This separation of the working lives of men and women contributes to the deep poignancy of 'The Condemned'. Dafydd Parry, dying slowly at home of cancer, hears the slow tread of his workmates as they pass the house on their way to the quarry, but gradually he becomes part of the routines of the household world as he watches the endless work of his wife, Laura. And, movingly, he begins to re-evaluate their marriage, to realize how work and routine have taken the place of affection – 'After marrying, people began to live, not to love' (111). Now, as he has time to watch Laura, Dafydd begins to realize how isolated from each other they have been: 'By now, Dafydd was sorry that he had not spent more time talking to Laura. How much better it would have been.'

These, then, are tales of domestic loneliness – for while Evans's tales are of the fields and woods, Roberts's stories are primarily of the interior, domestic (and thus female) world. Indeed, the house in which the woman labours becomes a small area which *can* be ordered and controlled, in a world which in general seems indifferent to human control, the home a place of relative security in a universe which affords little sign of reassurance, physically or spiritually, to the human individuals who inhabit it. Storm Jameson's comment that the solitude she detects in the stories is 'not always and never only physical' (*A Summer Day*, 11) is thus an acute one. The women's endless domestic labour (and, indeed, the men's grim work in the quarry) becomes emblematic of a more universal need for human resilience in a world which seems empty of meaning. The point is illustrated in 'Sisters': Meri Ifans is almost comically obsessive in her domestic cleaning, but the tone of the story darkens when, after a series of strokes, Meri can no longer cope and the house becomes increasingly filthy; her married sister, with such time as she can spare from her own home, manages to keep Meri herself and her bed 'white as driven snow', but beyond the lamp, beyond this island of cleanliness and order, there is in the 'surrounding gloom . . . dirt and disorder' (*A Summer Day*, 102). The scene takes on a clear metaphorical resonance, and the same emblematic quality is present in a scene to which Evans draws attention in her review. In 'The Quilt', the wife of a couple whose small shop has finally gone bankrupt sits huddled with a quilt clutched around her, clinging to the only thing in her life which is beautiful and colourful and transcends mere utilitarian value, while, in the words of Evans's review, ' . . . the removers rummage away her life . . . The Removers! The justified, the hostile, the overpowering forces!'

Occasionally, in reading these stories, one is reminded of Thomas Hardy's narratives of working communities in the grip of inexorable shifts of value, and of his bleak awareness of a universe without plan or order. Roberts's characters at times suffer the cruel chances and coincidences which beset Hardy's rural characters: Meri Ifans being struck by her first stroke just as her last child leaves home, for instance, or Dafydd Tomos glimpsing Geini, his former love, staring at the wedding rings in a jeweller's window, only days after he has married someone else. And, as in Hardy, Roberts's landscapes can reflect the bleak indifference of the universe these men and women inhabit: in 'The Condemned', for instance, when Dafydd, in his last illness, ventures out for a walk, the earth is 'hard and colourless; all over it there were stones, alternating with lumps of dried dung' (*A Summer Day*, 109). In fact, we find nothing in Roberts of the lyrical, detailed evocation of the natural world which is such a presence in Evans's stories and which, ultimately, gives her intimations of a spiritual wholeness. In 'A Summer Day', even as the girls lie in the shade of the trees in a sun-filled landscape, there is 'no time for looking at things minutely' (*A Summer Day*, 64): the thematic focus of the story comes only when they enter a nearby cottage, another domestic interior.

In the final letter from Margiad Evans to Kate Roberts which survives (10 August 1952), Evans comments, evidently in response to something Roberts has written in a letter which has not survived, 'My childhood world has disappeared too. Horses & traps, lanterns, white lanes, sunbonnets & wooden hay rakes like combs. I see nothing so interesting now but I suppose if I were a child I should.' Here we glimpse the lyrical countryside of childhood, recaptured in such stories in *The Old and the Young* as 'Solomon' and in the title-story; Roberts's memories of the quarrying villages of Caernarfonshire in which she sets her stories are clearly very different. In fact, the stories of both writers are haunted by a sense of change and process, and frequently centre on memory as the means by which the individual maintains his/her sense of a continued identity, however vulnerable, through time. In a number of Roberts's stories, memories are stirred at moments at which life changes – retirement ('The Last Payment', 'Folded Hands'), bankruptcy ('The Quilt'), final illness ('The Condemned') – and the character looks back and takes, often painful, stock of his/her life. Other memories are triggered by a simple incident, as when watching his granddaughter making toffee in the kitchen reminds Dafydd of his beloved Geini doing the same thing and revives the whole sad memory of losing her.

It is such simple domestic tasks and smells that trigger memories most frequently in Roberts, usually with a poignant sense of how the stability and content associated in childhood with 'home' have been replaced by a life which has turned out to be anything but secure. Unhappy in her marriage, Annie in 'The Loss' remembers her old home, 'the scents of a farmhouse kitchen on a Sunday afternoon – a mixture of farmyard, dairy, potatoes baking in the oven, and apple tart' (*A Summer Day*, 42). 'Old Age' is constructed of layers of memory: the narrator at the side of his evening fire remembers back thirty-two years to his friendship with Twm at school, the same Twm who has been buried that day, dead in his forties. The narrator remembers Twm more recently, in his illness, watching his wife tap the bottom of the loaves as she removes them from the oven and reminding Twm in turn of his mother doing the same thing when he was a boy. The narrator remembers her as a busy, energetic mother, doting on her son. But when he breaks the news of Twm's death to the now elderly and confused old lady, she merely comments: 'Which Twm? Don't know him' (62). To lose one's memory is to lose one's sense of who one is, is to lose one's struggle with time.

Margiad Evans's stories are, if anything, even more dominated by time and memory.[27] And again there is often the longing for a lost sense of stability and security of self that is associated with 'home'. The narrative of 'The Boy Who Called For a Light' is wholly a recollection by the narrator of his childhood fear of being out in the dark, and of his knocking on doors 'in a kind of concentrated friendliness' in search of reassurance (again, a lonely figure surrounded by blackness). But before he begins his story the narrator, seemingly inconsequentially, remembers the routines of his boyhood home: 'and the queer thing is that after the first, the first one you remember, there's never another, not even when you're a man, married, with your own children, living somewhere' (*The Old and the Young*, 62). In a lovely, epiphanic moment in the volume's title-story, fragile, eighty-nine-year-old Tilly, recalling a few steps from her own girlhood, dances with some village children, including the narrator, then a girl; the narrator, entranced by the scene, recalls saying to herself 'I'll remember this . . . I'll *always* remember this' (162), though now, years later, she also thinks, 'When did she die? Where's she buried? Where's everybody? And what has happened to us?' (150).

Memory is the resistance of the individual consciousness to the inexorable flow of time, but in the stories of Margiad Evans – as in those of Kate Roberts – it is memory that colours the lives of so many of the characters with a profound sense of loss. Emily, in 'The Lost Fisherman', yearns in the stress of wartime for the sense of freedom and happiness she had as a girl on her aunt's farm, a clear echo of the way Evans's own memory of the year at Benhall at the age of eleven becomes talismanic of the peace she has lost, the world she is now outside.

As we have seen, Evans was acutely aware of her situation as an outsider. Drawn to the cultural continuity and rootedness she identified with Wales, she is always aware that she could never be other than on its margins. Indeed, she seems to relish the separateness, the liminality, geographically and culturally, of her situation: '*I am the border.*' Ultimately, her creative imagination draws on more uniquely personal circumstances than those of Roberts: a lack of family security, constant movement, financial anxiety, albeit these also serve to sensitize Evans to the wider cultural uncertainties and restlessness of the times. Her sense of human vulnerability, the fragile thread of memory and identity in the face of time, is registered in essentially lyrical tones: personal, emotional and ardently responsive to the rural world which surrounds her. And ultimately that world provides Margiad Evans with a more comforting vision; she reaches out beyond solitude to some sense of spiritual at-homeness. But Kate Roberts finds no such comfort. As her letter to Evans makes clear, it was the pain inflicted on her family by the First World War that had hurt her into writing; that loss gave her an anguished new insight into the nature of the universe she and her community inhabited and which through her writing she sought to confront: 'I had to do it or die.' Her fiction records the dogged resilience of Welsh working people, but the local struggle also becomes emblematic of a more universal struggle –'the ripples of very great tragedies' – underlying which there always remains, as Derec Llwyd Morgan has pointed out, that painful and essentially modern question: 'for what?'[28] In the final story of *A Summer Day*, Beti watches her elderly husband hacking at thorns in the fields and looks back over the years: 'If all that work were piled together into one heap, it would surely reach to the sky, a monument of monotony' (*A Summer Day*, 120). It is this wider vision which ultimately marks a distinction between the work of the two women. They both write about fundamental human experiences – youth, age, suffering, death – but while the voice of Margiad Evans is a distinctive, poignant, lyrical voice, Kate Roberts expresses an awareness of human struggle, individual and communal, that is deep and tragic. In the words, again, of Evans's review: 'It is not only the weather of Welsh mountains but the weather of mankind that rages in *A Summer Day*.'

Notes

[1] Margiad Evans MSS 875/1–4, National Library of Wales. The correspondence between Kate Roberts and Margiad Evans is currently being edited, with a commentary in Welsh, by Dr Ceridwen Lloyd-Morgan. I am most grateful to Dr Lloyd-Morgan for supplying me with a draft of her paper and for commenting on an earlier version of the present paper.

[2] The point is made by Ceridwen Lloyd-Morgan in her forthcoming paper: 'Ysgrifennai [Kate Roberts] ati gan gymryd yn ganiataol y gallai ymddiried ynddi, ac am hynny mentrai ddadlennu ei hofnau a'i gwendidau; gallai droi at Margiad Evans fel confidante am y rheswm nad oedd hi'n rhan o'r gymuned Gymraeg.' ('[Kate Roberts] could write to her taking it for granted that she could trust her, and because of that she ventures to disclose her fears and her weaknesses; she was able to turn to Margiad Evans as a confidante because she was not part of the Welsh-language community').

[3] Ceridwen Lloyd-Morgan in her invaluable study, *Margiad Evans* (Bridgend: Seren, 1998), pp. 106–9, notes the correspondence and suggests some similarities between the two writers' work. Clare Morgan, 'Exile and the Kingdom: Margiad Evans and the Mythic Landscape of Wales', *Welsh Writing in English*, 6 (2000), 89–118, briefly notes the connection and Dr Lloyd-Morgan's comments but sees the two writers' treatment of themes and settings as 'radically distinct' (113).

[4] *A Summer Day and Other Stories* (Cardiff: Penmark Press, 1946). Further references will be included in the text. For a detailed account of the publication of *A Summer Day*, including the genesis of the translations, see John Harris, 'A Long Low Sigh Across the Waters: The First Translations of Kate Roberts', *Planet*, 87 (June/July 1991), 21–9. Storm Jameson, a native of Yorkshire, had lived in Wales since 1942.

[5] *Welsh Review*, 5 (1946), 217–18, 220.

[6] NLW MS 20062B.

[7] NLW MS 20062B, and see Lloyd-Morgan, *Margiad Evans*, p. 23. Ifor Williams, Professor of Welsh at Bangor and an expert on Old and Middle Welsh, lived in Pontllyfni in the 1930s; Kate Roberts had referred to his scholarship in her letter.

[8] The short novel was published in its entirety in *Welsh Short Stories* (London: Faber, 1937). It is possible that Kate Roberts read it there, since the collection also included a translation of her own story 'A Summer Day'. In her letter to Evans, Roberts says, 'I want to say how much I enjoyed your "Wooden Doctor" [1933], which I read years ago and still remember and your short stories'.

[9] Clare Morgan, 'Exile and the Kingdom'.

[10] See Lloyd-Morgan, *Margiad Evans*, pp. 8–9, and Moira Dearnley, *Margiad Evans* (Cardiff: University of Wales Press, 1982), pp. 2–3. Evans first visited Benhall at the age of nine in the year that her father was forced to leave his job with an insurance company, subsiding thereafter into chronic alcoholism; the family, financially insecure, lived with relatives for two years.

¹¹ Letter to Gwyn Jones, 28 January 1946, Prof. Gwyn Jones Papers, NLW.
¹² Letter to Gwyn Jones, 6 March 1946, Prof. Gwyn Jones Papers, NLW. Quoted in Lloyd-Morgan, *Margiad Evans*, p. 32. Robert Herring was the editor of *Life and Letters To-Day*, which published a number of Margiad Evans's stories and essays in the 1940s. See Meic Stephens, 'The Third Man: Robert Herring and *Life and Letters To-Day*', *Welsh Writing in English*, 3 (1997), 157–69.
¹³ A selection of stories from the later volumes, as well as from the period of *A Summer Day*, have been translated into English by Joseph Clancy in *The World of Kate Roberts* (Philadelphia: Temple University Press, 1991).
¹⁴ *Life and Letters To-Day*, 51 (November 1946), 54–8.
¹⁵ Evans had long been fascinated by Emily Brontë, and two years after her review of Roberts she published an essay on 'Byron and Emily Brontë' in *Life and Letters To-Day*, 57 (June 1948), 193–216. See Lloyd-Morgan, *Margiad Evans*, pp. 33, 58, 112–13.
¹⁶ Margiad Evans MSS 875/1–4, NLW. Quoted in part in Ceridwen Lloyd-Morgan, *Margiad Evans*, p. 107. Kate Roberts's brother had been killed in the First World War.
¹⁷ Letter to Kate Roberts, 14 November 1946, NLW MS 20062B.
¹⁸ Letter to her husband, Michael Williams, 14 March 1946, Margiad Evans MSS 864, NLW.
¹⁹ *The Old and the Young*, with Introduction and Notes by Ceridwen Lloyd-Morgan (Bridgend: Seren, 1998). Further references are included in the text.
²⁰ In her Introduction to Clare Hanson (ed.), *Re-reading the Short Story* (London: Macmillan, 1989), Hanson argues that the short story is a genre which loans itself to the expression of the experience of the outsider. For an application of Hanson's ideas to the Welsh situation, see Tony Brown, 'The Ex-centric Voice: The English-Language Short Story in Wales', *North American Journal of Welsh Studies*, 1 (Winter 2001), online journal at *http://spruce.flint.umich.edu/~ellisjs/Vol One*.
²¹ Lloyd-Morgan, *Margiad Evans*, p. 78.
²² Margiad Evans herself wrote almost daily to her husband during his time in the navy; many of the letters are in the Margiad Evans MSS, NLW.
²³ Lloyd-Morgan, *Margiad Evans*, p. 83.
²⁴ Margiad Evans, *Autobiography* (Oxford: Basil Blackwell, 1943), p. 10, Evans's italics. Further page references are included in the text.
²⁵ On the disappointment of marriage in Roberts, see Katie Gramich, 'Gorchfygwyr a Chwiorydd: storiau byrion Dorothy Edwards a Kate Roberts yn y dauddegau', *DiFfinio Dwy Lenyddiaeth Cymru*, gol. M. Wynn Thomas (Caerdydd: Gwasg Prifysgol Cymru, 1995), pp. 80–95, esp. p. 85.
²⁶ Ceridwen Lloyd-Morgan has suggested that 'The Loss' may have unconsciously influenced Evans's writing, in 1946, of 'The Ruin'. See *The Old and the Young*, 209.
²⁷ On memory in *The Old and the Young*, see also Lloyd-Morgan, *Margiad Evans*, pp. 102–3.
²⁸ Derec Llwyd Morgan, *Kate Roberts*, new edition (Cardiff: University of Wales Press, 1991).

4
'Gartref – bron': Adversity and Refuge in the Jewish Literature of Wales

JASMINE DONAHAYE

In the annual National Eisteddfod lecture in 2003, Jane Aaron argues that the perpetuation of Welsh culture 'has depended to such an extent on developing a resistant spirit which insists on survival . . . that a mental pattern has evolved conditioning the Welsh to respond in this way', and in his equally provocative essay 'The Jewish Ideology of Affliction' Bernard Susser examines the similar role that an adversity-centred world-view has played in Jewish cohesion and continuity: 'A sense of being embattled and beset – the perennial victim – is perhaps the most prevalent and familiar of Jewish attitudes', he claims. 'If there is a paradigmatic Jewish tale . . . it is one of the embattled Jews suffering for their beliefs, resisting the pressures of a hostile world and prevailing nonetheless.'[1]

Like Aaron, Susser argues for the value that such a survival instinct has had in Jewish culture, but he also suggests that it now undermines rather than serves Jewish identity.[2] In Welsh Jewish writing, evidence supporting his arguments is prominent. Nevertheless, an awareness of *Welsh* adversity qualifies and, in some cases, moderates this affliction-centred world-view, both in the work of Jewish writers who were born in Wales and left, and in that of writers who have temporarily or permanently made their home here. This movement into and out of Wales illustrates another signature of Jewishness, which is that of the cultural imperative to leave and to search for new refuge.[3]

Bernice Rubens and Dannie Abse are perhaps the most familiar of the group of Jewish writers who left Wales, which also included

Maurice Edelman, Mervyn Levy, Sonia Birch Jones, Barbara Hardy and Lily Tobias. Their movement towards the English metropolitan centre (from where Tobias subsequently left for Palestine) expresses their dual cultural identity, for it echoes the movement of Jews from the ghetto and shtetl (isolated Jewish villages) to the dominant cultural centre at the time of Jewish emancipation and the Welsh movement towards England and London. As at the time of emancipation, it is in pursuit of opportunity, of modernity and of high art culture that Jews leave, in a way that implicitly consigns Wales to the cultural status of shtetl.[4]

Paradoxically, many of those who left describe Wales as being virtually free of anti-semitism, yet an awareness of Jewish affliction is central to their identities. Nowhere is Susser's description of the deeply enculturated attitudes to adversity more clearly illustrated than in Bernice Rubens's novel *Brothers*, which was published in 1983.[5] While its didacticism and historicism are atypical of Rubens's popular novels, *Brothers* nevertheless stands as her encapsulating statement both on the Jewish experience and on the Jewish experience in Wales, and its message of a permanently hostile world almost serves as a case history for Susser's thesis.

Brothers follows the misfortunes of several generations of a wandering Jewish family, and utilizes a structure common to all Rubens's fiction, which is the deployment of a central, bizarre motif around which the narrative is organized and to which it repeatedly returns. In *Brothers* this motif consists of an anti-semitic threat and, in response to that threat, the ritual enculturation of the sons of the next generation with a creed of anti-semitism and Jewish survival. Whether a major event or a passing anti-semitic remark has jogged the fathers out of their complacency, they take their sons aside and explain:

> There are always such men . . . and always will be. Wherever you are. As long as you are a Jew. Such men will attack you in many disguises. They will do it in the name of the Czar, or they will assault you in the name of freedom . . . They will use all kinds of ideologies, but whatever they are called, and with whatever sweetness, they are made, each one of them, of Jew-hate and oppression.[6]

Passed down through five generations of Jewish brothers, the fathers' doctrine of survival gives their children permission to abandon, if necessary, the appearance of Jewish practice in order to survive: 'I want you to live . . . I want you to survive', they say. 'There is no cause on earth worth dying for . . . no God worth one's dying breath, no country worth one's sacrifice. Only in the name of love and friendship is Death worthy.'[7] This doctrine is described as the boys' 'sure and sublime inheritance'.[8]

It is both the story of the Jews suffering oppression and this process of enculturation that so closely illustrates the argument Susser makes, for he claims that:

> As no other feature of Jewish civilisation, the conviction that oppression is permanent and reconciliation is illusory has been faithfully passed on from generation to generation. Deeply encoded and primordial, it often outlives even the decline of Jewish knowledge and the erosion of Jewish commitment . . . The sense of embattlement is perhaps the only Jewish remnant that persists when all else has been sloughed off.[9]

This is true of each generation of the family in *Brothers*, in which one brother moves towards assimilation but is returned to Judaism by anti-semitism.[10] However, this family's typical experience of affliction is qualified during its brief sojourn in Wales, for Rubens compares Jewish suffering and survival with that of a mining community. Here it is not anti-semitism that triggers the enculturation of the next generation; on the contrary, because Wales provides a place of respite from anti-semitism, the value of passing on this legacy – and indeed the value of Jewish survival altogether – is called into question.

The two brothers of the Wales generation, Aaron and Leon, arrive in Cardiff in the 1870s. Leon, appalled by the toll that being Jewish has taken on his family, abandons Jewish practice, takes up a pedlar's route in the Valleys and marries a Welsh woman, announcing: 'My children will not be the Chosen, either by God or the Czar.'[11]

Although Leon is accepted in the valley, the marriage breaks down, in part as a result of cultural differences, and on the day their son David ought to have had his bar mitzvah, Leon's wife Mary takes him to chapel, precipitating the crisis in reaction to which Leon imparts to his son his 'minstrel's song of survival'. However, Leon wonders to what end:

this is Senghenydd . . . a sleepy village in the Aber valley, far from Czar, ignorant of pogrom, a village in which he, Leon Bindel, was the only Jew. What relevance was his legacy to a child to whom his bar mitzvah day was no different from any other birthday?[12]

Nevertheless, his son responds to the family story by comparing it with that of a mining family's tragedy, and Leon thinks 'that his son had understood him after all'.[13]

The parallels between Welsh and Jewish suffering are made explicit when Leon explains to his brother Aaron the reasons for his son becoming a miner: 'David has a history almost as long and as oppressed as our own. His grandfather was a collier, so was his father before him.'[14] However, Rubens limits the possible sympathy between the two cultures: earlier, listening to miners singing, Leon 'turned away his ear from the name of the son of God whom they praised . . . he stood here on alien soil amongst men who were strugglers and survivors like himself and still that name jarred in his ear.'[15]

In *Brothers*, the absence of anti-semitism in Wales and the comparison Rubens makes between the Welsh and Jewish histories of adversity are particularly striking, given that the 1911 riots in Tredegar have been widely interpreted as being anti-Jewish and symptomatic of a general Welsh anti-semitism. Neither Rubens, nor indeed any of the writers considered here, construes the disturbances in Tredegar as being indicative of an underlying hostility to Jews, which some historians have been eager to do.[16] On the contrary, because of its own troubled history, Rubens constructs her south Wales valley as a haven, albeit one that in its very safety poses a threat to Jewish survival through the possibility of assimilation.

It is the emptiness of this assimilated life that initiates Leon's return to Judaism, and this re-entry is secured by the trauma of a pit explosion that takes his family's lives. Subsequently the narrative shifts to Germany and Wales recedes for, as with other locations in *Brothers*, it has been no more than a temporary – if exceptional – resting point in the Jewish odyssey. As if to indicate its incidental nature in the larger sweep of anguished Jewish history, Wales becomes subsumed under England.[17]

The formulation of a survival identity in *Brothers* effectively illustrates Susser's argument, that an adversity-centred world-view undermines a viable Jewishness because it 'artificially resuscitates a moribund ethno-religious consciousness although it cannot tell those who are affected why they ought to survive as Jews'.[18] Although *Brothers* certainly provokes questions about the purpose of surviving as Jews in the absence of a creative engagement with Jewish culture and Jewish ethics, it provides no answers, and such questions need in similar fashion to be asked of Welsh culture, lest the 'survival despite oppression' identified by Aaron becomes, like Rubens's formulation, essentially survival *because* of oppression.

In contrast to that of Rubens, the adversity-centred world-view of Lily Tobias is moderated by a sense of purpose. The inevitability of anti-semitism and, consequently, the inevitable failure of attempted assimilation are dominant themes in her work, but, unlike the virtual reification of Jewish wandering in *Brothers* or recent scholarly arguments that might be termed post-Israel positions, which reject the importance of a geographical centre, Tobias argues that the only solution to Jewish oppression is a homeland in Palestine.[19]

Tobias espouses an optimistic pre-Holocaust Zionism, and although she pleads for a national home that would be a haven from anti-semitism, the dominant hope that her work expresses is for a model society with a larger international peacekeeping purpose.[20] Her sense of Jewishness is ethnic and national as much as religious and cultural, and hence her expectations of refuge are in a different register from those of Diaspora-centred Jews: indeed, although she constructs Welsh-speaking Wales as a philo-semitic haven, it can clearly be no *home*.[21]

In an early story 'The Nationalists', which was written before the First World War, the Jewish protagonist Leah agrees with the nationalist Idris that the Jews are treated well both in Wales and in England, but she protests that this is not the same as having freedom in one's own country.[22] Sheba, Leah's counterpart in another early story exploring the class tensions of second-generation Jewish immigrants in Wales, concludes that 'if there was a Jewish country, one wouldn't have to worry'.[23] Expanding this story, Tobias's first novel, *My Mother's House*, explores the social and psychological cost of attempted Jewish and attempted Welsh assimilation in English society, but despite the sympathetic parallels she draws between Welsh and Jewish dilemmas in four of her five books, her Zionist focus is almost always dominant.[24]

Unlike Bernice Rubens and Dannie Abse, both of whom were born in Cardiff and had minimal contact with Welsh-speaking

Wales, Tobias grew up in the largely Welsh-speaking town of Ystalyfera. In the 1920s she lived in the tenants' cooperative of Rhiwbina, which was the site of a thriving intellectual enclave of socialist and nationalist thought.[25] Her attribution of a general Jewish sympathy to Welsh speakers and her situating of Zionist arguments in a Welsh context reflect not only her sympathies with Welsh-language culture and tradition but also the influence that this environment had on the formation of her socialist and pacifist Zionism.[26]

The optimism and idealism of her pre-Holocaust Zionism moderate the expectation of affliction which Tobias's work, like that of Rubens, clearly expresses. Although she writes of anti-semitism in Wales, she attributes it almost exclusively to the English and to the socially climbing Anglicized Welsh, such as the Anglophilic shop-girl Miss Howells, whose casual contempt for 'greasy old Jews' is equal to her contempt for all things Welsh.[27] She reserves for Welsh-speaking nationalists, such as the characters Lloyd Patagonia and Christmas Jones, not only a strong sympathy with Jews but also support for Jewish national aspirations.[28] However, in the dominant argument for the necessity of a Jewish return to Zion, this Welsh-speaking nationalist Wales can serve only as a place of political sympathy and a temporary and inadequate refuge; it cannot be a permanent home.

In contrast, Tobias's nephew Dannie Abse argues that Wales is virtually free of anti-semitism.[29] However, his experience of this 'tolerant Wales' does not appear to moderate the expectation of adversity that defines his sense of Jewishness. In *Goodbye 20th Century*, in which he discusses the development of his Jewish identity, Abse claims that, on the whole, as a child he had

> but the vaguest conception of the difference between Christian and Jew . . . It was all rather baffling. 'Who's Jesus Price, mama?' I asked. 'Not Price, son,' my mother said . . . 'A good man,' [she] insisted, as if she knew him personally. 'But not divine, not the son of God.'[30]

In the same vein, typical both of his motif repetitions and humour, Abse describes his mother's insistence that he should be proud to be Jewish: ' "Why?" I demanded, in a voice perpetually stranded on top doh. My mother would simplify for me our ancient traditions, pronounce on our heritage of high moral codes, and finally, defeated, resort to name-dropping.'[31] On the whole, he concludes, echoing his brother, 'if you were a schoolboy in South Wales, being Jewish had advantages'.[32]

Despite the absence of anti-semitism, Abse absorbed an adversity-centred world-view, a process of enculturation described in the fictional *Ash on a Young Man's Sleeve*:

> Thousands of years of faith leaned with the men as they leaned – these exiled Jews whose roots were in the dangerous ghetto and in dismayed beauty . . . One received a hint, even as they prayed, a hint of that unbearable core of sensual suffering . . . I saw in their large dark eyes that infinite, that mute animal sadness, as in the liquid eyes of fugitives everywhere. I was eleven years old then: I could not have named all of this but I knew it . . . I knew it all.[33]

Abse's growing adolescent atheism was informed by an awareness of events in Europe and 'unemployment and dole queues in the Welsh valleys', but the increasingly anti-semitic environment of the 1930s informed his secular Jewish identity. A counterpoint to Leon in *Brothers*, his mother is to be heard succinctly articulating Susser's adversity thesis: 'Chosen People', she says bitterly. 'Chosen to be persecuted.'[34]

Echoing his mother, Abse's formulation of Jewish identity in terms of anti-semitism and Auschwitz is one of the few places where he can be said to be taking an unequivocal position rather than, as M. Wynn Thomas puts it, 'constantly playing one of his identities off against another'.[35] His statements 'Auschwitz has made me more of a Jew than Moses did' and 'as I take in more fully the unbearable reality of what happened in Europe . . . then gradually I feel myself to be more of a Jew than ever' illustrate what has come to be called a 'Holocaust identity', and as such may be usefully compared with the similar 'negative' Jewish identity formulated by Auschwitz survivor Jean Améry.[36] In an essay examining the different responses to Auschwitz by Améry and Primo Levi, Nancy Wood compares the 'memory of the offence', described by Levi, with the formative memory of the '*social* designation as a Jew' and hence a Nazi victim, described by Améry.[37] According to Wood, what binds Améry to this identity is 'the *memory* of the abandonment that had condemned him to this physical fate and his subsequent loss of "trust in the world" '. It was society's failure to defend him against persecution rather than the actual injuries he sustained that formed Améry's 'irreducible identity as a victim'.[38] Like Améry, Abse is a secular Jew; he claims that he, too, is a survivor and, like Améry (and indeed like Rubens), expresses a loss of trust in the world:

> I came to realize that what had happened . . . was something that could not be irrevocably suppressed from consciousness, that in one sense I, too, was a survivor . . . The realisation of the destruction of the Jews . . . changes, poisons subtly, one's attitudes to other people. I am aware that ordinary, decent people one has met, with ordinary passive prejudices, could be, under other circumstances, the murderers of one's children . . .[39]

If, as a very real and direct victim of Nazism, the position statements of Améry have been challenged and found wanting, those made by Abse at such a remove must also be called into question. Indeed, Abse's statements are the more remarkable for his repeated claims that his upbringing in Wales was virtually free of antisemitism. Susser indicates that the lack of trust expressed by both Abse and Rubens is typical not of the post-Holocaust Jew per se, but of what he argues has become a defunct form of Jewish identity, for he claims that

> historical memories often conspired to regard cordiality with suspicion, to believe that it was tentative and exceptional. The image of Jewish life as insecure, of antisemitism as a permanent threat, and of violent onslaught as *the* residual condition, was so deeply entrenched in Jewish intuitions and perceptions that . . . it prevails even in periods of relative tranquillity and prosperity.[40]

Although Abse asks 'how can we be anything but (neurotically?) afraid of anti-semitism seeing what happened in Europe?',[41] it seems that in his assimilated state he now depends upon antisemitism to remind him that he is a Jew, for he remarks: 'I think it was Ehrenberg . . . who declared that he was a Jew as long as there was one anti-semite alive. To this sentiment I assented and still assent.'[42] Like Rubens's character Leon who, because of the *absence* of anti-semitism in Senghenydd, runs the risk of wholly losing his Jewishness, which has been reduced to a negative credo of oppression, Abse too must rely on the threat of anti-semitism to maintain his sense of identity as a Jew.

To query Abse's construction of himself and, by implication, of all Jews as survivors, and hence also as victims, is not to query the impact or significance of anti-semitism or the Holocaust. On the contrary, the purpose of such questioning is to highlight a widely held defensive formulation of secular identity that, arguably, is not only no longer sustainable but also threatens a viable Jewishness. As Susser expresses it: 'embattledness as an instinct has outlived embattledness as a reality. And this discrepancy has created a major crisis of credibility.'[43] If Susser is criticizing Israeli attitudes as much as those of Diaspora Jews, the statement by Abse that 'when Israel is threatened, I become a conscious Jew'[44] suggests how this crisis of credibility extends to all of us who let our Jewish cultural legacy of adversity hold our more important cultural legacy of humanitarianism hostage.

That this Holocaust awareness, which at times dominates Abse's poetry, and the expectation of affliction, expressed by Rubens, are not inevitable but *elective* formulations of Jewishness is indicated by the very different response of the German-Jewish refugee writer, Kate Bosse-Griffiths. Like Améry, Bosse-Griffiths grew up in a Christian household with one fully assimilated Jewish parent, but although she acknowledged her background, unlike Améry, her response to Ravensbrück, where her mother died, was a refusal to allow the 'memory of the abandonment' to define her. Instead, as Heini Gruffudd expresses it, after fleeing Germany, she closed the door on what was unassimilable and launched herself into a new life in Wales.[45]

While this might be viewed as a pathological response to a traumatizing experience, in the case of Bosse-Griffiths it is perhaps more accurately to be seen as a creative survival strategy, for her experiences determined her attitude to life in positive ways. As Gruffudd writes: 'dihangodd [hi] yn fwyaf dianaf [o'i theulu], er na all neb mesur anaf i enaid. O hynny ymlaen mesurai anawsterau bywyd yn ôl graddfa Ravensbrück, a bach iawn oedd ei phwys ar foethau materol' (She escaped the least harmed [of her family], although the injury to her soul cannot be measured. From then on she would measure life's difficulties according to the scale of Ravensbrück, and she had little concern with material luxuries).[46]

Robat Gruffudd observes that Bosse-Griffiths retained a joyful and irreverent disposition and had little time for formal religion; he suggests that she 'embraced Welshness partly as an anti-German reaction' and does not believe that she 'in any sense defined herself in terms of anti-semitism'.[47] Bosse-Griffiths learned and wrote in Welsh, and the Welsh location and social context of her fiction provide the largely unmarked background to her explorations of social relationships.[48] Her published work does not address Jewish matters or the Holocaust and her experience of persecution did not return her to Judaism or a conscious engagement with Jewishness. However, her experiences did inform her fundamental pacifism, which in part was expressed through her involvement both with Plaid Cymru and with the pacifist literary group *Cylch Cadwgan*, which she founded with her husband.[49]

As her status as a fully assimilated Jew in Germany gave Bosse-Griffiths no protection against the betrayal of Nazism, her ability to embrace Welsh culture wholly, despite her experiences and the fate of her family, constitutes, on the one hand, a remarkable act of trust, but it also suggests that the absence of overt anti-semitism in Wales, upon which other Jewish writers have commented, meant that she was not forced to confront a past and a social designation that were too painful to contemplate.[50]

Bosse-Griffiths's engagement with Welsh culture differed from that of her fellow refugee Josef Herman, who made his home in Wales for eleven years. In his diary and other writings, Herman reflects on Wales as a refuge and a creative source, and celebrates the quiet of his environment in Ystradgynlais: 'I came to cherish the dullness of peace', he writes. 'I came to cherish the dullness of uneventful days. I find comfort in the quiet of shadows'.[51] His description of Wales as a peaceful and simple refuge echoes his idealized imaging of miners, which has been strongly criticized for its reductionism.[52] In *Mae'r Galon wrth y Llyw*, Kate Bosse-Griffiths's discussion of the painter Evan Walters highlights the comparisons made by Peter Lord between insider and outsider visual imaging of industrial Wales and, by its sensitivity to the local and particular in Walters's work, reinforces the problems that have been identified in Herman's depiction of the miner as a 'walking monument to labour'.[53] The universalizing of Herman's miner-painting is reflected in his writing, for he renders those around him in simplified and representative terms, citing 'those splendid Welsh voices and their primitive veracity'[54] and describing how 'it is this traditional passion, this monumental appearance, that broadens the local and incidental, and the once individual becomes typical and symbolic'.⁵⁵ Perhaps as suggestive of the reductionism of his attitude is his assertion that 'what makes the group so singular outside is but the strong similarity within the group'.⁵⁶

In 'A Strange Son of the Valley' Herman's sensitive description of a Jewish miner named Moishe differs significantly from that of his Ystradgynlais miners: Moishe is 'bony and hard with blue scars on face and hands, his appearance . . . not unlike other old miners'. Heredity, Herman informs us, 'makes no man as typical as a job does'.⁵⁷ In contrast to his written and visual depiction of Welsh miners, his telling of Moishe's story individualizes him, and his description of a Yiddish book published by the Swansea Jewish Debating Society in 1904 and shown to him by Moishe suggests his sensitivity to Jewish history: 'The pages of cheap paper were yellowish and smelt like wet chalk, yet they breathed as if alive, sounded alive like an echo of times that never really disappear, for they are layers in the mountain of our history.'⁵⁸

Herman's description of Moishe and his Yiddish book reinforces the reductionism of his construct of the Welsh. Nini Herman, his second wife, claims that Herman 'lost his heart to Wales – where his memory is enshrined as a legend, part of the folklore, a myth'.⁵⁹ It is this mythical 'Joe bach', now deployed in the projection of 'tolerant Wales' by Tony Curtis and others, which is problematic, for while the refuge that Wales offered Herman is rightly to be celebrated, the limitations of his response to its social complexity ought not to be obscured.⁶⁰

Other Jewish writers who have come to Wales have tended to respond thoughtfully to the complexity of Welsh society and, like Kate Bosse-Griffiths, to engage with Welsh-language culture. In her collection of essays *Hen Wlad Newydd*, Judith Maro, for example, provides a more nuanced construct of Wales-as-refuge than Herman.⁶¹ Maro left Israel in 1949 and, while she celebrates the peacefulness of her new home in rural north Wales, she also engages with it critically. Responding to the geographical parallels between a Wales whose ubiquitous Hebrew place-names reflected a still-living Biblical tradition and her original home in the source of that tradition, she writes: 'teimlais ar unwaith rywfaint o berthynas rhwng Cymru ac Israel . . . a dyma beth y byddwn yn dod i sylwi arno dro ar ôl tro, atsain rhwng fy ngwlad fy hun a'r wlad roeddwn yn mynd i fyw ynddi . . . Roeddwn i gartref – bron' (I felt at once some connection between Wales and Israel . . . and that's what I would notice time and again – a resonance between my own country and the country I had gone to live in . . . I was home – almost).[62]

Maro comments on how her new home is remarkable for the refuge from conflict that it offers, but she qualifies this observation in an interview with Ned Thomas, which was published in *Planet* in 1976.[63] Thomas, invoking the construct of Wales-as-refuge, compares its 'exceptionally peaceful history' to the violence of Israel, and asks if it isn't dangerous to compare the two. Maro responds: 'Living in Wales, I am deeply conscious of the inherent peace. It is a thing to be cherished. But if Wales is to remain Wales, it is not to be taken for granted.'[64] Similarly, Stevie Krayer, a more recent arrival and one who, by settling in Ceredigion, encountered the language tensions of rural Wales, indicates in her poem 'Displaced Person' that she has not taken refuge from complexity or ambiguity:

> I'm not the only one; there are so many
> Ways to be an exile. You don't even
> Have to leave the country.
> Invaders come and then you are
> The outsider; progress rumbles in,
> Bulldozing the old hills, the old skills.
> You may survive instamatically –
> A figure in a pastoral idyll, snapped
> Just before your metamorphosis
> Into a chambermaid.[65]

Krayer is a Quaker, but her work is infused with Jewish imagery and concerns. In the poem 'Teifi Pools' she observes that 'this is my Canaan', using a biblical image that is perhaps as much a response to the biblical landscape of Wales explored by Maro as an expression of her Jewish poetic vocabulary. Nevertheless, Wales as Canaan is not a construction of Wales-as-refuge, for the poem continues:

> Yet I have felt at times an Africa, a limitless veld
> unfurl within me, and it's there
> that I must take my chances, when I dare.[66]

Despite her conversion, Krayer expresses something of the mistrust that characterizes the work of Abse and Rubens, for in the poem 'Voices from a Burning Boat', whose title points both to the boat that she herself burns by her conversion and to the whole Jewish past that she – and the world – is losing, she observes that, despite conversion, 'The Nazis would have given me a star'.[67] Similarly, in 'Displaced Person' she writes:

> Not that my family was unaware
> How quickly a jackboot on the stair
> Could give me back the old identity . . .

Nevertheless, although this invocation of a residual adversity-defined Jewishness resonates with the attitudes of Abse and Rubens, her poem argues that this Jewish identity is

> Not for some dream of safe anonymity
> But for a nobler idea – a covenant
> That the whole world, renascent
> From the flood, would be my native land,
> Instead of a selfish ghetto.[68]

Krayer does not comment upon anti-Semitism in Wales, and her work indicates that, despite Wales being her 'Canaan', it is the intimacy of the Friends' Meeting that is her true refuge. It would appear that it is this experience of refuge, along with the internationalism of her upbringing and her own young adulthood, which moderates her expectation of anti-Semitism.[69]

The sensitivity to the political and social complexity of Welsh-speaking Wales expressed by Krayer, Maro, Bosse-Griffiths and Tobias contrasts with reductionist constructs of industrial south Wales. Herman, Abse and Rubens reinforce the manner in which, among those who left, the construction of Wales-as-refuge is also one of Wales-as-shtetl. While Abse, for example, finds it natural 'to claim both traditions', in his description of his return to his Welsh roots and 'to the refreshments a writer can gain by returning to his birthplace' it is 'Welsh comic portentousness', the boastful and fabricating poetic 'heirs of Iolo Morganwg' and the peaceful scenery of Ogmore by Sea that he cites.[70] Rather than being an expression of Welsh identity, this return by Abse to a simple and stereotypical Wales – and by Rubens to ideas of Welshness[71] – might, paradoxically, express more of a Jewish identity, for these returns appear to arise from a typically Jewish restlessness rather than from a re-engagement with Welsh culture.

The undercurrent of mistrust common to the writing of Abse and Rubens, which their construct of Wales-as-refuge does not appear to moderate, and the more qualified mistrust expressed by Tobias and Krayer, appears to be absent from the work of Maro, Bosse-Griffiths and Herman, despite the fact that all three were far more directly affected by what could be termed Jewish adversity. Indeed, it would appear to be exactly that direct experience of adversity which predisposes them to accept refuge. This refuge that Wales offers them mediates an ideology of affliction, and allows these writers to remember the blow, rather than to suffer 'mistrust in the world'.

Notes

[1] Jane Aaron, *The Welsh Survival Gene: The 'Despite Culture' in the Two Language Communities of Wales* (Cardiff: Institute of Welsh Affairs, 2003), p. 2, and Bernard Susser, 'The Ideology of Affliction: Reconsidering the Adversity Thesis', *Diasporas and Exiles: Varieties of Jewish Identity*, ed. Howard Wettstein (Berkeley: University of California Press, 2002), pp. 221–33 (221).

[2] For an alternative (religious) view to that of Susser see also Lionel Rubinoff, 'Jewish Identity and the Challenge of Auschwitz', *Jewish Identity*, eds David Theo Goldberg and Michael Krausz (Philadelphia: Temple University Press, 1993), pp. 130–51.

[3] See Gabriel Josipovici, 'Going and Resting', *Jewish Identity*, eds Goldberg and Krausz, pp. 309–21.

[4] Mervyn Levy's description of the attraction of Paris and London illustrates this shtetl status of Wales. See interview with Peter Lord, National Library of Wales, *The Visual Culture of Wales Research Project* deposit.

[5] Bernice Rubens, *Brothers* (London: Abacus, 1988).

[6] Rubens, *Brothers*, p. 106.

[7] Ibid., p. 49.

[8] Ibid., p. 109.

[9] Susser, 'The Ideology of Affliction', p. 224.

[10] Nicholas de Mesurier, 'Surviving the Earthquake', *New Welsh Review*, 18 (Autumn 1992), 26–9.

[11] Rubens, *Brothers*, p. 188.

[12] Ibid., p. 210.

[13] Ibid., p. 211.

[14] Ibid., p. 219.

[15] Ibid., p. 203.

[16] W. D. Rubinstein challenges this dominant view in 'The Anti-Jewish Riots of 1911 in South Wales: A Re-examination', *Welsh History Review*, 18 (1997), 667–99.

[17] See Rosalind Elbogen Harries, 'A Million Miles From Odessa', *New Welsh Review*, 38 (1997), 62–4.

[18] Susser, 'The Ideology of Affliction', pp. 228–9.

[19] For Diaspora-centred arguments see Wettstein (ed.), *Diasporas and Exiles*. For Tobias see Jasmine Donahaye, 'Hurrah for the Freedom of the Nations', *Planet*, 147 (2001), 28–36, and 'Wales in the Work of Lily Tobias', *British Jewish Women Writers*, ed. Claire Tylee (forthcoming).

[20] Lily Tobias, 'Zionism and Militarism; Some Other Considerations', *Zionist Review*, 4, 5 (1920), 89–90.

[21] See Donahaye, 'Hurrah for the Freedom'. For discussion of the problematic use of the terms anti-semitism and philo-semitism see, for example, Bryan Cheyette, *The Construction of the Jew in English Literature: Racial Representations 1875–1945* (Cambridge: Cambridge University Press, 1993), p. 8.

[22] Lily Tobias, *The Nationalists and Other Goluth Studies* (London: C. W. Daniel, 1921), p. 17

[23] Tobias, *The Nationalists*, p. 49.

[24] *My Mother's House* (London: George Allen & Unwin Ltd, 1931). The exception is *Eunice Fleet*, in which Welsh and Jewish questions are peripheral to the central pacifist message ([1933] Aberystwyth: Honno Press, forthcoming).

[25] Iorwerth Peate, *Rhwng Dau Fyd* (Dinbych: Gwasg Gee, 1976). Also Leo Abse, personal interview, 1 May 2002.

[26] See Donahaye, 'Hurrah for the Freedom'.

[27] Tobias, 'Glasshouses', *The Nationalists*, p. 31.

[28] See 'Glasshouses', in Tobias, *The Nationalists*, and *My Mother's House*.

[29] For example, Dannie Abse, *Ash on a Young Man's Sleeve* ([1954] London: Penguin, 1982), pp. 22–3 and *Goodbye 20th Century* (London: Pimlico, 2001), pp. 15, 195.

[30] Abse, *Goodbye 20th Century*, p. 13.

[31] Ibid., p. 15.

[32] Ibid., pp. 15–16. For Leo Abse, see Jasmine Donahaye, 'Cultivating Irreverence', *Planet*, 160 (2003), 7–17. Here, 15.

[33] Abse, *Ash on a Young Man's Sleeve*, p. 33.

[34] Abse, *Goodbye 20th Century*, p. 17.

[35] M. Wynn Thomas, 'Prints of Wales: Contemporary Welsh Poetry in English', *Poetry in the British Isles: Non-Metropolitan Perspectives*, eds Hans-Werner Ludwig and Lothar Fietz (Cardiff: University of Wales Press, 1995), pp. 97–114 (101).

[36] For discussion of Holocaust identity see Jon Stratton, *Coming out Jewish: Constructing Ambivalent Identities* (London: Routledge, 2000), p. 11.

[37] Nancy Wood, 'The Victim's Resentments', *Modernity, Culture and 'the Jew'*, eds Bryan Cheyette and Laura Marcus (Cambridge: Polity Press, 1998), pp. 257–62.

[38] Ibid., p. 258.

[39] Abse, *Goodbye 20th Century*, pp. 67–8.

[40] Susser, 'The Ideology of Affliction', p. 223.

[41] Abse, *Goodbye 20th Century*, p. 68.

[42] Ibid., p. 67.

[43] Susser, 'The Ideology of Affliction', p. 225. For an alternative depiction of the legacy of the Holocaust see also Art Spiegelman, *Maus: A Survivor's Tale* (New York: Pantheon Books, 1986).

[44] Abse, *Goodbye 20th Century*, p. 213.
[45] Heini Gruffudd, personal interview, 5 June 2003.
[46] 'Cofio Kate Bosse-Griffiths', *Taliesin*, 102 (1998), 100–9 (105).
[47] Letter to the author, 25 February 2001.
[48] See for example Kate Bosse-Griffiths, *Mae'r Galon wrth y Llyw* (Aberystwyth: Gwasg Aberystwyth, 1957) and *Cariadau* (Talybont: Y Lolfa, 1995).
[49] Heini Gruffudd, personal interview.
[50] This is not to suggest, however, that Wales is free of anti-semitism.
[51] *Notes from a Welsh Diary 1944–1955* (London: Free Association Books, 1988), p. v.
[52] Peter Lord, *Industrial Society* (Cardiff: University of Wales Press, 1998).
[53] Bosse-Griffiths, *Mae'r Galon*, p. 77, and Herman, *The Early Years in Scotland and Wales* (Llandybië: Christopher Davies, 1984), p. 85.
[54] Herman, *Notes from a Welsh Diary*, p. xi.
[55] Herman, *The Early Years*, p. 89.
[56] Ibid., pp. 85–6.
[57] 'A Strange Son of the Valley', *The Jewish Quarterly*, 21, 1–2 (1973), 131–2 (131).
[58] Ibid., p. 133. Moishe was not the only Jewish miner – see also Morris Silverglit of Aberfan, audiotape, Museum of Welsh Life oral history archive, 6017.
[59] Josef Herman, Foreword, *Related Twilights: Notes from an Artist's Diary* ([1975] Bridgend: Seren, 2002), p. 10.
[60] Tony Curtis, Introduction, *Related Twilights* (2002). See also Ozi Rhys Osmond, 'Epiphany in Ystradgynlais', *New Welsh Review*, 48 (Spring 2000), 9–11. The use of Herman in this way is not dissimilar to that made of Paul Robeson.
[61] Judith Maro, *Hen Wlad Newydd: Gwersi i Gymru* (Talybont: Y Lolfa, 1974). The title is a translation of Theodor Herzl's Zionist work *Altneuland*. Maro's work is translated into and published in Welsh.
[62] Ibid., pp. 16–17.
[63] Ned Thomas, 'Israel/Wales', *Planet*, 31 (1976), 16–20.
[64] Ibid., p. 19. For an examination of pacifist movements in Wales see K. O. Morgan 'Peace Movements in Wales 1899–1945', *Welsh History Review*, 10, 3 (June 1981), 398–430.
[65] Stevie Krayer, *Voices from a Burning Boat* (Salzburg: University of Salzburg Press, 1997), p. 46.
[66] Ibid., p. 77.
[67] Ibid., p. 15.
[68] Ibid., p. 46.
[69] Stevie Krayer, personal interview, April 2003.
[70] Abse, *Goodbye 20th Century*, p. 204.
[71] See Michael Parnell's interview with Rubens in *New Welsh Review*, 9 (1990), 46–54.

II
ENGENDERING WALES

GILLIAN CLARKE

The Accompanist
for Wynn

A glass to help us listen
to the word,
to hear the poem speak
from the silence of the page.
Father and daughter,
piano and voice.

Hard to say who leads,
who follows,
poet, composer,
singer or listener,
the reader or the page,

the voice or the piano
as she sings Fauré's *Lydia*
in a house by the sea
to the steadying sound
of his hands on the keys,
the tide on the shore,

and her voice becomes bird,
takes flight
and she is Lydia
haunting the evening
with something like grief, like joy,
and is more than music.

6
En-gendering a New Wales: Female Allegories, Home Rule and Imperialism 1890–1910

KIRSTI BOHATA

From the French Revolution to the early twentieth century, allegories of nations in female form were commonly employed in nationalist iconography. The long nineteenth century was also a period in which the nation-state came to be imagined according to the model of the bourgeois family, with its strict division of labour along gender lines. In international relations, too, the familial trope was frequently employed to represent supremacy and dependence – as in allegorical depictions of an imperial power as the paternal protector of a maidenly and vulnerable colony, or perhaps as the guiding husband or father of a dependent wife or child. While the use of a female form to represent a nation does not necessarily mean that such allegories are coded female – Britannia could be androgynous or symbolize masculine prowess – these figures could easily be slotted into established gender-roles of wife, mother, virgin and so on, thereby symbolically placing subordinate nations within a political hierarchy that reflects a patriarchal social order.[1] If female allegories of nation were used by imperialists to suggest the weakness, vulnerability or even the alluring exoticism of colonized countries, they were also employed by anti-colonial nationalists. Addressing a very different audience, these images depicted the subjugation of the nation, with the aim of engendering the manly valour of patriots keen to rescue the nation as 'damsel in distress'. Furthermore, some feminist studies have suggested that women themselves might also adopt female allegories of nation as feminist-nationalist icons. In this brief essay I will focus on Welsh representations of nation in female form alone. This discussion explores how far such allegories might conform to a feminized (weak and subordinate) Wales, 'married' to a masculine (strong and guiding) England, or how an equally male-centred discourse might picture an alluring, feminine Wales in order to engender masculine Welsh valour. I will also, however, briefly consider the potentially feminist agenda of some of these images.

The figure of woman-as-nation is inevitably inflected in Wales by the nineteenth-century construction of the Welsh people as a feminine race, who would naturally benefit from the masculine guidance of the (racially distinct) English. The feminization of what was inscribed as racial otherness was, of course, a common feature of British colonial discourse, but was employed and inflected in various ways in different countries. In Wales, for instance, the significance of women as emblematic figures is complicated by the national cultural debate emanating from the Welsh response to the Blue Books of 1847, when women became contested icons of the national character subject to the discourse of both 'colonizer' (or hegemonic power) and 'colonized' (or subordinate nation).[2] A popular version of woman-as-nation in Wales was the one which pictured the nation as a mother; indeed, sanctifying the role of the mother in nationalist discourse is a very common one, especially where 'language, culture [and/or] ethnic descent are seen as the binding elements of nation'.[3] The implications of being confined to the role of mother by nationalist discourses and the different ways women have reinscribed and empowered the role of mother are now the focus of a plethora of new international feminist and postcolonial studies, which are transforming the often more limiting notions of motherhood imagined by western feminism. More abstractly, however, the allegory of nation-as-matriarch – the mother who must protect her children – might still be utilized by anti-colonial nationalism without necessarily transgressing the bourgeois familial model employed by imperial nations, since this mother figure could simply be interpolated into the dominant discourse as subservient to the imperial patriarch.[4]

Perhaps the best-known female allegory of the Welsh nation is that created by the cartoonist for the *Western Mail*, J. M.

Staniforth, in 1900. Staniforth's 'Dame Wales' was a matronly figure who, although she might fiercely champion the cause of her 'children' on minor domestic issues, generally supported the status quo, often appearing as a faintly ridiculous peasant.[5] She might be compared with C. L. Innes's description of Mother Ireland, who 'as Catholic peasant mother . . . is shrewd and kindly enough, but limited and limiting in her vision, which is entirely pragmatic and domestic in its concerns'.[6] Rather more regal versions of Dame Wales had been scripted into various national pageants, most famously, perhaps, in the Welsh National Pageant of 1909. Hywel Teifi Edwards has described how this pageant was intended to secure the status of Cardiff as an important and enterprising Welsh/British city and of Wales as an important nation within the British Empire, and also to teach the people of Wales of their heroic past and thus engender self-respect. Thousands of schoolchildren from across Wales were brought to Cardiff to witness the spectacle, which was staged daily for nearly two weeks and included members of the Welsh nobility among its cast of thousands. The Dame Wales of this Pageant, played by Lady Bute, was a regal figure rather than the national-costumed peasant of Staniforth's cartoons, yet perhaps her role was not all that different.

Lady Bute's commanding figure appeared in the Prologue and Finale of the National Pageant. The prologue might be seen as enacting Wales's own 'empire-building' or, as it was represented in the Pageant, the reclamation of rightful territory. Dame Wales calls her counties, each represented by a woman, together by name (incidentally, calling 'Glamorgan, to the front'[7]). She beckons to Monmouthshire (which was widely regarded as annexed to England due to legal and administrative arrangements) to join the group:

> And thou, dear Monmouth, stand beside thy kin;
> For though great England claims thee for her own,
> Cymric thou art, and Cymric thou shalt remain.[8]

Although the assertion of Welsh unity and this irredentist speech were immediately undermined by comic bickering amongst the counties over who might rightfully claim as their own each of the Welsh heroes to be celebrated in the Pageant, the finale attempted some form of closure with the assertion of the territorial unity of the Welsh nation. After the final scene of the central historical drama, Dame Wales, surrounded by her shires and a multitude of other women dressed as the *tylwyth teg* (fairies), formed a map of Wales with their bodies, constituting a living, all-female emblem of the nation.

Yet, for all the National Pageant's irredentist 'frame' and its patriotic procession of heroes, it seems to have underwritten loyalist rather than separatist national feeling in Wales, concerned more with proving Wales a worthy partner (a wife to England's royal consort, perhaps) in the British imperial enterprise than attempting to extricate Wales from any perceived status as a colonized nation within Britain. The final historical scene ended with an assertion of Welsh loyalty to the United Kingdom, as Henry VIII announces, amid a 'general uproar' of joyous shouts and pealing bells, the Act of Union between England and Wales: 'My kin and faithful liegemen, I have harkened to your prayer and granted your petition. Here is the Act of Union between England and Wales for ever.'[9] Thus Wales's loyalty within the United Kingdom is reaffirmed in terms which are highly suggestive of a marriage ceremony. (Dame) Wales is unified – 'made one' – with England, embodied here by the hypermasculine Henry. The marriage vows, ironically, or perhaps rather appropriately in this context, include the woman's promise to 'love, honour and *obey*' the man, and a comedic closure to the Pageant is achieved. The Welsh may claim to have contributed to the greatness of the United Kingdom – the penultimate scene, for example, shows the crowning of 'Harry Tudor' on Bosworth Field, and a note reinforces not only his Welsh ancestry but the fact that this Welshman is regarded by 'scholars . . . as the founder of the British Empire'[10] – but this participation is limited to that of a minor partner, aptly suggested in the figure of the weaker sex.

An earlier and much more radical, if lesser-known, allegory of Wales-as-woman may also be productively read in terms of the romantic model described above. 'Lady Gwen, or the days that are to be', by 'A Welsh Nationalist', is a fascinating story, which promotes full citizenship for women in an independent Wales. This fictional fusion of the goals of the women's and the nationalist movements in Wales was serialized in the bilingual periodical *Cymru Fydd: Cylchgrawn y Blaid Genedlaethol Gymreig* between 1890–1. I have been unable, so far, to discover the identity of 'A Welsh Nationalist'.[11] In an important preface to the story, the author describes 'his' intentions: 'Under the disguise of a romance, he wishes to offer to his countrymen an ideal which, if they choose, they can realize for themselves.'[12] In the context of this study, however, the 'romance' elements of the plot may be shown to have a rather more significant bearing on this utopian home-rule narrative than may at first be obvious. If we remember that Gwen is clearly the embodiment of the nation, as we shall shortly see, then the person to whom she is wed or otherwise romantically linked is of great importance to the nation.

Before going on to look at the romance plot and at Gwen as an allegory, a brief outline of this little-known work is necessary. Ten chapters of 'Lady Gwen' appeared but, unfortunately, the novel was incomplete when *Cymru Fydd* was discontinued in March 1891. The plot is of fairly minor importance in the available fragment, not least because there is no opportunity for the development of the potentially complex sub-plots. Briefly, the story is set in Harlech, in AD 2000, on the last day of the National Eisteddfod, at a banquet to celebrate the victorious role of Wales in a war between America and the Empire of Greater Britain. Sir Roland Wynne-Hughes, a lawyer, opposition politician and the most popular man in Wales, having just returned a soldier-hero from a war against America, finds himself drawn into a plot to bring down the government headed by his much-beloved cousin Gwen, all because of his inappropriate and unrequited love for Miss Herbert. As a further consequence, Sir Roland seems set to become the dupe of another plot to bring the whole of the Empire of Greater Britain under the sway of the Roman Church. Lady Gwen is also threatened by the arrival of her estranged half-brother, who appears in disguise, bent on destroying Gwen out of an old enmity and in revenge for his ruin in America during the recent war. 'Lady Gwen' is hardly a major work of fiction, but it is nevertheless a textually rich narrative which offers no fewer than thirteen pieces of verse (in English and Welsh) of up to thirteen stanzas each, along with a number of lengthy speeches, demonstrating in form what it declares in prose: that the Welsh are a people who thrive on rhetoric and song, poetry and hymns. Its political messages dominate the narrative, and the emphasis is on historical and social comment rather than depth of character or plot. There is a substantial commentary on the land question of nineteenth-century Wales, the cruelty of landlords, the tithe wars and disestablishment, while the success of this future Wales is shown to be the result of the influence of uniquely Welsh Calvinist principles in private and public life. Its purpose, as a piece of utopian writing, is to encourage its Welsh nationalist readers to fight for home rule, disestablishment, votes for women and a federated empire.

The first mention of Gwen herself appears at the end of the first chapter, which until then has sketched the state of Wales and its pivotal role in the Empire. Gwen is the leader of the progressive party, 'a second Cymru Fydd', that aims to push through the agenda of a new wave of Welsh radicalism.[13] She is now prime minister of Wales and at the height of her popularity, but also, clearly, an embodiment of both idealized womanhood and idealized woman-as-nation.

> The leader of the reforming party was a woman, – and this accounts, to some extent, for the purity of ideals and chivalric behaviour of the party which recognised in her the most perfect example of an *ideal Welsh womanhood*. No one reproached the reforming party for being led by a woman. It had been clearly understood that all great periods in the history of the world had been characterized by the presence of heroic women. Welsh literature is characterised by what one may call a worship of woman; Dafydd ap Gwilym and Dafydd Nanmor and Ceiriog, the popular singers of Wales, are at their best when they describe the influence which woman exercises, – *a modifying, purifying, ennobling influence*. In Lady Gwen Tudor the new Welsh movement found an ideal leader, typical of what was best in the past of what would be in the future, – a new Lady of Snowdon or Joan of Navarre.[14]

Here, essentially feminine qualities are linked with the Welsh social successes through the form of Gwen. If the link between Gwen and her country is not obvious enough in this passage, then the following chapter makes the connection explicit: 'An aristocrat in taste and feeling, but a Calvinist in religion, Gwen seemed to combine in her own person every feature of Welsh nationality.'[15] Gwen's credentials as a representative or embodiment of this particular version of Welsh nationalism are authenticated by her rural origins and she is toasted with the cry of *'ein gwlad, ein hiaith, ein cenedl*, (our country, our language, our people) never so honoured as by its union with the name of Lady Gwen'.[16]

Gwen is the embodiment not only of radical religious and nationalist ideals (in terms of nineteenth-century Welsh politics); she also symbolizes a feminine ideal which needs to be considered in the light of her supposed function of promoting female suffrage. We might question, for instance, how the prominence of conservative and perhaps rather limiting traditional feminine traits might be reconciled with her potential as a feminist icon. Gwen is single, but she is beautiful – although it is interesting to note that, while she is described as embodying Welsh womanhood, her beauty is of a distinctly Anglo-Saxon variety: she has blonde hair and blue eyes, rather than the dark Welsh features of most of the other beauties described in the story.[17] Gwen's talents do not end with her grasp of politics, but extend to include the more traditional feminine accomplishments, such as music and singing; she even breaks off her busy preparation of an important speech in order to entertain her cousin (Sir Roland Wynne-Hughes) with tea, song and the playing of a 'traditional' small Welsh harp. In the figure of Gwen we are presented at once with a feminist ideal – a woman prime minister in a country that has benefited enormously from the input of women – and also with a traditional, harp-playing, pious, feminine angel in the Victorian mould. The assumption that this angelic figure was necessarily antithetical to the cause of feminist independence would be wrong, however, and in terms of Anglo–American New Woman discourse it could be viewed as anticipating a feminist strategy advocated by Sarah Grand. In 1893, Grand argued that New Women should make every effort to appear as feminine and attractive as possible, so as to undermine the efforts of anti-feminists to portray the New Woman as 'unnaturally' mannish and ugly.[18] In portraying Lady Gwen as being ultra-feminine and highly desirable, as well as an intelligent and capable politician, the narrative presents an iconic figure who should appeal to as wide an audience as possible – to Welsh nationalists and feminists alike – while undermining the criticism of those who saw professionally active women as desexed and dangerous.

The narrative of 'Lady Gwen' might, however, be read as conforming to rather more conservative pictures of Welsh womanhood than this feminist interpretation suggests. Since we know from the outset that this story is a romance, it is highly significant that we are told that if our heroine were to marry she would have to retire from politics. The traditional ending of a romance plot would thus be a dubious one from a feminist perspective. Apart from the problem of the marriage disqualification, there is the question of how far the allegorical Gwen may be regarded as offering any positive models to real women at all. Marina Warner has emphasized the 'tabula rasa' qualities of the female form as national allegory, but she also notes that allegories offer 'the potential for affirmation not only of women themselves but of the general good they might represent'.[19] Classical feminine allegories were indeed used by various women's movements of the *fin de siècle*, often as personifications of Victory. In a discussion on Ireland, Margaret Ward offers a national framework for this use of allegory. While she acknowledges that Cathleen ní Houlihan and the other female personifications of the nation were primarily constructed by male-orientated discourses that presented Ireland-as-woman as a victim, needing to be rescued by Irish men, Ward also points out that women might respond to these images of Cathleen ní Houlihan in a different way: 'unlike their male comrades, the women were not undertaking some chivalric rescue but were fighting on their own behalf – they were Cathleen ní Houlihan just as much as Cathleen was the personification of the ideal.'[20] Thus Cathleen symbolized 'individual as well as national freedom'.[21]

Although the figure of Lady Gwen seems to conform to a male-centred discourse and, in all likelihood, was the creation of a man, she too might still be seen as appealing to Welsh feminists as well as being an alluring figure for male readers. The themes of temperance and disestablishment prominent in 'Lady Gwen' were, for example, widely supported by various women's movements which, although not primarily established with a national(ist) agenda in view, nevertheless reinforced a sense of 'connection . . . between temperance, womanhood, the Welsh language and the sense of belonging to a Welsh nation'.[22] Gwen's uncompromising stance on the sale of alcohol (demonstrated by her refusal to allow celebrating regiments access to alcohol and her diatribe on the social evils of drink) is just one of the ways in which we might see her as acting as a role-model for real Welsh women engaged in real social and political campaigns during the late nineteenth century. Furthermore, the insistence on the ability of women to benefit the nation through politics is sustained, and the unhappy lot of women forced to exist within the narrow constraints of nineteenth-century polite society with only a meagre education is forcefully outlined.

If Gwen may be a double-coded icon in terms of her role as allegory of nation, then the way in which she seems to embody the best of Welsh culture, with her singing, harp-playing and, indeed, her eisteddfod-winning essays, is equally complex. The role of women as the keepers and conveyors of national culture, usually as mothers, has generally been regarded as conservative and limiting. Such a view is, however, problematized in the Welsh context. An article in *Young Wales* in 1898 illustrates the point. 'Patriotism and the Women of Cymru', written by 'Un o'r ddau Wynne' (Mallt Williams), has been interpreted by Ursula Masson as reflecting the Cymru Fydd movement's drift away from radicalism and towards a more romantic and conservative phase.[23] Mallt Williams urges women to show their patriotism by rediscovering and passing on to their children the language, poetry, history and legends of Wales, and advocates the revival and preservation of spinning – preferably whilst wearing the Welsh costume![24] Any assessment of this article as purely reactionary is complicated, however, by Williams's comment about the importance of passing on the '*mother*-tongue' of Wales (the emphasis is in the original). Here the language is claimed as a matriarchal gift to be bestowed by women, thus elevating the status of motherhood in national terms.

The importance of the mother tends to be undermined by some western models of feminism which often dismiss calls for women to find their national role through motherhood as being reactionary and inhibiting (although, interestingly, New Women in the 1890s could often represent motherhood as a positive regenerative force). Significant strands of postcolonial feminism, however, while not ignoring the restrictions which may be imposed upon women expected to fulfil the role of conveyors of culture, often consider the passing of stories and language from mother to daughter as potentially opening up sites of 'contest [and] revolutionary struggle', where motherhood may incorporate anti-colonial resistance.[25] The idea that the domestic as opposed to the public sphere may constitute an important site of resistance is also recognized in studies of diasporic peoples, and home may become the only place where a subaltern culture may be transmitted.[26] Passing on an unofficial, 'native' language such as Welsh, at a time when parents were actively choosing *not* to pass on the language to their children, can be viewed as an explicit act of resistance to cultural imperialism.

To return to the romantic details of this utopian narrative, Gwen's allegorical function renders the question of her marriage of crucial importance, not only to female emancipation, but also to the state of the nation. Here the question is not so much what happens to her career after she marries, but *who* she marries. Since the novel is incomplete it is impossible to discuss the conclusion of the story, and yet there are a number of potential romantic and symbolic unions in the ten published chapters. Since 'Lady Gwen' is a highly derivative story, we may also draw on comparisons between the Welsh narrative and its sources to illuminate this discussion. The declared source for 'A Welsh Nationalist' is an 1889 novel by the ex-prime minister of New Zealand, Sir Julius Vogel, *Anno Domini 2000; or, Woman's Destiny*.[27] 'A Welsh Nationalist' follows Vogel in many aspects of plot – the war with America is acknowledged as lifted straight from Vogel – but the most appealing feature of Vogel's utopian novel was the vision of Imperial Federalism which offered, as 'A Welsh Nationalist' notes, a world order with all the benefits of autonomy without the need to sacrifice the advantages of empire.[28]

'A Welsh Nationalist' also follows Vogel closely in depicting the array of female politicians in 'Lady Gwen'. Gwen herself is modelled on Vogel's Hilda Fitzgerald, the young premier of New Zealand, but with one important difference. The romance plot of *Anno Domini 2000* is based on a love triangle between Hilda and the Emperor of Greater Britain – the two legitimate lovers – and the dastardly Lord Reginald. This latter not only kidnaps Hilda and tries to force her to marry him but also masterminds the treacherous plot by which Australia tries to leave the Empire. In thwarting Lord Reginald's treachery and marrying the Emperor, Hilda – or 'Zealandia' – affirms New Zealand's loyalty to the Empire. 'Lady Gwen' differs significantly from *Anno Domini 2000* in that the Emperor (who is also the King of England in the Welsh version) does not feature prominently at all, although a number of loyal toasts are made. Whether 'A Welsh Nationalist' intended to follow Vogel in marrying his heroine to this imperial monarch is impossible to tell, but although Wales is loyal to the Crown in this utopia, a similar union would obviously have more problematic implications for the Welsh story's primary aim of asserting the desirability of Welsh autonomy. Indeed, marrying outside the Welsh race (for it is described in such terms) is shown to be highly undesirable in this narrative. Roland's unrequited love is for Lucy Herbert, 'the daughter of a Denbighshire gentleman, from a family of English extraction, which had resided in Wales for generations'.²⁹ Gwen identifies her as thoroughly unsuitable for Roland in the following terms:

> She is essentially earthly and common-place, the fault, perhaps, of her Saxon blood. Roland is essentially Welsh. He has the soul of a Ceiriog or of a Dafydd ap Gwilym, and, unhappily, his imagination has transformed Lucy Herbert into a Myfanwy or a Morfudd.³⁰

It is hard to imagine, then, Gwen falling for the English king. Rather, the most appropriate romantic partners insinuated in the text are Sir Roland himself, or, perhaps more abstractly, the hero of Welsh Calvinism, Howel Harries. Both of these men are presented as great military heroes, religious patriots and, interestingly, enthusiastic imperialists. While the missing text prohibits any conclusive analysis of this novel, the allegorical nature of Gwen and the importance of asserting Welsh military valour, in the form of these two Christian soldiers, lead inevitably to the implied union of this feminine allegory of Wales with the balancing masculine valour of its founding father, Howel Harries, and his later 'incarnation' in Sir Roland. In one passionate speech, Gwen recalls the glories of the eighteenth century in Wales, describing a painting of Howel Harries who 'prays from the canvas, and who, though he wears a sword at his side, wears the features of a saint'.³¹ She links this image of the Christian soldier to an explicitly anti-colonial nationalism, as he shares the canvas with other Welsh soldiers who 'may soon have to meet the invading French'.³² Yet Gwen makes him the ardent champion of Empire, the hero of this future Wales and federal imperialism:

> Was not Howel Harries a soldier, and is he not also a canonised saint in our church. The age in which he lived witnessed the foundation of our colonial empire, and no man's heart beat more proudly than his when the news of the glorious victories which the genius of Lord Chatham had planned, reached our Cambrian shores. The ignorant critic has described Welsh Methodism as narrow and provincial. I tell you that Howel Harries was the first man who brought home to the children of Wales their privileges and duties as co-heirs with Englishmen of an Empire on which the sun never sets. When I say to-night of the British race and Empire, -
> > 'We sailed wherever ships might sail,
> > We founded many a mighty state,

Pray God our greatness may not fail
Through craven fears of being great,'-
I know I am saying nothing more than what the great Methodist preacher would have said had he been in your midst.[33]

Leaving aside the ambiguity of this imperialist vision, which seems to echo rather than refute late nineteenth-century jingoism, the point I want to emphasize is that in 'Lady Gwen' the only romantic connections which appear to be available to our female allegory are thoroughly masculine *Welsh* heroes. Far from 'marrying' an English king, as in the loyalist National Pageant of 1909, or looking outwards to find marital union with the federated Empire, as in Vogel's novel, in 'Lady Gwen' 'A Welsh Nationalist' looks into the Welsh past in 'his' imagining of a glorious military and imperial Welsh future.

It has been possible to look at only a small number of examples of the use in Wales of female allegories of nation, and there is scope for a much larger study. It would be interesting to look at representations of Wales-as-woman which originate from outside Wales and, perhaps more relevantly, to consider why there is a relative dearth of such images, in comparison to the numerous sketches of Erin, or Hibernia, which were used to depict Anglo–Irish relations. More importantly, perhaps, would be an extended study which considered Welsh national allegories, from Rebecca to the various personifications of Wales which appear in historical pageants well into the twentieth century, and discussed further their national, imperial and feminist significance.

Notes

My thanks to Tony Brown for his valuable comments on an earlier version of this essay.

[1] See Marina Warner, *Monuments and Maidens: The Allegory of the Female Form* (London: Vintage, 1996), pp. 250–1.

[2] See, for example, Siân Rhiannon Williams, 'The True "Cymraes": Images of Women in Women's Nineteenth-Century Welsh Periodicals', *Our Mothers' Land: Chapters in Welsh Women's History: 1830–1939*, ed. Angela V. John (Cardiff: University of Wales Press, 1991); Jane Aaron, 'Finding a Voice in Two Tongues: Gender and Colonization', *Our Sisters' Land: The Changing Identities of Women in Wales*, eds Jane Aaron, Teresa Rees, Sandra Bettes and Moira Vincentelli

(Cardiff: University of Wales Press, 1994); Gwyneth Tyson Roberts, *The Language of the Blue Books: The Perfect Instrument of Empire* (Cardiff: University of Wales Press, 1998); and, most recently, Harri Roberts, 'Embodying Identity: Class, Nation and Corporeality in the 1847 Blue Books Report', *North American Journal of Welsh Studies*, 3, 1 (Winter 2003), 1–22.

[3] Ruth Roach Pierson, 'Nations: Gendered, Racialized, Crossed With Empire', *Gendered Nations: Nationalisms and Gender Order in the Long Nineteenth Century*, eds Ida Blom, Karen Hagemann and Catherine Hall (Oxford: Berg, 2000), p. 47.

[4] Rodanthi Tzanelli has described how Greek mimicry (in Bhabha's sense) of British imperial discourse produced a forked dialogue, in which Greece played to a split audience of 'Britons and subjected Greeks': 'When addressed to the British, the Greek discourse would present the mother figure as a weak degraded creature. When addressed to the non-native Greeks of the Ottoman Empire, the very same maternal image would become the patron, which all the unredeemed Greeks ought to love and respect.' Tzanelli's descriptions of the two versions of Mother Greece presented to two very different audiences might perhaps offer a model for exploring the way in which Welsh allegories of nation could signify different things to different audiences. See her unpublished thesis 'The "Greece" of Britain and the "Britain" of Greece: Performance, Stereotypes, Expectations and Intermediaries in Victorian and Neohellenic Narratives, 1864–81', Lancaster University, 2002.

[5] See Hywel Teifi Edwards, *Codi'r Hen Wlad yn ei Hôl: 1850–1914* (Llandysul: Gomer, 1989).

[6] C. L. Innes, *Woman and Nation in Irish Literature and Society, 1880–1935* (London: Harvester Wheatsheaf, 1993), p. 48.

[7] G. P. Hawtrey and 'Owen Rhoscomyl', *National Pageant of Wales: Book of the Words*, Preliminary Edition (Cardiff: Western Mail, 1909), p. 2.

[8] Quoted in Edwards, *Codi'r Hen Wlad yn ei Hôl*, p. 256.

[9] Ibid., p. 56.

[10] Ibid., p. 54.

[11] The periodical was edited at this time by O. M. Edwards, who was responsible for the Welsh-language material, and Revd R. H. Morgan, who was responsible for the English language material. The title translates as *Future Wales: The Periodical of the National Party of Wales*.

[12] *Cymru Fydd*, 3, 6 (June 1890), 335–44 (335).

[13] Ibid., p. 344.

[14] Ibid., my emphasis.

[15] *Cymru Fydd*, 3, 7 (July 1890), 385–96 (385).

[16] *Cymru Fydd*, 4, 1 (January 1891), 28–40 (40).

[17] I am grateful to Jeni Williams for drawing my attention to Gwen's appearance.

[18] Ann Heilmann, *New Woman Fiction: Women Writing First-Wave Feminism* (London: Macmillan, 2000), p. 31.

[19] Warner, *Monuments and Maidens*, p. 66.

[20] Margaret Ward, 'National Liberation Movements and the Question of Women's Liberation: The Irish Experience', *Gender and Imperialism*, ed. Clare Midgely (Manchester: Manchester University Press, 1998), p. 106.

[21] Margaret Ward, quoting Belinda Loftus; ibid., p. 106.

[22] Ceridwen Lloyd-Morgan, 'From Temperance to Suffrage?', *Our Mothers' Land*, p. 148.

[23] Ursula Masson, 'Nationalism and Feminism: Women Liberals and Cymru

Fydd', Mamwlad/Motherland 2000 conference, Trinity College, Carmarthen, April 2000. On this subject see also Emyr W. Williams, 'Liberalism in Wales and the Politics of Welsh Home Rule 1886–1910', *The Bulletin of the Board of Celtic Studies*, eds Dellis Evans, J. Keverley Smith and Robin G. Livens, 37 (1990), 191–207, and Ursula Masson's essay, ' "Hand in Hand with the Women, Forward We will Go": Welsh Nationalism and Feminism in the 1890s', in *Women's History Review* (forthcoming).

[24] Mallt Williams (Un o'r Ddau Wynne), 'Patriotism and the Women of Cymru', *Young Wales*, 4, 5 (May 1898), 115.

[25] See, for example, Susheila Nasta (ed.), *Motherlands: Black Women's Writing from Africa, the Caribbean and South Asia* (London: The Women's Press, 1991).

[26] See bell hooks, *Yearning: Race, Gender and Cultural Politics* (London: Turnaround, 1991).

[27] Although Vogel's novel was not the great popular success the author and publisher had hoped for, it has since gained prominence in New Zealand as a radical feminist text and also for its surprisingly accurate prophecies of technological development. For more information, see entries on 'Science fiction', 'Utopianism', 'Vogel, Julius' and 'Women's Suffrage' in the *Oxford Companion to New Zealand Literature* (Auckland: Oxford University Press, 1998); and see Lawrence Jones, 'The Novel', *Oxford History of New Zealand Literature in English*, ed. Terry Sturm, 2nd edn ([1988] Auckland: Oxford University Press, 1991). See also Roger Robinson's introductions to Vogel's novel, in editions from Exisle Press, Auckland, 2000, and University of Hawai'i, 2002.

[28] This aspect of 'Lady Gwen' is discussed further in the special edition of *Journal of New Zealand Literature: NZ in UK*, 21 (2003), 140–6, in an article co-authored by myself and Roger Robinson entitled 'Vogel in Wales: *Anno Domini 2000*, "Lady Gwen" and the Federated Empire'. It is also discussed in Bohata, *Postcolonialism Revisited: Writing Wales in English* (Cardiff: University of Wales Press, 2004).

[29] *Cymru Fydd*, 3, 9 (September 1890), 529–36 (531).

[30] Ibid.

[31] *Cymru Fydd*, 4, 3 (March 1891), 171–83 (173).

[32] Interestingly, Lady Gwen reinforces gender boundaries by retaining military valour as a male domain; thus the Fishguard Invasion is repelled by male Christian soldiers, and the legend of local women scaring off the invaders by using their red petticoats or mantles to mimic soldiers' red coats is ignored. My thanks to Jeni Williams for pointing this out.

[33] *Cymru Fydd*, 4, 3 (March 1891), 173–4.

7

'There's a change come over the valley': The Crisis of Masculinism in Early Twentieth-century Welsh Drama in English

ALYCE VON ROTHKIRCH

This chapter is partly a response to and a dialogue with M. Wynn Thomas's essay 'All Change: The New Welsh Drama before the Great War'.[1] It is also written in acknowledgement of the great influence which that particular essay and – later – many more pieces by M. Wynn Thomas had on me. Indeed, it may be said that 'All Change' effected one of the most important 'changes' in my own life, namely my tearing up a letter to him, in which I had wanted to ask for more information about early Welsh drama in English, and writing a proposal for a Ph.D. thesis instead – with him as my supervisor.

M. Wynn Thomas argues in 'All Change' that the development of Welsh writing in English might have been different if J. O. Francis's work had been taken as its beginning, rather than the controversial work of Caradoc Evans.[2] This is certainly true, and it would also have meant that drama would have been at the heart of a canon of Welsh writing that today is – in my personal, highly biased opinion – dominated by poetry and novel-writing to the detriment of other forms, like drama, the short story or the essay. However, this is not another instalment in the never-ending debate about the (lack of) status of drama in Wales. Instead, I want to re-engage with the play which M. Wynn Thomas places at the centre of a new canon of Welsh writing in English: J. O. Francis's *Change* (1912). This chapter argues that it is useful to read the conflict within the family portrayed in *Change* in terms of a 'crisis of masculinism'. *Change* is compared with two plays written in the late 1930s: Jack Jones's *Land of My Fathers* (1937) and E. Eynon Evans's *Cold Coal* (1939). It is argued that, by the end of the 1930s, the 'crisis of masculinism' had reached pathological levels, as the change in economic and social circumstances had not resulted in a change of prevalent notions of how 'masculinity' was to be defined.

The concept of a 'crisis' with regard to the gender constructions called 'masculinities' is controversial, of course. R. W. Connell argues that

> [a]s a theoretical term, 'crisis' presupposes a coherent system of some kind, which is destroyed or restored by the outcome of the crisis. Masculinity... is not a system in that sense. It is, rather, a configuration of practice *within* a system of gender relations. We cannot logically speak of the crisis of a configuration; rather we might speak of its disruption or its transformation.[3]

Masculinities as such cannot be in 'crisis', although different masculinities may be in competition with femininities or with other masculinities. However, it is not masculinities per se I am concerned with here. Indeed, one cannot discuss masculinities without taking the power relations not only between the genders but between competing masculinities into account. Thus, it is the hegemonic masculinity – the ideology of the most powerful masculinity – which Arthur Brittan has termed 'masculinism' that I am interested in, for it is 'masculinism' and its increasing failure to represent the reality of Welsh men in the beginning of the twentieth century that forms the subtext of the plays under discussion.[4] The plays document the painful processes through which an older generation of men realize that their sons are not following their example, and through which the younger generation struggle and fail to generate a new set of hegemonic masculinities to which they can aspire.[5]

J. O. Francis's play *Change* was written in 1912 and won the Howard de Walden prize – an award for a play of national importance which was meant to encourage professional playwriting in Wales – in the same year.[6] It is a play which, put simply, deals with the destruction of a south Walian family as the parent generation fail to realize how social and personal changes have caused their children to be considerably different from themselves.

Change was to prove remarkably prescient in the way it addressed the great social upheavals that were to engulf south Wales, for the Edwardian period was, according to D. Gareth Evans, still relatively prosperous.[7] Even though the play remains vague about the exact nature of the cause and effect of the changes he describes, Francis successfully charts the demise of the hegemonic image of the classless male Welsh identity, embodied in the *gwerin* ideology,[8] and the helplessness of the younger generation who do not succeed in carving out a new masculine identity for themselves.

What does this hegemonic masculinity consist of? As in most traditional realist drama, the characters of the play are characterized by the stage-setting, and nothing could better illustrate the father generation's world-view than the furnishings of John Price's living room.[9] The room exudes an air of faded respectability – 'the furniture is humbly serviceable, and has seen long usage'.[10] A Welsh dresser occupies a central position and on

> the lowest shelf stands a row of well-worn books, and two small bookshelves, well-stocked, hang on each side of the dresser . . . At the back, one on each side of the dresser, are pictures of Gladstone and C. H. Spurgeon. In other places are pictures of Henry Richard and some of the well-known Welsh preachers.
>
> (*Change*, 8)

This is the home of a man who is clearly meant to be an urban representative of that often-described Welsh phenomenon, the *gwerin* (see Hywel Teifi Edwards in this volume). Gwyn A. Williams has given one of the most comprehensive descriptions of the *gwerin*:

> The *gwerin* was a cultivated, educated, often self-educated, responsible, self-disciplined, respectable but on the whole genially poor or perhaps small-propertied people, straddling groups perceived as classes in other, less fortunate societies. Welsh-speaking, Nonconformist, imbued with the more social virtues of dissent, bred on the Bible and good practice, it was open to the more spiritual forms of a wider culture and was dedicated to spiritual self-improvement . . . The *gwerin* deeply respected learning . . . [11]

This ideal citizenry – and it is described in such terms by Williams – came into being partly as a result of the respectable Welsh middle-class's response to the 'outrage of the Blue Books' (described in this volume by Kirsti Bohata) and in part as an expression of Welsh Victorianism, although its roots go back further.[12] John Price is signified as belonging to the *gwerin* because he values learning, as his small library of well-thumbed books suggests, although he is not well-educated himself (*Change*, 10).[13] He is a man who works hard for his family: even though his first-born son, Lewis, has followed him into the mine, he has managed to send his second son, John Henry, to university to study for the ministry, he can afford to send his ailing third son, Gwilym, to Australia and he employs their 'poor relation', Lizzie Ann, as a maid. Yet, he is also a man who is very conscious of the many sacrifices he made, and this knowledge has made him demanding and not just a little hard towards his sons. He is also a man whose Nonconformist belief tends towards the dogmatic, and the arrival of the so-called 'new theology' in south Wales is greeted by him with derisory criticism (*Change*, 29).[14] His criticism of the labour movement and trade unionism is equally scathing – being a Nonconformist Liberal, he does not understand society in terms of class, as his firebrand son Lewis does, but in terms of individual responsibility before God (13). It emerges in the opening scene of the play that John Price is a more or less exact copy of his father, described by Gwen as 'a hard man' and by John as 'a respectable, God-fearing man, [who] died without anyone being able to say he owed so much as a ha'penny' (14). While his *gwerin* values have served his father and himself well, the play argues that his sons cannot create an identity for themselves out of the same ingredients.

The play is constructed as a tragedy and thus every act brings a new blow to the family, which, in the end shatters to smithereens. Firstly, John Henry arrives back from university in Cardiff. He has given up studying for the ministry because his belief 'just slipped away . . . It seemed so easy up here in Aberpandy after the Revival' (45). The emotional frenzy the revival had provoked seems to have rapidly disappeared in the metropolitan atmosphere of Cardiff, where the chapel boy was introduced to new books, plays and concerts. John Henry's faith probably never went very deep and thus did not withstand any serious intellectual probing. John Price, however, sees John Henry's very painful loss of faith as an act of wilful rebellion against the foundations of his way of life and, thus, against himself and his authority over his sons. Unable to accept that the hegemonic masculinity – which for him and his father had been indissolubly bound up with a rigid, dogmatic Nonconformism –

cannot provide the same basis for values, meaning and identity for his son, he pushes him away: 'if my eye offends me, I can pluck it out' (68).[15] John Henry, an essentially weak character, retaliates by acting in direct opposition to Nonconformist conceptions of respectability: he goes to London with a male-voice choir and stays there to find a job on the stage. While probably effective in causing a maximum of pain to his father (and mother), John Henry's actions can hardly be said to constitute the beginnings of the forging of a new identity.

His elder brother is more open about his rebellion. Unlike John Henry, Lewis left school early to go to work in the mine. However, he continued in education and has presumably attended classes at a local miners' institute – classes which were quite often organized by the Workers' Educational Association or other organizations, like the South Wales Miners' Federation. It is never explained where his political convictions come from but it is quite likely that his political outlook was formed at work and at the night-classes he attended. Steeped in the certainties of his Communist 'belief', he openly challenges his father's political opinions, telling him and Isaac Pugh, a family friend: 'Labour and Capital are at grips, always, always! . . . And you're not in the fighting line. You're prisoners of the past' (33–4). Price is essentially powerless against his son's eloquence and his call of 'I won't have this ungodliness in my house' (35) is feeble at best. He wrestles back control over his unruly son, however, when his youngest son Gwilym dies in unfortunate circumstances when a strike turns into a riot, by calling him Cain – the biblical son who killed his innocent brother, Abel.[16] It is a measure of Lewis's feelings of deep guilt that he accepts the label for himself and leaves the house a broken man. However, beyond the human drama lies the tug-of-war of two political creeds: Liberalism against the labour movement. Both John Price and Lewis embody the political identities of their respective generations, but neither can see it as such. John Price is all the more bitter because he instinctively knows that his time has gone, as his failure to engage with any of Lewis's arguments shows. However, while his side is clearly winning (49), Lewis personally is unhappy. Underlining the essentially humanist, non-partisan message of the play, Lewis realizes that he chose to be active politically primarily because he wanted the power that went with it (125–6). Socialism is not shown as a movement on which the young generation can build its identity.

M. Wynn Thomas has interpreted the death of the poet with the weak bodily frame, the clear-sighted third son Gwilym, as sacrificial.[17] What is being sacrificed is, amongst other things, the hope for a reconciliation between the generations. Gwilym's role as the peacemaker in the family suggests that Francis advocates compromise and the reconciliation of old and new values as the basis for a new identity – however, Gwilym's fate in the play shows that Francis does not believe that the Gwilyms of this world stand much of a chance in the new Wales. That he fails to create a character based on a radically new concept of masculinity, one that is not based on what has been named 'traditional' masculinity,[18] should not, maybe, come as a surprise, given his political convictions.[19] What is more surprising is the consistent failure of new generations of playwrights to engage in the imagining of a new masculine ideology.

I would now like to look at two plays which have been neglected in both the teaching of and the research into Welsh drama in English: Jack Jones's *Land of My Fathers* (1937) and E. Eynon Evans's *Cold Coal* (1939).[20] They are both coalfield dramas written in the late 1930s and they show how the crisis of masculinity has deepened without a hope of a change for the better. The 'traditional' hegemonic masculinity that had been based on *gwerin* values had, in the manner of patriarchal ideologies everywhere, gained a large part of its real power from its dominance in the world of work: even though the means of production might not have belonged to the *gwerin*-miner, his 'identity revolve[d] around notions of the traditional breadwinner, [and around] the assumption of mature adult responsibilities in terms of a wife and children, the settling-down into respectability, duty and security'.[21] In many ways the extreme separation of male and female spheres in the mining communities only reinforced this dominance, and a miner like John Price would have taken pride in this characterization. However, as Applebee points out in a different context: 'The departure of "work" from "working class" communities has affected not only the local economy but also the culture of family and society.'[22] With the ever-deepening economic depression, the 'breadwinner ethos' became obsolete as more and more men became dependent on the dole and as more and more women entered employment.[23] The two plays under discussion reinforce the notion that no new hegemonic masculinity had been forged and that the men were left stranded, without role-models and without self-respect.

Evan Eynon Evans was born in Glamorgan in the beginning of the twentieth century. He had a lower-middle class background and wrote numerous comedies, mainly for amateur theatre. He became a professional playwright in the 1940s and had some success on the London stage – even though his drama always remained connected to south Wales. *Cold Coal* is his only tragedy and it is in many ways remarkably similar to Francis's *Change*. In *Cold Coal*, too, the most sensitive and likeable character, who also happens to be a poet, dies in tragic circumstances – however, here the younger son, Wensley, dies in a colliery disaster, and the incident is not the pivotal structural element it had been in *Change*. Wensley's tragic death is merely a further blow to a family which has already suffered much. Indeed, the play is best summarized as a tale of the suffering that prolonged unemployment brings to a family.

The play focuses on the bitterness and despair of the young generation. The young generation is represented by the eldest son, David, and his friend, Arthur Davies, fiancé to the daughter of the house, who have both been unemployed for more than three years. Contrary to Wensley, who is in line for promotion and who neglects his fiancée for the sake of attaining it, it is as if the lives of the other young men have been put on hold, as if they are prevented from living. Mair, whose marriage to Arthur has been postponed for those three years, voices the bitterness of the young generation thus:

> MAIR . . . Getting a job is a matter of unlimited patience, persistence, perhaps a little influence, indifference to the hopes and feelings of other job-seekers, and a good deal of what people call luck. The job-seeker must have no pride, forget that he is a man or that he has the right to do anything but beg.
>
> (*Cold Coal*, 9)

Mair describes how the unemployed man loses his dignity, his pride and, crucially, his 'self', as work is a crucial element of 'traditional' hegemonic masculinity. In Mair's words, he does not get a 'chance to become responsible' (13) and to grow up to become a real man. Indeed, Evans is not the only playwright to describe the unemployed as men who are prevented from growing up. Jack Jones uses the same metaphor in *Land of My Fathers*. In the play, Jones, who is more famous for his novels (for example, *Rhondda Roundabout*, 1934, or *Bidden to the Feast*, 1938) and who is one of the few writers of Welsh plays in English from a working-class background, describes the ups and downs of the Huws family who live in 'a Heartbreak Valley' which has been depressed for many years. Written in the style of what Dic Edwards would later disparagingly call 'slice-of-life' drama,[24] the play does not have much plot to speak of and can be imagined as continuing indefinitely, as a kind of soap opera of 1930s Valleys' life: the play does not so much end as simply stop after three acts, and one half expects to go back to the theatre in the following week to see the next instalment. However, the analysis of society in the microcosm of an extended family is perhaps more complex than this characterization would give the play credit for. The Huws family consists of the grandfather Howell Rees, Will Huws and Mari Huws, their five children Lemuel, Frank, Jack, Gwen and Ike, their respective partners and the children's aunt Marged Huws and her husband Dai. All the men except Frank, who is a teacher, and Ike, who is in the army, have been unemployed for years. And, as in Evans's play, the most important characteristic of the unemployed young men, Lemuel and Jack, is that they have not grown up to accept responsibility for themselves and their actions. Jack is a Communist agitator who, in the course of the play, is caught by the police and imprisoned for six months. Prison only hardens his convictions, and, with the unconcern of the true fanatic, he walks all over his family in the pursuit of 'class consciousness' (*Land of My Fathers*, 76ff. *passim*). However, he is very dependent on his family: he does not seriously consider moving out and patently cannot exist without the ministrations of his long-suffering mother ('It would be just your price if you were all left to the mercy of capitalism – A clean collar mam?', 90). Lemuel's case is even more striking. He is the eldest son and '*very, very fat. The years of unemployment have aided his happy-go-lucky disposition to produce a Falstaffian figure which strains at a cheap blue-serge suit*' (21). He cuts a ridiculous figure; he gambles, drinks and dotes on his racing greyhound, Gyp, but 'forgets' to pay towards the child he has with Katie, and ignores her pleas to marry her and take the stigma of the unmarried mother off her. He is unwilling and unable to accept any responsibility for his actions: when his mother finds out that he has been withholding the baby's money for nine weeks – money that she has given him to give to Katie – he can only hang his head and cry (25). 'Childish' is the adjective most often used to characterize Lemuel, and his behaviour alternates between the childishly clever and devious and the childishly pathetic. But his brother Frank remembers the time when Lemuel had gone into the pit every day with Will and Dai, when he was working extra hard to enable Frank to go to secondary school and then university, in the days before 'the rot set in' (42). In *Cold Coal*, too, the idea of unemployment as a 'rotting away' of a man's sense of self-worth is voiced by David, who, after a particularly frustrating day of pushing his bike up and down the country in search of work, concludes that he will give up looking for a job because he is 'fed up with the hunting and the hoping, the creeping and the cringing'. But of course an existence on the dole is just as bad and he concludes that 'if this wave of prosperity eventually arrives, let them come back and look for me and they'll find me – find me damn well rotted' (*Cold Coal*, 21).

Another recurring image is, as mentioned above, the one of young people unable to get married because they lack the money to establish their own household. In *Land of My Fathers*, this means not only that Lemuel cannot get married to Katie, but that Frank cannot get married to Olwen. Both Frank and Olwen are in full-time employment and it is the money they contribute to the upkeep of their respective families that keeps the 'means-test man' away. Setting up their own household would mean subjecting their families to the indignity of having an official looking at the family's finances – an indignity that Marged describes in these terms: 'it's rotten for a man like my Dai to have to sit recitin' his poverty about once a month before the likes o' them chaps' (18). Furthermore, in both plays the long wait leads to considerable (sexual) frustration and, maybe inevitably, to children conceived out of wedlock, considerably heightening the sense of desperation. In *Cold Coal*, Mari's increasing bitterness becomes understandable when she reveals that she is pregnant. This also explains Arthur's otherwise inexplicable decision to become a 'blackleg', a strike-breaker. Not feeling that he is able to tell the family of his desperate need to have money quickly in order to get married, he has a vicious argument with David:

ARTHUR . . . What I am going to sell is my labour, the strength of my hands and the will to work . . .

DAVID   No, you sell your soul, you sell your right to look another man in the face, your right to equality with another man who has strength and labour to sell and the will to work. You sell your self-respect, you become a robber of rights and privileges. In other words, a blackleg, a damned blackleg...

ARTHUR All right, a damned blackleg. Well, I would rather be a blackleg than a damned parasite!

(*Cold Coal*, 61)

The word 'parasite' stings badly. Furthermore, the general loss of what might be described as 'standards' – not getting up early in the morning, not taking care of one's personal appearance, and a general inertia of body and mind – described in both plays, added to David's disappointment in himself, also contributes to his decision to turn blackleg too. Indeed, his father understands his motivations clearly:

JOHN   ... David knows he is doing wrong, knows it as well as I do. He has become bitter, he is getting his own back, a kind of revenge against circumstance. He can't think clearly about the harm he is doing, because he is blinded by the harm that has been done to him.

(*Cold Coal*, 72)

David becomes a 'blackleg' out of a perverse desire to get back at a society which has robbed him of the chance to be the responsible, grown-up man the hegemonic masculinity demands him to be. Indeed, it is the very impossibility of living up to this ideal that sets him up as a rebel against his former beliefs.

The older generation of men can only watch helplessly. Will Huw is unemployed and John Llewellyn becomes unemployed in the course of *Cold Coal*, but they never lose their sense of self or their vigour. They belong to the industrial brothers of the *gwerin*: Nonconformist and apparently without political convictions, they feel strongly about issues of solidarity with their fellow men – a solidarity based not necessarily on class but on a code of decency and personal responsibility.[25] They do not give in to circumstances: Will goes to the slag heap to fetch coal every few days (his sons do not even think of helping him) and John believes that 'using [your] leisure to good purpose' will keep men alert and ready for work when 'the change comes' (*Cold Coal*, 35). The crucial difference is that they have been able to live up to the ideal of 'traditional' masculinity for most of their lives, whereas the young men have had to come to terms with, in David's words, 'the fact that [they are] not wanted, that [they are] redundant, that there is no place for [them] in the scheme of things' (34).

Both plays end without resolutions to the problem of masculinities. In *Cold Coal* John Llewellyn is left with the agony of seeing his children turn their backs on a way of life he believes in without having a future they can face (87). By contrast, *Land of my Fathers* ends on a positive note. The young people get married, even in the face of poverty, and – deus ex machina-like – the news of new employment opportunities is made public in the final scene of the play. Suddenly Dai and Lemuel sound a bit like their former selves – Dai to the extent that he even manages to be 'masterful' towards his chatty wife, Marged. Thus even the prospect of work leads to a certain reassertion of traditional power-structures within patriarchal society (*Land of My Fathers*, 109). A new spirit of optimism lightens the mood in the family and Will speaks for all when he says that 'it'll be a joyful resurrection after years of living death' (110).

R. W. Connell points out that '[t]o recognize gender as a social pattern requires us to see it as a product of history and also as a *producer* of history'.[26] It is a tribute to the power of the 'traditional' masculinity as hegemonic ideology, which, in Wales, had for a long time taken the form of the male *gwerin*, that, after the ideology had ceased to be productive, consecutive generations of men (and women) failed to change this ideology to one which could accommodate the social and economic changes of the twentieth century. The realistic plays I have discussed above are testimony to the staying power of an outdated masculinism and the pathological consequences this has had for young men and women – an ideology which, in many parts of Wales, still exists, even though it was shown to have failed all those years ago.

Notes

[1] M. Wynn Thomas, 'All Change: The New Welsh Drama Before the Great War', *Internal Difference: Literature in 20th Century Wales* (Cardiff: University of Wales Press, 1992), pp. 1–24 (1).

[2] Thomas, 'All Change', p. 1. See Hywel Teifi Edwards on Caradoc Evans in this volume.

[3] R. W. Connell. 'The Social Organisation of Masculinity', *The Masculinities Reader*, eds Stephen M. Whitehead and Frank J. Barrett (Cambridge: Polity, 2001), pp. 30–52 (45).

[4] Arthur Brittan, *Masculinity and Power* (London: Blackwell, 1989), p. 4.

[5] The 'crisis' of male identities described here is, of course, accompanied by a similar upheaval in female gender constructions. However, in this chapter I will concentrate solely on the changes in masculine gender identities. For an excellent introduction to feminine Welsh identities see Jane Aaron, 'Women in Search of a Welsh Identity', *Hard Times*, 63, available at *http://www.erzwiss.unihamburg.de/sonstiges/hardtimes/63Aaron.htm*. See also Deirdre Beddoe, 'Images of Welsh Women', *Wales: The Imagined Nation. Studies in Cultural and National Identity*, ed. Tony Curtis (Bridgend: Poetry Wales, 1986), pp. 225–38.

[6] Angela M. Coyne, 'The Growth of Drama in the Early Twentieth Century in Wales and the Work of J. O. Francis', unpub. MA dissertation (Swansea: University of Wales Swansea, 1991), p. 3.

[7] D. Gareth Evans, *A History of Wales, 1906–2000* (Cardiff: University of Wales Press, 2000), p. 9.

[8] My definition of 'ideology' is based on Hansjörg Bay's definition. He argues that an ideology is a coherent series of images and narratives which help the individual shape his or her identity. Only when ideology ceases to be productive and enabling does it become as negative and limiting as the popular understanding of the word 'ideology' suggests; 'Erzählpanzer: Überlegungen zu Ideologie und Erfahrung', *Ideologie nach Ihrem 'Ende': Gesellschaftskritik zwischen Marxismus und Postmoderne*, eds Hansjörg Bay and Christof Hamann (Opladen: Westdeutscher Verlag, 1995), pp. 17–41.

[9] See Manfred Pfister, *Das Drama: Theorie und Analyse* (9th edn, München: Fink, 1997), p. 348.

[10] J. O. Francis, *Change: A Glamorgan Play in Four Acts* (4th edn, London and New York: Samuel French; Cardiff: The Educational Publishing Co., n.d.), p. 7. Hereafter referenced as *Change*.

[11] Gwyn A. Williams, *When was Wales? A History of the Welsh* ([1985] Harmondsworth: Penguin, 1991), p. 237.

[12] See the rich literature on the *gwerin*, for example, Frank Price Jones, 'The Gwerin of Wales', *Studies in Folk Life: Essays in Honour of Iorwerth C. Peate*, ed. Geraint Jenkins (London: Routledge & Kegan Paul, 1969), pp. 1–13; or, less uncritically celebratory, Prys Morgan, 'The Gwerin of Wales – Myth and Reality', *The Welsh and their Country: Selected Readings in the Social Sciences*, eds Ian Hume and W. T. R. Pryce (Llandysul: Gomer, 1986), pp. 134–52.

[13] His son Gwilym sees him as such: 'He belongs to the old valley. At heart he is of the agricultural class – slow, stolid, and conservative' (*Change*, 50). The *gwerin* were largely associated with rural Wales, although the ideology did transplant to the industrial centres of Wales to an extent (see Williams, *When was Wales?*, p. 239).

[14] The new theology tried to appeal to groups estranged from the largely middle-class, Liberal Nonconformism. The movement gained influence from *c.*1907 and one of its most vocal supporters was the Reverend R. J. Campbell, whose book *The New Theology* was published in 1907. Campbell was a supporter of socialism and a close personal friend of Keir Hardie. See Evans, *A History of Wales*, p. 39.

Masculinism in Early Twentieth-century Welsh Drama in English   83

[15] John Price's faith is clearly based on tradition rather than close reading of the Bible, for he misunderstands Mark 9: 1 to mean 'if one part of me is diseased I will cut it off to prevent other parts of me from becoming diseased'. The full quotation reads, however, 'if your eye *causes you to sin*, pluck it out; it is better for you to enter the kingdom of God with one eye than with two eyes to be thrown into hell' (Bible, Standard Revised Version. Italics added). The misquotation is crucial, for John Price uses it to exonerate himself when he, in fact, is meant to reflect on the way he himself is sinning.

[16] On the historical basis for the strike and its symbolic value for the plot see Thomas, 'All Change', p. 15.

[17] Ibid., p. 20.

[18] David H. J. Morgan, 'Family, Gender and Masculinities', *The Masculinities Reader*, eds Whitehead and Barrett, pp. 223-32 (226).

[19] Thomas, 'All Change', p. 14.

[20] E. Eynon Evans, *Cold Coal: A Drama of Welsh Life* (London: Samuel French, 1939), hereafter referenced in the text as *Cold Coal*, and Jack Jones, *Land of My Fathers* (London: Samuel French, 1937), hereafter referenced in the text as *Land of My Fathers*.

[21] Morgan, 'Family, Gender and Masculinities'.

[22] Elaine Applebee, 'Inclusive Learning – A Community Approach', North of England Education Conference, Bradford, 5-7 January 1998 (n.p.).

[23] This is not to say that women had not always made up a certain percentage of the workforce. However, women generally expected to stop working (or be sacked) once they got married. This started to change only with the outbreak of the two world wars. See Angela V. John (ed.), *Our Mothers' Land: Chapters in Welsh Women's History 1830-1939* (Cardiff: University of Wales Press, 1991).

[24] Dic Edwards, 'A Dereliction of Duty', interview with Hazel Walford Davies, *State of Play: Four Playwrights of Wales*, ed. Hazel Walford Davies (Llandysul: Gomer, 1998), pp. 82-7 (82).

[25] The exception to this rule is Dai Huws, who has gone the way of Lemuel.

[26] Connell, 'Social Organization', p. 42. Italics in original.

8
Valleys' Women Writing

JANE AARON

One unexpected finding apparently to be extracted from the 2001 Census data is that between 1991 and 2001 more people left the south Wales Valleys, particularly the Merthyr Tydfil area, than has hitherto been supposed. Taking the history of the Valleys in the twentieth century as a whole into consideration, though, the greater wonder must always be that so many people have remained for so long in this part of Wales. From 1926 on, the gradual decline of heavy industry left industrial south Wales a 'problem' area, with its social life first created, then to all intents and purposes destroyed by the history of capital in the region, its initial profitability and then its decline. A distinguished heritage of men's writing, like the poetry of Huw Menai and Idris Davies, and the novels of Lewis Jones, Rhys Davies, Glyn Jones, Gwyn Jones, Gwyn Thomas and the Welsh-language writer Rhydwen Williams, virtually all of them today out of print, provides an authentic record of the political struggles and achievements of the Valleys' people, of the sufferings they endured during the long period of industrial depression and of the emigration of many of their numbers. But nowhere does this body of writing adequately explain why so many people did in fact stay in the area, when for so many decades hopes of gaining profitable employment there had faded, why the Valleys did not become one vast ghost township, suffering the same fate as the ghost villages of the lead-mining industry in mid-Wales, left deserted a century or so earlier. The social and cultural, as well as economic, growth of the Valleys is very insistently tied up in these literary records with its industrial growth: it is the patterns of human relationship established by the heavy industries which create the area's politics and its leisure activities, the socialism, trade unionism, male-voice choirs and rugby loyalties which play so enduring a role in the image of Valleys' communities. And yet these communities and their culture did not pass away with the closure of the industries which created them. They survived. Why?

That question appears to be about as perplexing as the problem which occupied the mind of a Valleys' woman writer some thirty years ago. Elaine Morgan, born in Pontypridd in 1920, published in 1972 her answer to the question of why a certain species of the hairy ape evolved into the hairless early human, walking upright, by focusing on female, rather than male, experience. Her book, *The Descent of Woman*, famously took as its central premise the disputed hypothesis, initially put forward by Sir Alister Hardy in 1960, that the ape had undergone an era of aquatic life, of living in water, as it evolved into the human. But we do not have to accept the hypothesis of the aquatic ape to find many of the original solutions produced by Elaine Morgan to the details of human evolution convincing. Take, for example, her account of the development of the female bosom in humans as opposed to flat-chested female apes. According to earlier evolutionists like Desmond Morris, who had considered the question solely from the point of view of the male, females developed breasts in order to retain their appeal to the male after the evolution of man the hunter, and the subsequent need for every male, and not just the dominant male of the pack, to be equally motivated for the hunt by the offered reward of a woman. Hence pair-bonding developed, and the personalizing of sex, face to face now, and in need of greater female attractiveness to the front than the physiognomy of the ape had to offer. But as Elaine Morgan says, '[s]urely, if you are considering a process as strictly functional as lactation, and you notice a modification in the arrangements for it, it would be reasonable to think about the primary beneficiary of the process – namely, the baby – rather than trying to relate it to the child's father's occupation'.[1] The baby of a hairy ape could cling to its mother's flat chest by gripping on to her hair while it sucked from the nipple. But once the human anthropoid had lost her chest hair (as, of course, she must at some stage have done, whether or not we believe in the aquatic explanation), in order to suckle comfortably, at rest in its mother's lap, the baby needed the nipple brought lower and it needed something to hold on to, 'a lump of something less bony, something pliant and of a convenient size for small hands to grab hold of'. And since the baby is what evolution is all about, what it needed, Elaine Morgan says, is what it ultimately got – the female breast, which only afterwards became an object of sex appeal. This makes good sense, along with many other explanations like it in *The Descent of Woman*.

It would appear that solutions to some of the mysteries of evolution can indeed convincingly be posited by attending to the experience of women and the relations of reproduction, as opposed to concentrating purely on men and the relations created by changing processes of material production. Encouraged by Elaine Morgan's audacious example, then, we may ask ourselves whether similar solutions cannot be found to the puzzle of why the communities of the south Wales Valleys endured after the demise of those industries which had brought them into being, by focusing on female rather than male experience.

From the literary critic's point of view, one obstacle to this investigation presents itself in the fact that, compared to men, Valleys' women writers are few and far between. It cannot be denied that the heavily polarized nature of the roles the two genders were forced to play out in the Valleys' communities was not conducive to women becoming writers. As Deirdre Beddoe has recently reminded us in her volume on twentieth-century Welsh women, *Out of the Shadows*, the human cost of maintaining the late nineteenth- and early twentieth-century industrial communities of Wales fell particularly heavily upon the shoulders of the womenfolk.[2] Valleys' women were the essential and overworked servants of the industrial machine, as they struggled to rear and maintain healthy manpower in the overcrowded and unsanitary terraces. Life expectancy was lower for women than men in the Valleys, for all the health hazards of the men's employment; women died earlier, worn to the bone by childbirth and the incessant effort to maintain standards of hygiene before the establishment of pit-baths or domestic-water supply.[3] And women's exclusion from the paid workforce of the heavy industries, and their marginality within the labour movement which fuelled much of the creative cultural activity of the period, made it difficult for them to imagine themselves as suitable spokespersons for their communities. It is not surprising, therefore, that few Valleys' women had the leisure or the self-confidence necessary to become authors, and that some of those who did were amongst the migrants who moved away from the area.

When I was hunting for stories by Welsh women, published before 1950, for a short-story collection, I was pleased to find two good tales located in the south Wales Valleys, Rhian Roberts's 'The Pattern' and Dilys Rowe's 'A View across the Valley', the second of which gave my collection its title. But I had difficulty finding out much about these two writers because, as it transpired, both of them had long since left not only Wales but also the UK. Rhian Roberts, born in Abercynon in the 1920s, the daughter of a coalminer, published a few stories located in the Valleys in the early 1940s, but then emigrated to Ontario to work as a teacher before marrying and settling in New Mexico. Dilys Rowe was born in 1927 in Landore, an industrial village in the Swansea valley, her father a clerk in the local steelworks. In her early twenties, she moved to London to work as a journalist (she was the editor of the *Observer*'s women's page in the 1960s) before finally settling in the south of France. Why such women left is explained, perhaps, in the story 'A View across the Valley'. In it an unnamed thirteen-year-old girl escapes on a blazingly hot afternoon from the claustrophobia of her tight-packed Valleys' town to the surrounding hills to brood on the industrial scene below her:

> The valley had life as a wound has microbes . . . She was high above it where woods had been, where there was nothing to wreck . . . but sometimes a piece of slag would have the print of a fern stamped deep into it . . . When it was two o'clock the hooter sounding between hills sent packs of soiled and sweating men moving through the valley . . . The girl was dappled in sunshine and hatred for wilful destruction.[4]

She is in search of an alternative perspective of her own on the steelworks, the dirty canal, the slag-heaps, the chapels and the terraced streets which make up her world. And she finds it, but at the cost of her life, as the sun ignites a circle of fire about her on the scrubby hillside. In a sense, both Dilys Rowe and Rhian Roberts could be said to have escaped the Valleys at the cost of their creative lives, in that neither developed careers as creative writers after they left Wales, though their early stories located in the Valleys show much promise.

But what of those who did remain, like, for example, Elaine Morgan herself, now living in Mountain Ash? In her 'Prologue' to the volume *Struggle or Starve: Women's Lives in the South Wales Valleys between the Two World Wars*, Elaine Morgan suggests one possible solution to the puzzle of why, after their industrial decline, the Valleys' communities survived. She refers to the mythic figure of the Welsh Mam and asserts that for her that icon was no romance but a reality, in the shape of her own mother, Olive:

> I have sometimes been asked whether the traditional picture of the Welsh Mam – the backbone of her family, the peace-keeper, the self-sacrificer, the tower of strength – was just a romantic myth. I don't think so. Olive's own mother was certainly no role model but she had a better one in her Welsh mother-in-law who was all of those things – and Olive followed her example. My childhood memories of a household of four adults and a child, run on two dole packets, are of a life of comfort and ease and harmony . . . She was the strongest character in the household, and within those four walls could have got her way over anything she set her heart on; but what she had set her heart on was keeping the peace.[5]

A character who can create 'a life of comfort and ease and harmony' for the inhabitants of a household, without one wage-packet coming into it, is clearly not going to be defeated by the absence of work in the neighbourhood. It is precisely in that absence that her strengths really come to the fore.

Historians seeking to delineate the social and historical processes which went to construct such strong female personalities have suggested that it was the Welsh Nonconformist culture which shaped their characteristic concern with good order and high standards of cleanliness against the odds. Maggie Pryce Jones, born in Trelewis and now living in Treharris, Merthyr Tydfil, notes in her autobiographical volume *Kingfisher of Hope*, sections of which are also reproduced in *Struggle or Starve*, that 'tidy' was 'the most important word' in her mother's vocabulary. Like Elaine Morgan she attests to the strength of character of such 'tidy' women, saying, '[i]f only Mam and her peers had known and recognized the power they held. They were the strong ones, not the men. They had the iron hands in their velvet gloves.'[6] A fictional Mam of the same type is portrayed in a novel by Menna Gallie, born in Ystradgynlais in 1920 and reared in Creunant, in the Dulais valley, and perhaps the most significant female contributor to the tradition of Valleys' writing. Flossie, in *The Small Mine*, is a 'dark, darting little woman

... bouncing with energy'. That she takes her household duties as seriously as any male could take his paid labour is indicated by the reference to 'the curlers in her greying hair' which 'would assert their plastic discipline until that cloth had been lifted, for combing out her sausage curls was Flossie's clocking-off signal'. 'Long since out of patience and passion for her slow, kindly, insensitive husband', Flossie's devotion is reserved for her son Joe, 'the worshipped, centred-on, axis, pivot of their unspoken, unverbalised, unfettered regard'. *The Small Mine* is set in the early 1960s, after the nationalization of the coalmines, and the introduction of pit-head baths and household bathrooms. But when Joe gives up his Coal Board job and becomes a fireman in a privately owned small mine, Flossie welcomes his move because it restores to her one aspect of the traditional Valleys' Mam role. The small mine has not installed pit-head baths, and Flossie enjoys the energetic bustle of dealing with her son when he returns home to her, black with coal. She says to him, '[i]t's like old times, Joe, to see a collier looking like a collier, honest. Am I a bit daft, or what? – but I feel you're more of a man in your dirt, like.' And though she can now run a bath for him rather than carry water from the street pump and heat it on the stove, Joe makes sure she still gets her share of the grime:

> Getting the coal off in a bath he found surprisingly more difficult than getting clean under the showers at the pit-head . . . He pulled the plug out of the bath, but made no attempt to clean it of the coal; cleaning baths was a woman's work and there are no greater respecters of the division of labour than the colliers.[7]

Flossie's zeal for good order in her home and for that cleanliness which is proverbially next to godliness cannot, however, be understood in this novel as motivated primarily by Welsh Nonconformity. Though she's a chapelgoer, her faith seems to be a matter of lip-service, for when Joe is subsequently killed in the small mine, religion is of no comfort to her. And, indeed, it cannot historically have been the case that Welsh Nonconformity and its inculcated standards alone supplied the motivation which drove the Valleys' women to make of their homes such unshakeably social anchors that they were difficult to leave, even when no work presented itself in the area. The women of the mid-Wales lead-mining communities and of the slate-quarrying villages of the north, during the mid-

and late nineteenth century, were equally Nonconformist, but their communities were quickly depopulated when the industries on which they depended were deemed unprofitable and closed down. So we must look to more than Nonconformity alone to account for the peculiar characteristics of the women of the Valleys.

One way in which they differed from the womenfolk of the lead-mining or slate-quarrying communities was in their number. So very heavily populated were the packed terraces of the Valleys' townships during the peak of industrial activity in the area that a critical mass of Welsh Mams must have accumulated in the area, making it difficult for any individual woman to escape the influence of the all-pervasive role-model, whatever her original cultural affiliations. As we have seen in the case of Elaine Morgan's Olive, for example, her own English mother was not a Welsh Mam role-model, but her mother-in-law was. Had she not been, then a neighbour might have served the same purpose, a neighbour whose life would have impinged much more closely on her own in the terraces than in the more far-flung smallholdings of the typical slate-quarrying or lead-mining community. Just as the number of men massed in the pits and undergoing a shared discontent at their working conditions served to make the Valleys the crucible of socialist evolution, so the numbers of women and the similarities of their domestic struggle must have intensified the need to evolve a way of life capable of triumphing over their accumulative discontent, or at least of making it bearable.

What is more, within the mining communities women's experience of the tensions of the shared domestic struggle would have been further heightened by the ever-present possibility of the sudden death of their menfolk in the pit. A woman born in Llwynypia in 1904 recalled in later life that, during her childhood,

> [w]e were more or less living with death every day. Because there wasn't a week passing by, there wasn't someone being injured, someone being killed. There was always that tragedy hanging over . . . That was my experience. I felt that as a child. That there was something hanging over us all the time.[8]

Women like Elaine Morgan's mother Olive, who created homes redolent of ease and harmony, did so despite this persistent dread, as well as despite poverty. Another woman writer, a poet this time, born in Seven Sisters in 1922, muses in some of her poems on what it means to live with such a dread. Ruth Bidgood is not commonly thought of as a Valleys' writer, as her family left the Valleys in her childhood, and she has now for many years been settled in rural mid-Wales, in the Abergwesyn area. Yet her preoccupations in such poems as 'Heol y Mwyn' and 'Slate-Quarry, Penceulan' appear to me clearly to reflect her formative childhood experiences in the coalmining community of Seven Sisters. In 'Heol y Mwyn' she describes herself and a friend taking shelter in the mouth of an old, long-deserted mine-shaft during a wet walk in the old lead-mining area:

> Butting the wet wind, we stumbled
> along Heol y Mwyn. The sky
> trawled for us with nets of drizzle,
> grey as the lead mined once
> in the wilderness upstream.
> Soaked, blinded, we crouched for refuge
> in an old adit.
>   'Listen!' you said.
> Now we could hear not only
> the shush of rain over the shaggy surface
> of the hill, but somewhere far within it
> the hollow fall of water into water,
> the unceasing enigmatic speech
> of depth and darkness.
>   The wind veered,
> the sky drew in its nets, empty.
> Freely we walked up a sunny valley.
> Our lightest words had now
> more gentleness, since we had known,
> together, the chill uneasy sound
> of the hill's hidden waters, falling,
> falling, for ever into dark.[9]

Dread knowledge of the hollow darkness in which men had worked far down below adds depth and gentleness to the friends' surface exchanges. To me this poem speaks of what it must have meant to an imaginative child to know that the men and boys of her locality were daily living and working in dangerous dark tunnels, far below the ground's surface. The knowledge of how their daily bread was earned may well have pressed upon the imaginations of the female inhabitants of the coal villages more hauntingly than it did on the miners themselves, precisely because the women had no actual experience of pit work. The strangeness of the men's daily disappearance down the mine-shaft was not for them demystified and rendered 'normal' by the day-to-day routine and camaraderie of the workplace. Certainly, Ruth Bidgood, for one, returns again and again in her poems to the contrast between life in the light, on the surface, and the never-to-be-forgotten darkness below. In 'Slate Quarry, Penceulan' she is again preoccupied with this contrast:

> I had known the quarry for years –
> dark hills of broken slate: round hole,
> high up, of an adit: a black
> unfenced shaft down by the river:
> and, reassuringly, above it all
> a strip of untroubled green catching the sun.
>
> When I spoke of the place to a man
> who well knew it, that bland field
> was the danger he warned of, not the tunnel's whisper
> of shift and sag. The high field,
> said he, spoke no word of its peril.
> He had seen horses, dogs, men
> skeltering along it, and no harm done.
>
> But he had been inside the hill. He drew
> no chart; from his words I read
> the unfading map spread in his mind.
> I know the three-branched tunnel now,
> the water-barrier, the fall-blocked road,
> the third way with its rusty rails
> reddish in torchlight, opening out
> into a chamber whose functional hugeness
> amazes, whose dark hollowness
> rears up close under sunny grass.
>
> My mind makes a tree, rising out of the dark
> of that hidden hall, breaking the shell
> of the hill, flowering high in the air,
> binding blackness to light. Its petals cling
> in the manes of horses that innocently go
> galloping on the green brittle hill.[10]

The hill is brittle because the huge man-made cavern beneath it comes up so close to the earth's surface. Its brittleness suggests the fragility of mortal life itself, so easily crushed and darkened. But in spite of that dread, the poet in her imagination constructs a tree which will flourish on the earth's surface, even though its roots dangle over the cavern underground. It will 'bind blackness to light' and so make the darkness tolerable without repressing it. In the same way, it could be said that when a miner's wife and mother succeeded in creating for her family 'a life of comfort and ease and harmony', to use Elaine Morgan's words again, then she did so despite her knowledge of the darkness below in which the men worked, and her creation was at once all the stronger and more gentle, more humane, because of that knowledge. It was a civilizing triumph over brutal circumstances, and one strong enough to retain its grip even during periods of strikes, lock-outs and closures. At least, at those times when the pit-wheels were still, the women had the compensation of knowing that the persistent threat of sudden underground death was lifted, though economic hardship came instead.

Recently the playwright Ed Thomas has coined the term a 'despite culture' to describe the achievements of Welsh theatre in the late 1980s and 1990s, which succeeded, as he sees it, despite little support from the establishment and despite the absence of a national theatre.[11] The term can yet more tellingly, perhaps, be applied to that social and domestic culture which Valleys' women evolved despite poverty, despite the strikes, lock-outs and industrial decline, and despite their harrowing knowledge of the nature of the men's employment. To participate in a 'despite culture' is invigorating in a special way; it gives an energizing sense of accomplishment achieved in the face of limiting conditions. That 'despite everything' vitality was apparent in, for example, the women's support groups of the 1984–5 Miners' Strike and is to be heard in the oral testimonies transcribed in Jill Miller's book about Welsh women and the Strike, *You Can't Kill the Spirit*. An activist called Gwyneth recalls, for example, that

> The [women's] group gave me a lot more confidence to express my feelings, thoughts and ideals. My ideas became much clearer, and as a result I was more determined than ever that we shouldn't and wouldn't give in to this government which was trying to destroy a community that

took generations to build . . . I'm proud to be a miner's wife, I'm proud to be part of that community. I'm proud to be Welsh too.[12]

The warmth and resilience of a 'despite culture' is also evident in the work of the popular novelist Catrin Collier, born Karen Jones on the Graig in Pontypridd, who now lives as Karen Watkins in Swansea, and who publishes also under a second pseudonym, Katherine John. Her series of popular fictions about the valiant women of Pontypridd during the Second World War years have won fans as far afield as New Zealand and South Africa and have recently been televised. For all their overtly romantic plots these novels are deliberately constructed as a memorial to the women Catrin Collier grew up amongst, as her notes to the sixth novel in the series, *Past Remembering*, indicate:

> There are women living in the Welsh valleys now, who still bear the scars and cope with the loss of limbs and blindness that occurred as a result of 'minor incidents' in munitions factories during the war. In one accident alone between thirty and forty workers were killed, two-thirds of them women. Up until September 1942 more civilians than servicemen were killed and injured as a result of the war. *Past Remembering* is their story.[13]

Pontypridd in these novels is a haven of warmth in a harsh world – 'heart-warming' is the adjective most frequently used by reviewers to describe these books – a haven made up of loyal family networks, of sensuality tempered (more or less) by self-respect, of practical energy and of resourceful good sense. It is an essentially caring world, bravely sufficient unto itself and largely made up of strong female characters, who bid their warring menfolk good-bye on the long Pontypridd station platform, and then return up the Graig terraces for a brief weep before they pull themselves together and get on with life for the sake of the children. The tough love ethos of the Welsh Mam is their modus vivendi and is all-pervasive in these sagas.

But Catrin Collier's novels are marketed as popular romances, for all the degree of historical detail they contain. A recently published and much more harrowing account of existence in today's Valleys initially suggests that, whether or not she was in the past a reality, the Welsh Mam is by now defunct, defeated by the severity of unemployment and the erosion of old value-systems in a Wales without miners. In her novel *In and Out of the Goldfish Bowl* Rachel Trezise, born in the Rhondda in 1978, portrays Rebecca, the central protagonist and narrator of the text, as having endured an unremittingly bleak and destructive childhood on the Penrhys estate above Tonypandy, here described as 'the drug and crime capital of the Valleys', 'a prison for the innocent and a haven for the criminal'. Abused by her stepfather and unprotected by an alcoholic mother, Rebecca escapes to a squat in Nottingham but, much to her dismay, is caught and returned to the Rhondda by the police. 'I saw the "Welcome to the Rhondda" board on the Bwlch', she says, 'I'm sure the police driver slowed passing it, to prolong my displeasure.' It would appear that by the 1990s the Welsh Mam has finally laid down her burden, her 'despite' spirit vanquished by the cumulative effects of disastrously planned housing estates, continuing unemployment and drug availability. Yet Rebecca finally manages to tell her tale and, in so doing, to make sense of her life, because of the influence upon her of a figure who could have come straight out of the most heroic pages of *Struggle or Starve*. 'My grandmother', the narrator of *In and Out of the Goldfish Bowl* tells her readers, 'was a strong woman':

> Born in Carmarthen, she left for London at fourteen to nanny. She worked through the war, driving buses, driving troops around Britain . . . She moved to the Rhondda when she met my Grandfather, and she cleaned every pub in Treorchy. Her children were the best fed and dressed; and they were the first family in the Rhondda with a television and a car . . .

It is through her relation to this woman, still undefeated in old age, that Rebecca gains a sufficient sense of self-worth to want to live and to write her account of her struggle. Her grandmother 'gave me the person who is writing this sentence', she tells her reader: 'She gave me treasured stories and examples and standards to live by, reasons to fight my way to where I want to go. Reasons to get up in the morning and make the day a success.' For all that, there seems little to hope or plan for in the 1990s Valleys, in which 'more than half the population are living dead, walking wounded', yet 'the memory of my Grandmother pinches my arm and it's back to the fight'.[14] Rebecca survives, despite the obstacles ranged against her, because of her grandmother, a Welsh Mam par excellence.

Circumstances may have been too much for Rebecca's own mother, but her grandmother has succeeded in passing on to a new generation her resilience and strength.

Is the Welsh Mam only a memory now or is she still a real force? Certainly, she still exists in the pages of writing by contemporary Valleys' women. The gritty realism of *In and Out of the Goldfish Bowl*, as much as the romance fictions of Catrin Collier or the documentary material contained in *Struggle or Starve*, suggests that more than one afflicted generation has survived and flourished, despite the odds, in the industrial valleys because of the fighting spirit of their Mams. If that is indeed the case, then it is not illogical to conclude that it is predominantly to female experience that we must look to account for the continuity in adversity of the south Wales Valleys' communities.

Notes

[1] Elaine Morgan, *The Descent of Woman* ([1972] London: Souvenir Press, 1985), p. 37.

[2] Deirdre Beddoe, *Out of the Shadows: A History of Women in Twentieth-Century Wales* (Cardiff: University of Wales Press, 2000), pp. 85–97.

[3] See Dot Jones, 'Counting the Cost of Coal: Women's Lives in the Rhondda, 1881–1911', *Our Mothers' Land: Chapters in Welsh Women's History 1830–1939*, ed. Angela V. John (Cardiff: University of Wales Press, 1991), pp. 109–34.

[4] Dilys Rowe, 'A View across the Valley', *A View across the Valley: Short Stories by Women from Wales 1850–1950*, ed. Jane Aaron ([1955]; Dinas Powys: Honno, 1999), pp. 262, 264–5.

[5] Elaine Morgan, 'Olive', *Struggle or Starve: Women's Lives in the South Wales Valleys between the Two World Wars*, eds Carol White and Siân Rhiannon Williams (Dinas Powys: Honno, 1998), pp. 5–6.

[6] Maggie Pryce Jones, *Kingfisher of Hope*, reprinted in White and Williams (eds), *Struggle or Starve*, pp. 104, 266.

[7] Menna Gallie, *The Small Mine* ([1962]; Honno: Dinas Powys, 2000), pp. 3–4, 42, 45–6.

[8] Llwynypia woman, born 1904, quoted in Bill Jones and Beth Thomas, *Coal's Domain* (Cardiff: National Museum of Wales, 1993), p. 37.

[9] Ruth Bidgood, 'Heol y Mwyn (Mine Road)', *Selected Poems* ([1982] Bridgend: Seren Books, 1992), p. 106.

[10] 'Slate Quarry, Penceulan' [1986], ibid., p. 137.

[11] See Steve Blandford, 'Making *House of America*: An Interview with Ed Thomas and Marc Evans', *Wales on Screen* (Bridgend: Seren Books, 2000), p. 71.

[12] Jill Miller, *You Can't Kill the Spirit: Women in a Welsh Mining Valley* (London: Women's Press, 1986), pp. 106, 110.

[13] Catrin Collier, 'Notes', *Past Remembering* (London: Arrow, 1998).

[14] Rachel Trezise, *In and Out of the Goldfish Bowl* (Cardiff: Parthian Books, 2000), pp. 117, 119, 121.

III
AMERICAN PERSPECTIVES

MENNA ELFYN

Perlïo Geiriau

A geiriau yw'r unig falm a feddwn,
Fel yr eli y bydd y wennol
Yn ei roi i'w chyw, o sudd llygaid Ebrill,
Neu'r crwban sy'n llowcio o fintys y graig,
Neu'r wenci sy'n gwella'i hun drwy flodau,

Felly'r ddynol ryw, yn dda, a di-nod,
Wrth gasglu llysiau a'u glesni rhad.

Dail Whitman. Y wig yn Walden.
Tafell o oleuni Emily,
Eu gosod arnaf fel tintur, yn hael,
Morgan Llwyd a'i wawl,
A minnau'n ddall yn ymbalfalu
O gwmpas muriau'r byd.
Moddion yw geiriau ar wely'r claf,
Tudalennau beunyddiol – Mihangel o ha'.

*

Ac ofni'r gair 'gwyn' a wna ein dyddiau ni,
Er gwyn eu byd y rhai a feddylia amdano,
Cans nid croen a'i enwa, eithr enaid a'i fendithia,
Ac mae gwynfydau i'w blitho o hyd yn ein byd,
Glân i orfoleddu drosto, i wylo amdano,
Glân fel cynfasau sy'n dallu ein nos,
Glân yn yr ewyn fel carreg Arthur
Yn sychedig am fedydd y môr ar ddiwedd y dydd,
Glân, fel lili'r maes rhwng sgroliau'r gwlydd.

I hyn y mae perlau'n eiriol, a throi weithiau yn 'wynn',
Yn ddisglair halen o leuad ger distyll y don.
Gwyn a dryloywa'n meidroldeb. Ein curiad. Ein sawr.
I'r gwynfyd, deled teyrnas a'i llithoedd yn wawl,
Yn lluwch i'r dihalog, tu hwnt i blant y llawr.

The Worth of Words

And words are the only balm we have,
Like the salve the swallow gives
Her chicks from figworts' sap,
Or the tortoise gorging on marjoram,
Or the weasel healing itself with flowers,

So humankind, unremarkable and good,
In gathering herbs and their gracious freshness.

Whitman's leaves, the woods at Walden,
A sliver of Emily's light,
Spreading them over me lavishly like a tincture,
Morgan Llwyd and his enlightenment,
As I blindly fumble
Around the walls of the world.
Words are medicine for a sick-bed,
Daily pages – an Indian summer.

*

And our days fear the word 'blessed',
Though blessed are those who can imagine it,
Since flesh will not name it, but spirit sanctifies it,
And beatitudes still have their place in our world:
It's holy to rejoice in it, to weep for it,
Holy as sheets that blind our night,
Holy in the foam, like Arthur's Stone
Thirsty for the sea's christening at day's end,
Holy, like the lilies of the field among the scrolls of stems.

To these, pearls are wordy, and turn at times to winnings,
The moon's bright salt near the ebb of the white wave
That transparifies our mortality. Our pulse-beat. Our savour.
Into the bliss, may the kingdom come, its readings radiant,
Drift enter the undefiled, beyond the children of earth.

Translated by Joseph P. Clancy

10
Under Milk Wood: Lists, Made and Undone

HELEN VENDLER

This chapter is offered in homage to Professor Wynn Thomas, whom I have prized as a friend for many years. I should tell here the story of our acquaintance. The editor of the journal *American Literature* sent me, for comment, an essay on Walt Whitman by a person named Wynn Thomas. I had tried to write a book on Whitman myself, and failed. I did not know why I had failed; there was something I could not understand about how Whitman chose words and put them together. And then there came in the mail the brilliant essay that accomplished what I could not: it spoke about Whitman 'from the inside' (as I put it to myself) – from that place I had never been able to reach. I was moved to send a letter to the author of this revelatory piece, urging him to write a book on Whitman; he, rather surprised, wrote back, and the book on Whitman – an incomparable view of Whitman's style and politics – came out a few years later. Someone in Wales who had never yet visited the United States had comprehended Civil War Washington like a native, had understood the literary and social urgencies of Whitman's work and had seen their results in the poet's style. Wynn Thomas had mastered in his research (as I had not) all the underpinnings of Whitman's culture – the newspapers, the stump speeches, the editorials, the war dispatches – and therefore his study moved in historical synchrony with Whitman's mind. To his book on Whitman, Wynn Thomas brought the profound feeling for imagination and for language which has inspired all his work in Welsh, English and American literature. He sees in all literature that drive toward the most musical and complex representations of the inner and outer worlds in which it awakes to consciousness. His own books and articles are marked by empathy, curiosity and a vivid rendition of literary contexts, expressed in the cadences of the born writer. He has been especially tireless in making known the literature of Wales to both the academic world and the public world. He has contributed to the survival of modern poetry in selflessly agreeing to become the literary executor of his friend R. S. Thomas. Most of all, he has given to his friends and students, as to his family, a care and generosity almost superhuman in a life burdened by professional responsibilities, during a difficult time for universities in England and Wales. He has kept a natural gaiety of response that rises above the trials of existence to meet the possibilities of personal happiness. Among my own life's joys and privileges I count my friendship with Wynn Thomas. Because he showed me Dylan Thomas's house in Swansea and took me to the Boathouse in Laugharne and the Gower peninsula, I wanted to write on Dylan Thomas for his festschrift. My own interest in Thomas goes back fifty years, but I have not had the occasion to write on him before and am glad to find myself doing so now.

In May of 1953, as a girl of twenty, I entered the basement of Harvard's Fogg Museum to hear Dylan Thomas read – by himself – all the voices of his new radio play *Under Milk Wood*. A few years earlier, in my teens, I had heard him read in Boston, and his poems – not entirely new in effect to someone as steeped in Hopkins as I then was, but new in their risky sense-making – had captivated me. When I discovered that the Lockwood Memorial Library at the University of Buffalo owned many of Thomas's manuscripts and that they were available on microfilm, I spent my Saturdays in the Boston Public Library reading the Thomas drafts. Eugene Magner, the Curator of the Lockwood Library, once he saw my attachment to the poems, began sending me all sorts of other Thomas material – special Thomas issues of little magazines, various British publications not owned by the Boston Public Library. Finally, I came, with intense regret, to the end of all the microfilm. After Thomas's death, I sent a letter and a week's wages (twenty hours a week at 50 cents per hour for working at a branch library) to the Curator to thank him for his kindness. He wrote back to me, saying (so far as I remember), 'Dear Miss Hennessy, You are an unusual scholar; most scholars do not thank us with contributions.' It was the first time I had ever been called a scholar; he did not know I was an undergraduate. He added that he would buy a book for the library and put my name in it on the bookplate. The book he had chosen, he said, was *Under Milk Wood*, newly issued in England. Perhaps that copy is still in Buffalo. In any case, I felt linked to the play because of having heard Thomas read it, and because my name had become attached to a printed copy of it.

What was it that made the evening at the Fogg so unforgettable? Although I already knew the Thomas voice and the Thomas presence, I had not really registered Thomas's social imagination; of his prose, I knew only the playful *A Child's Christmas in Wales*. I was a provincial girl who had scarcely ever left Boston and had rarely given a thought to Wales, but as Thomas read *Under Milk Wood*, a town and its population gradually took shape. I was aware of the fairy-tale aura of the play and of the spell-casting power of Thomas's imagination, but for all I knew, some place in Wales was actually like Llareggub (I did not catch the reversal in the title). I had none of the personal investment that made some Welsh hearers feel either simplified or betrayed by Thomas's portrait of a mythologized Laugharne. I was not surprised by the irregular behaviours in Thomas's town – drunkenness, infidelity, promiscuity and bigamy were, after all, the very stuff of literature. So the play entered my mind like a Polaroid snapshot slowly coming into clearer and clearer focus, deeper and deeper colour. The buoyancy and tenderness and comedy of Thomas's words made me happier and happier; his own infallible intonations gave the characters' speeches all the right cadences and the winning tonal interplay of indulgence and satire pleased my ear. The tempo, the pacing, the staccato and the rubato, the crescendo and decrescendo of the voice, put the whole audience in Thomas's power. There was sustained applause when his voice fell silent. Afterwards, Thomas stood dazed and tired in the foyer as congratulations washed over him. I saw a blowsy young woman, untidily dressed, with a weedy flower threaded through her hair, approaching Thomas and saying confidentially, while sliding her hand out of sight, 'Oh Mr Thomas, I've put my poem in your pocket.' I backed away and left.

The news of Thomas's premature death came to me, as to so many others, as a disorienting shock. I had seen pictures of the golden-haired children and the forcefully beautiful wife, but had no idea of their tormented and hapless life with their driven and alcoholic poet – a life revealed only later with the publication of Thomas's marvellous and appalling letters.

How does *Under Milk Wood* seem to us now, fifty years later? Some readers have thought that the play suffers from sentimentality; they prefer the more surreal and difficult Thomas of the early poems, poems made irresistible by their conviction and pressure, their conjunction of fleshly biology and visionary dream, their potent metaphors and biblical resonance. *Under Milk Wood* is altogether looser and more diffuse than those close-packed youthful poems. That *Under Milk Wood* exists at all – especially after Thomas twice lost it in manuscript – is surely one of the kindnesses of fate. Its reception was in one sense all its author could have wished; it became instantly popular. But it also attracted hostility (most of which proved to be transient) for its alleged immorality and for its characterization – stereotype or caricature, depending on the critic – of the population of Llareggub.

Professor Walford Davies, in his comprehensive Introduction to the edition of *Under Milk Wood* that he co-edited with Professor Ralph Maud, tracks the earlier writings and broadcasts of Thomas that bear a relation to *Under Milk Wood*, gives a reception history of the play and offers a persuasive account of its virtues, emphasizing – as I also want to do – its constantly varied inclusive play of light and dark, life and death, joy and mourning.[1] Rereading the play, I became interested in how Thomas manages the inclusiveness and chiaroscuro remarked on by Davies and others. As I see it, *Under Milk Wood* is, from beginning to end, a compendium of lists. Thomas's lists – his chief means to inclusiveness – accumulate in striking ways, contributing to the play's major and minor keys. The descriptive lists are chiefly (but not exclusively) produced in voice-over by the Narrator (called on the page 'First Voice'). His omniscience makes us trust his perceptions; and although we see the summoned characters with some irony, we do not ironize the First Voice, who is himself the eiron of the play. But beyond the Narrator's descriptive lists (to which I'll return) there are the 'lists' of appearances of characters: these scenes are called up, as all critics have noticed, not by the demands of plot (there is no plot except the gradual decline of the day from morning to evening) but by the exigencies of imagination. A list has only two structural requirements: that it should consist of at least two things, and that it should end. To understand the lists of *Under Milk Wood*, we need to ask not only their function in the ongoing play, but also when and why they stop. Against the plenitude of his lists, intimating the immemorial continuation of the archetypal life of the town, Thomas sets, as we shall see, the necessary truncation of every aspect of that life, superimposing elegy on comedy.

At the very beginnning of *Under Milk Wood*, we see the processional appearance of the five drowned sailors, who appear to Captain Cat in a rigidly ordered succession: First Drowned, Second Drowned, Third Drowned, Fourth Drowned and (identified by First Drowned) Fifth Drowned (*Under Milk Wood*, 4–6). After their first individual speeches, the floating Drowned could presumably have voiced their subsequent utterances in any random order. But they do not: they maintain their original sequence. We recognize Thomas's adaptation of the musical model of the round (in sequential, not overlapping, mode) as we hear, in the second appearance of the sailors, the same inflexible order: Second Drowned, Third Drowned, Fourth Drowned and Fifth Drowned (First Drowned was taken care of in his earlier moment of introducing Fifth Drowned). And the sailors' third appearance produces First, Second, Third, Fourth, Fifth again, as do the fourth and fifth sets of appearances. The Round of the Drowned ends with the First Drowned starting up again (presumably to begin a sixth sequence), but he is interrupted by Captain Cat ('Oh, my dead dears!') and the Drowned disappear for good.

Why does Thomas arrange the voices of the Drowned – five times – in the same order of appearance? He does so, I believe, to make musically identical sequences of voice-tones (this is a radio-play, in which the actors are not seen, but merely heard). The Drowned are not individually characterized: a line from one ('Bosoms and robins?') could be substituted for a line from another ('And sparrows and daisies?'). But the actors playing the Drowned must be individually musically toned: a dark voice, a thin voice, a sweet voice, a rough voice, a flat voice (for example). We hear them calling out, always in the same order, in this five-part, five-fold, quintet: dark, thin, sweet, rough, flat; dark, thin, sweet, rough, flat; dark . . . and so on, to the end of the first scene.

Thomas turns to a second musical model, that of antiphonal response, in the duet that follows, as the platonic lovers Mog Edwards and Myfanwy Price alternate their voices: male, female, male, female. One could remark that antiphony is inevitable in dramatic dialogue, and so it is; we perhaps do not sense it as a musical form in this, its first appearance, in which the antiphonal sentences are different in length, but in Thomas's next list of character-appearances antiphony is more intensely foregrounded as a musical effect, through the pointed stichomythic speech-fragments of the scandalous gossip of First Neighbour and Second Neighbour – soon to be followed, also in antiphony, by Third Neighbour and Fourth Neighbour. Once they disappear, First Neighbour and Second Neighbour remain off-stage; they do not emerge to join in the gossip of Third Neighbour and Fourth Neighbour. These successive briskly antiphonic neighbour-duets are followed by a trio in which the voices are those of the inseparably joined Mr Ogmore, Mr Pritchard, and Mrs Ogmore-Pritchard (who has been married, successively, to Mr Ogmore and Mr Pritchard). After the initial quintet of the Drowned, the antiphonal duets of wistful romance and slanderous gossip, and the trio of the preposterous Ogmore-Pritchards, *Under Milk Wood* becomes more choral and ample until it reaches a discordant quartet of women. This passage manifests itself first as a trio spoken by First Woman, Second Woman and Third Woman; only at the close does the Fourth Woman enter briefly, making the trio into a quartet with her two separate dark summary statements: 'There's a nasty lot live here when you come to think' and 'Men are brutes on the quiet' (35–6). I call this female quartet 'discordant' because the appearances of the four women lack the predictable regularity of the appearances of the Drowned. The women speak in no foreseeable sequence, and therefore – though the four of them, like the five Drowned, must have voices distinctly different in pitch or timbre – there is no repeated melody impressed on the brain in the manner of the sailors' inflexible round or the alternating antiphonies. A later sequence uttered by girls and boys is also 'discordant', since it sets a single voice ('Girl') against a choral group ('Girls' Voices'), but does not follow this pattern with its boys. By introducing three separate Boys (and no 'Boys' Voices') it creates an asymmetry of utterance that is, again, discordant rather than concordant.

Appearances in fives, in twos, in threes, in fours; this highly visible substructure of character presentation of *Under Milk Wood* makes us expect that when a given character appears, a vocal sequence, a procession of other characters, discordant or concordant, will be generated. This expectation springs from the very nature of communal life as musically represented (for example, in opera). Persons group and regroup to make a trio here, a quintet there; a regular organization at one juncture (the round of the Drowned), an irregular one at another (the quartet of Women); a symmetrical structure here (Mog Edwards and Myfanwy Pritchard) and an asymmetrical one there (Girl, Three Boys, Girls' Voices).

I have said that the truncation of lists is as important as their creation. In every case, Thomas is faced with the time-limits of the radio feature, and must decide the amplitude of each character-list as it surges into view: how many sailors? How many neighbours? How much time for the love-duet? How much time for the children? The harmony of the play depends on Thomas's willingness to sacrifice each of his appealing list-appearances in favor of the next, as melody succeeds to percussion, as concord slides into discord. Some endings of lists seem conclusive and 'planned', as we'll see in the hymn of the Reverend Eli Jenkins. Others seem arbitrarily cut off, as in Captain Cat's inventory of the passers-by in Coronation Street. Both forms of list-closing – the rounded-off and the arbitrary – are in a way betrayals of our expectation. We expect any list, once it is set in motion, to be capable of continuing indefinitely.

Besides his successive lists of sequentially appearing characters, Thomas creates another list-plane in *Under Milk Wood*, that of the songs scattered through the play. The archetypal list-song (in this list-play) is, naturally, its first one – the nursery rhyme, 'This little piggy went to market', which finally exhausts its enumeration with the fifth little piggy (8–9).[2] The most serious list-song, and the one I want to dwell on, is the morning hymn of the Reverend Eli Jenkins (20–1), which lists the beauties of Wales in general and Milk Wood in particular. This daily and invariant ritual of praise has been seen variously by critics as a parody of amateur verse or as a heartfelt lyric. I am in the heartfelt faction, myself, while not denying that elements in the song may imitate popular verse. But no hack-poet ever constructed a list of lists as cunning as that of the Reverend Jenkins, who (as Davies points out) may be conceived partly in the image of Thomas's great-uncle William Thomas, whose poem 'Cân Mewn Cystudd' ('A Song in Affliction'), included an address to 'Dear Gwalia', the words opening Thomas's poem (p. 20, nn. on pp. 72–3).

Let me comment on the Reverend Eli Jenkins's morning hymn, his list of lists, as it evolves in quanta of two-stanza units. The first list, one of environmental beauties, is intended as a concession:

> Dear Gwalia! I know there are
> Towns lovelier than ours,
> And fairer hills and loftier far,
> And groves more full of flowers,
>
> And boskier woods more blithe with spring
> And bright with birds' adorning,
> And sweeter bards than I to sing
> Their praise this beauteous morning.

Towns, hills, groves, woods: elsewhere there exist, the poet concedes, better examples of these list-items than 'ours', and better bards to celebrate them. (We await the 'But' that is to follow this concession.) The Reverend Jenkins's hovering between nature and culture continues in the next two-stanza unit, where the 'molehill' of Llareggub Hill is compared, to its disadvantage, with a list of various mountains:

> By Cader Idris, tempest-torn,
> Or Moel y Wyddfa's glory,
> Carnedd Llewelyn beauty born,
> Plinlimmon old in story,
>
> By mountains where King Arthur dreams,
> By Penmaen Mawr defiant,
> *Llareggub Hill* a molehill seems,
> A pygmy to a giant.

Each of the mountains – as we would expect from Thomas – is differently characterized. The closest to a 'natural' object here is Cader Idris, but the metaphor in 'tempest-torn' humanizes the mountain. 'Glory' is a quality not intrinsic to mountains, but, like 'beauty', one conferred on them by human beings. The mountains are rendered mythological by the presence of King Arthur; and Plinlimmon, too, is made literary by being 'old in story'. Finally, Penmaen Mawr is anthropologically 'defiant' and allegorically 'a giant'. Critics who see this hymn as one that could appear in any country newspaper are mistaken; although the Reverend Jenkins must *seem* an amateur, real-life amateurs have no capacity for such perspectival list-variation. Nor can amateur poets achieve the satisfactory sound-cadences of the river-list in the Reverend Jenkins's next two-stanza unit:

> By Sawdde, Senni, Dovey, Dee,
> Edw, Eden, Aled, all,
> Taff and Towy broad and free,
> Llyfnant with its waterfall,
>
> Claerwen, Cleddau, Dulas, Daw,
> Ely, Gwili, Ogwr, Nedd,
> Small is our *River Dewi*, Lord,
> A baby on a rushy bed.

Davies informs us that this list employs the figure of ' "cymeriad" . . . whereby words are sometimes grouped by alphabetical sequence: hence "Claerwen, Cleddau, Dulas, Daw, Ely, Gwili" '. He adds that 'Thomas's relishing of the musical effect of this traditional close patterning of consonants is clear in his rendering of Eli Jenkins's part in the original New York recording' (p. 20, n. on p. 90).[3] Unlike the mountains preceding them, the rivers in this relatively unadorned list might seem almost entirely untransformed by the imagination – but the enchanting use of the alphabetical sequence pointed out by Davies confers visible linguistic intentionality on the list, and reminds us that the shadow-author behind the Reverend Jenkins is no novice in verse-making.

In the bardic song of the Reverend Eli Jenkins, we have seen a two-stanza list of generalities (trees, hills, groves, woods) followed by two two-stanza units of named specificities – particular mountains and rivers. The next list gave Thomas some trouble. Originally, like its predecessors, it occupied two stanzas: the first stanza spoke of the negligible age of a local architectural ruin compared with the ancientness of a castle; the second stanza described the comparatively small size of Llareggub's local promontory, Heron Head, against others more grand:

> By Carrig Cennin, King of time,
> *Our* ruin in the spinnet
> Where owls do wink and squirrels climb
> Is aged but half a minute[.]

> By Strumble or by Dinas Head,
> Our *Heron Head* is only
> A bit of stone with seaweed spread
> Where gulls come to be lonely.
>
> (p. 20, n. on p. 90)

These two stanzas are, in the final version of *Under Milk Wood*, 'conflated' (Davies's word) into one. Although continuing the comparison in the use of 'by', the resulting single list-stanza has not the coherence of its three two-stanza predecessors (noticing the general environment, mountains and rivers) since it compares an architectural ruin in its first half with a promontory in its second half. Breaking the mould both structurally and in rhyme, Thomas substitutes (for the draft double-stanza unit) a single stanza – the only one lacking a rhyme binding the first and third lines – which compares two unlike things, the venerable castle with the cliff to the humble Heron Head:

> By Carreg Cennen, King of time,
> Our *Heron Head* is only
> A bit of stone with seaweed spread
> Where gulls come to be lonely.

After this single-stanza, less rhymed anomaly, Thomas reverts to his 'normal' two-stanza unit to end the poem, but not without another anomaly: in the final stanza, Thomas departs from the regular hymn-metre (4–3–4–3) of the rest, extending lines two and four to four stresses each:

> A tiny dingle is *Milk Wood*,
> By golden Grove 'neath Grongar,
> But let me choose and oh! I should
> Love all my life and longer
>
> To stroll among our trees and stray
> In Goosegog Lane, on Donkey Down,
> And hear the Dewi sing all day,
> And never, never leave the town.

This nostalgic and self-extending close reveals the swelling affection to which all the earlier professions of modesty have been tending:

yes, there are 'towns lovelier than ours', yes, the Dewi is small in comparison with the 'broad and free' other rivers of Wales, yes, Milk Wood is 'a tiny dingle' – but, says the Reverend Jenkins, this is *my* singing river, this is *my* dingle, and I hope never, never, to leave the town. In this close, the tropes of pastoral – to stroll and stray in a golden grove and hear the waters singing – are gently parodied in Thomas's invented names for path and hill – 'Goosegog Lane' and 'Donkey Down'. These places, their names so securely inscribed on Thomas's hand-drawn map of the town,[4] give pastoral a new tonality, one of smiling affection on Thomas's part, which 'shows through' the sincerity of the Reverend Jenkins, to whom the names are 'normal'. The Reverend Jenkins's morning song is neither an imitation of newspaper verse nor simply parodic of such 'poetry': it is too clever to be the former and too moving to be the latter. Like some of the other songs in *Under Milk Wood*, it is a Blakean verse, a Song of Innocence composed (as such songs must always be) from an authorial vantage-point of experience. In this morning hymn, the humour of Thomas's experience ironizes the naive locutions of innocence ('I should / Love all my life *and longer* / To stroll among our trees'), without ceasing to believe in them. The love that says 'all my life' and 'all day' and 'never, never', is not, for Thomas, a subject for mockery.

The double-stanza lists of the Reverend Eli Jenkins observe a pleasing variety, justly proportioned and sweetly sung. The lists of the voice-over Narrator of *Under Milk Wood*, are, by contrast, quick, subtle and stealthy. They almost always begin innocently, and then insert a swift stab of subversion before returning, as though nothing had happened, to a blander level; they account for our sense that a darker Milk Wood lies under the pastoral one. The Narrator's first descriptive list presents us with spring, moonless night and silent cobbled streets before introducing 'the hunched, courters'-and-rabbits' wood limping invisible' down to the sea (3). Hunched and limping, Milk Wood casts a deformed shadow over its courting couples and its Wordsworthian rabbits. The Narrator's first sociological list, innocent with babies and predictable with postman, publican, drunkard and preacher, suddenly startles with its 'webfoot cocklewomen' (3). And toward the end of the Narrator's list of things dreamed by the town, we see, behind the eyes of the sleepers, not only the usual dream-scenery but also fall following flight, dismays succeeded by despairs. The darker words occur, as I have said, within the embrace of altogether more conventional items: 'Only you can hear and see, behind the eyes of the sleepers, the movements and countries and mazes and colours and *dismays* and rainbows and tunes and wishes and flight and *fall* and *despairs* and big seas of their dreams' (4; italics mine). As the Narrator lists the qualities of characters, comparable sly interpositions intrude: Mister Waldo is many things, but the devastating word 'quack' is dropped in expertly among his other more neutral characteristics: 'rabbitcatcher, barber, herbalist, catdoctor, *quack*, his fat, pink hands, palms up, over the edge of the patchwork quilt' (8; italics mine). Mog Edwards the draper, too, seems innocent as he outfits, in his imagination, the passers-by, until one ghastly item appears between the shirts and the blouses: 'Mr Edwards, in butterfly-collar and straw-hat at the doorway of Manchester House, measures, with his eye, the dawdlers by, for striped flannel shirts and *shrouds* and flowery blouses' (29; italics mine).[5] The peculiar Lord Cut-Glass seems, at first, merely an eccentric who has collected sixty-six clocks ('one for each year of his loony age', 49) but the initially innocuous clock-descriptions of the Narrator's list ('hourglass chimers, tu-wit-tu-woo clocks') soon become windows into the desolation of their owner's life: 'old time-weeping clocks with ebony beards, clocks with no hands forever drumming out time without ever knowing what time it is'. The Narrator's lists can be sardonically utopian when he eavesdrops on the dreams of pigs ('they dream of the acorned swill of the world, the rooting for pig-fruit, the bagpipe dugs of the mother sow, the squeal and snuffle of yesses of the women pigs in rut', 50), but his human subjects have no Utopia in Milk Wood. The darkest of the Narrator's comic lists reproduces the fantasies of the would-be wife-murderer Mr Pugh, as he 'cooks up a fricassee of deadly nightshade, nicotine, hot frog, cyanide and bat-spit for his needling stalactite hag and bednag of a pokerbacked nutcracker wife' (50).

The Reverend Jenkins's loving lists and the Narrator's subversive ones are not all we see by way of lists in the play. Thomas himself as the author is responsible for many lists, not only within the songs, but also within the speeches, of his characters. As 'This little piggy' is the ur-type of the list-rhyme, as 'pull him out, put him back' is the archetype of the list-song of alternatives, so Mae Rose-Cottage's daisy ritual is the ur-type of the list-speech: 'He loves me / He loves me not'. These minimalist versions of the list are interspersed among the more complex list-speeches of the play, of which the first is composed of the two-beat questions of the drowned sailors:

> How's it above?
> Is there rum and lavabread?
> Bosoms and robins?
> Concertinas?
> Ebenezer's bell?
> Fighting and onions?
> And sparrows and daisies?
> Tiddlers in a jamjar?
> Buttermilk and whippets?
> Rock-a-bye baby?
> Washing on the line?
> And old girls in the snug?
> How's the tenors in Dowlais?
> Who milks the cows in Maesgwyn?
> When she smiles, is there dimples?
> What's the smell of parsley? (6)

The hidden echo to each of these queries about conditions 'above' is the converse 'down here'. 'Down here' the Drowned have no rum or laverbread, no bosoms, smiles or dimples, no baby or washing, no tastes or smells. Sweet and familiar as the list appears, it is, in the mouths of the dead, an inventory of what is eternally missing, what the Drowned sorrowfully miss. With his usual inventiveness, Thomas suggests many categories of the missing: sense impressions (sounds, tastes, sights, smells), animate companions (dogs, 'tiddlers', 'old girls'), art (concertinas, tenors), actions (fighting, sex) and information ('Who milks the cows?'). By mixing categories within a single line ('bosoms and robins', 'fighting and onions'), Thomas implies the permeability of different experiences within the warm memories of the human mind.

Another kind of complex list-speech appears in the malicious conversations of neighbours. These display a competitive sort of list, in which each neighbour wants to outdo the other. We see the neighbours engaged in eager accusation of a local alcoholic husband:

FIRST NEIGHBOUR
What'll he do for drink
SECOND NEIGHBOUR
He sold the pianola
FIRST NEIGHBOUR
And her sewing machine
SECOND NEIGHBOUR
Falling in the gutter
FIRST NEIGHBOUR
Talking to the lamp-post
SECOND NEIGHBOUR
Using language
FIRST NEIGHBOUR
Singing in the w. (10)

The neighbours' competitive inclusiveness may enumerate sins (as above) or, in another instance, suggest potential punishments for a child, in which '[s]end him to bed without any supper', is countered by the worse '[g]ive him sennapods and lock him in the dark', which is itself topped by '[o]ff to the reformatory' (11).

The most informative of the complex list-speeches is that of Captain Cat, who describes the people going up and down Coronation Street. It is a list anthropologically interesting in the different ways the Captain identifies the characters: some are named conventionally ('Mrs Floyd'), some by their husband's first name ('Mrs Cherry [Owen]'), some by their bigamous status ('Mrs Dai Bread One'), some by their husband's trade ('Mrs Butcher Beynon'), some by their address ('Mrs Twenty Three'), some by their kin ('Mrs Rose-Cottage's eldest, Mae'), some by their function ('Ocky Milkman') (33). The Captain has many mental perspectives by which to classify his neighbours – or, we should say, Thomas is as careful in multiplying Captain Cat's social pigeonholes as he was in inventing the different list-items in the Reverend Jenkins's hymn or the elegiac memories of the Drowned.

How does it help us to see *Under Milk Wood* as a play of lists – of stage-setting lists by the Narrator, list-songs, list-speeches, list-rituals, list-competitions, population-lists? As the trope allegorizing plenitude, a list as such is theoretically endless. The Drowned could have gone on appearing ad infinitum, Polly Garter could have named more than four of her lovers, the neighbours could have competed further in spiteful commentary, Captain Cat could have continued his town census. We need to ask, about lists in literature, not only why they exist, but why and how they are limited. Thomas suggests many psychological motives for our accumulating items within a general category: we may do so to be master of all we survey (a motive we hear in Captain Cat's voice, recognizing every person who passes under his eye); to resume the past (as Polly Garter counts her lovers, as the Drowned enumerate what they miss); to perform a ritual (as in the lists of alternatives, whether taking out and putting back, or 'he loves me, he loves me not'); to characterize a person by his possessions (Lord Cut-Glass); to outdo our neighbour in competitive malice; to show complexity (as the Narrator's darker inserted qualities modify blander earlier ones); to typify bliss and satisfaction (as in the Reverend Jenkins's song and the dream of the pigs). The effect of lists as such in the play is to show the generativity of the town located 'under Milk Wood'; every item in the town has the potential to spawn a list, and what is offered in the case of one character, it is implied, could equally be offered with respect to another. We could have a list, perhaps, of the possessions of Polly Garter, or a competitive exchange between Mrs Dai Bread One and Mrs Dai Bread Two, or a gruesome list-song from Butcher Beynon. The ground is immeasurably rich in possibilities.

But the more interesting question about lists is the limiting of them. Thomas's aesthetic danger was always that of excess: his tendency (as can be seen in the prose) was to invent long ebullient lists which exfoliate into more and more fantastic and extravagant forms. The intrinsic time-limits of a radio feature, with which Thomas was well acquainted, demanded that any given list in *Under Milk Wood* be (in terms of Thomas's usual inclinations) cut short. We see just a sampling of the Coronation Street passers-by, only four of Polly Garter's lovers, only seventeen of Lord Cut-Glass's sixty-six clocks, only some of Rosie Probert's endearments to Captain Cat ('My little deck hand / My favourite husband . . . / My duck my whaler / My honey my daddy / My pretty sugar sailor' (52)). Presumably the Reverend Eli Jenkins could have found more elements to praise in Wales, but after his overture he makes only mountains and rivers (with brief mention of a ruin and a promontory) the substance of his song, decorously apportioning his two-stanza units to create a short and shapely whole. Thomas's creative hand is fully evident in the cutting down of the play's lists to harmonious size. Sentimentality would have lingered longer. And sentimentality would not have permitted the Narrator's subversions or the punitive neighbourly gossip. *Under Milk Wood* may present a 'genial dreamscape' (in Seamus Heaney's words),[6] but it displays an aesthetic control absent in dreams, and a geniality undercut by sadness, lunacy, frustration, eccentricity and death. By cutting off every list before we have had enough of its contents, Thomas makes his play enact the cruelty of the passing of time, in which moments vanish almost before we can savour them. The austere pacing of the play, the repeated disappearance of its successive plenitudes, allegorizes transiency itself. The richness of *Under Milk Wood* is a nourishment which slips away even as we bend to taste its nectar. It is our gradual sensing of the fated truncation of every list, just when we would want it extended, that makes *Under Milk Wood* so poignant in the hearing.

Notes

[1] Dylan Thomas, *Under Milk Wood: A Play for Voices,* eds Walford Davies and Ralph Maud (London: J. M. Dent & Sons, 1995); 'The Road to Milk Wood', pp. xi–xlviii. All subsequent quotations from the play will be identified by page number within the text.

[2] Other list-songs in *Under Milk Wood* include:
   (1) Captain Cat's song about Johnnie Crack, which contains the simplest form of list: alternative actions ab or ba ('One would pull it out and one would put it back . . . / O it's my turn now . . . /To take the baby . . . / And it's my turn now . . . / To . . . put it back . . . / One would put it back and one would pull it out' (39);
   (2) Polly Garter's song about her archetypically named successive lovers ('I loved a man whose name was Tom . . . / I loved a man whose name was Dick/ . . . And I loved a man whose name was Harry') which culminates with 'little Willy Wee', who outshone all the rest (p. 41).

[3] Thomas's evident pleasure in sound-patterning appeared in his Cambridge reading, too, though what I was most struck by was his tenderness in descending to 'A baby on a rushy bed'.

[4] Thomas, *Under Milk Wood*, p. 64.

[5] The anomalous subversive items in the Narrator's lists are frequently bound by alliteration to the 'harmless' items – 'catdoctor' to 'quack', 'shirts' to 'shrouds'. By this means the subversive items are made to seem 'indigenous' to the superficially 'harmless' lists.

[6] Seamus Heaney, from 'Dylan the Durable? On Dylan Thomas', *Finders Keepers: Selected Prose 1971–2001.* (New York: Farrar, Straus & Giroux, 2002), p. 340.

11
Web of Connection: Denise Levertov's Construction of Origins

BARBARA PRYS-WILLIAMS

Denise Levertov was the sort of writer who would have been delighted to find herself appearing in a *Festschrift*. In her autobiography, *Tesserae*, she celebrates the importance of warm human connection and of beneficent human influence.[1] Indeed, that she should feature in a work to honour M. Wynn Thomas would be to affirm a valued connection for her: while visiting Swansea in 1995, in an interview with him for the *Swansea Review*, she spoke of the importance in her make-up of what she saw as Welsh characteristics, derived from an unusual sort of upbringing in which her Welsh mother, Beatrice Levertoff, had played a crucial part.[2]

I

Described in her lifetime as 'America's foremost contemporary woman poet', Denise Levertov was also a high-profile campaigner for civil rights and against American global dominance.[3] Yet, when asked to write an autobiographical introduction to a selection of her poetry, she focused on her childhood: 'I've written only about my childhood [because] all that has taken place in my life since – all, that is, that has any bearing on my life as a poet – was in some way foreshadowed then.'[4] Feeling virtually an only child – her one surviving sibling, Olga, was nine years older than she was – Levertov was educated entirely at home until she was twelve by what she describes as 'her 100% Welsh mother'.[5] The nature of that upbringing moulded her. From much of her poetry and from *Tesserae* we see that her personal myth – the story that she tells herself about herself – is in part bound up with what she variously describes as 'some interesting genes'[6] and as a sense of colourful and courageous forebears. The fact that she was half-Welsh was a vivid strand in the weave of her being, just as the ancestry of her Russian-Jewish father was another, her upbringing in Essex a third and her experience in the USA, from the time when she emigrated as the wife of an American in 1948, yet another. Yet until one has understood the nature of Beatrice Levertoff's own formative experience, the thread of Welsh identity in the weave of her daughter's being may not be discerned for the distinctive element it was.

Beatrice Levertoff's decision to undertake the education of each of her daughters, in turn, at home, may well have had a significance that is not immediately obvious. In an analogous situation – where, for example, a child seems to refuse to go to school – it is nowadays a commonplace, in investigating the family circumstances of such a child, to discover traumatic early experience in life, endured by a parent who now compulsively retains a seemingly truant child at home for company.[7] Exiled from her culture of origin (like her husband) Beatrice Levertoff's determination to educate her children at home was probably a result of her own unconscious needs. Indeed, her own early life could be read as a bitter chronicle of grief and loss, parts of it retold in Levertov's biographical essay on her.[8] Beatrice's own mother died in childbirth when she herself was only two and a half. Her father, a doctor in a mining company in Merthyr, remarried not very happily. The stepmother, who neglected Beatrice, subsequently died and Beatrice's father died when she was only twelve. At this point she was transplanted from industrial Merthyr to Holywell, a country town in north Wales, to a maternal aunt's family where 'she always felt like "a poor relation"'.[9] Escaping to Constantinople as a teacher in 1910, at the age of twenty-five, she met and married Paul Levertoff, whose own Russian-Jewish family connections had been severed on his conversion to Christianity. Harsh bereavement and loss continued. Their first baby, 'a gift to be cherished as my orphaned mother / had not been cherished', died suddenly.[10] The family was put under house arrest in Germany during the First World War; they became Displaced Persons in Denmark once the war was over. Paul

Levertoff, ordained as an Anglican priest after his arrival in England, was appointed to a church in Shoreditch without a local congregation or vicarage, as it had been thought his interest would be in working with Jews in a highly Jewish area. When the family settled in nearby Ilford, Essex, they seemed like 'exotic birds in the plain English coppice'.[11] Looking back on a childhood lacking both the community links fostered by schooling and a local extended family, Denise Levertov as an adult reflects on 'how strong, in my case (where in others place and community often play a dominant part) were inherited tendencies and the influence of the cultural milieu – unsupported by a community – of my own family'.[12] At the living heart of that rather isolated family stood Beatrice Levertoff.

The refracting glass of memory operated with particular intensity for her. As her own childhood and early married life had involved a great deal of being uprooted and having to move on, it is not surprising that she seems to have taken great pleasure in rehearsing her locating myth to her children, through regular vivid tales of her life in Abercanaid and Holywell, memories which Levertov described as a 'fascinating oral storybook' which she persuaded her mother, in her old age, to write down.[13] In the interview with M. Wynn Thomas, many years later, she comments: 'So [my mother] gave me some sense of the Welsh background, and that's part of my psyche in some way.'[14] Indeed, in her own work, Levertov recalls the effect on her as a child of her mother's accounts. She recalls Beatrice Levertoff's tales of accompanying her own father on evening outings in Abercanaid:

> All along the street the men would be singing, sitting on their heels in the dusk after a long day down the pit. The music and the stars must have been mysteriously connected for the little girl, out and about when the other children of the village had been put to bed; as they were connected for me at the same age, listening to her tell about it.[15]

So tenderly has her mother depicted the loving kindness of the Abercanaid woman who would seek out the neglected child and gently, 'with the softest / of soft old flannel, / soaped and rinsed and dried / her grubby face', that Denise Levertov herself feels that she has lived that experience and 'shall carry towards my death / [the] memory' of those kind hands.[16] At times, it is as though Levertov has taken in with her mother's milk a sense of the beauty that comes from an awareness of transience and fragility. 'Nightingale Road' evokes a picture her mother often described of an Abercanaid family of beautiful children, all of whom were dying of tuberculosis, yet who sang and played the harp so wondrously that the night air was alive with their music until weeks before they died in quick succession.[17]

In the mid 1970s, Denise Levertov, then in her fifties, visited her mother's home village, accompanied by the African-American poet, Michael S. Harper. Harper, in a poem 'Visit to Abercanaid: for Denise Levertov' writes of the significance, as he sees it, for Denise of that visit.[18] An awareness, both of a 'coming home' for herself and a moving recognition of transience and continuing fragility in that beloved place, seems to have been powerfully evoked for her, as they absorb the impact of the 1966 Aberfan tragedy and its relation to the historical experience of dwellers in this former mining valley:

> Down the road is the shrine
> of Aberfan, site of the schoolhouse
> where children died in the arms
> of their teachers in great avalanches
> of rock humming to the mined gases
> of forebears who saw the sun only on Sundays.

Addressing Beatrice Levertoff, now aged ninety, directly, Harper writes:

> Beatrice Levertov: hearing your daughter
> Read your poem of childhood, of valley events
> ... I send you
> message greetings in homage to Denise
> whose images rise into clouds as triumph trumpets
> in the spoken utterance of growth and change
> for she has come home in her backtracking of you.

For Levertov, north Wales, too, is vividly real. In 'An Arrival (North Wales 1897)' she reveals a poignant empathy with her mother's newly orphaned state.[19] On her first arrival in Holywell:

> Nostrils flaring,
> she sniffed odors of hay and stone,
> absence of Glamorgan coaldust,
> and pasted her observations quickly
> into the huge album of her mind.

As she took in the new landscape, she came to terms with her new life 'alone',

> weeping only in rage or when
> the choirs in their great and dark and
> golden glory broke forth and the hills
> skipped like lambs.

Sometimes, these tales evoked the physical reality of particular places so intensely for Denise Levertov that she recreates in a poem an almost palpable picture, as in describing the play of light, the smell, the shifting colour in 'The Vron Woods (North Wales)':

> I was wholly there
> aware of each step
> in the hum of quietness.[20]

When Levertov, now living on a different continent, hears the sound of the wind in Scotch firs, what strikingly presents itself to her mind is the sea scene her mother very regularly imagined when she heard that sound on a north Wales mountainside:

> ... my now, her then
> intermingled as vision and sound
> mingle, and what is fleeting and what remains
> outside of time.[21]

In 'Link' Levertov conjures up a picture of her mother before her death, bequeathing childhood memories – 'transferring like earrings or brooches / her lapidary trove / into my vision' – as though these were the supreme inheritance.[22] In one remarkable poem, 'The Instant', Levertov as a child, on holiday in north Wales, is direct witness to the depth of meaning the Welsh landscape holds for her mother.[23] The poem builds to an epiphanic climax when a momentary parting of the mist reveals both the distant, high peak of Snowdon and, through her reaction, its deeply charged significance for her mother:

> 'Look!' she grips me, 'It is
>   Eryri![24]
>   It's Snowdon, fifty
> miles away!' – the voice
> a wave rising to Eryri,
> falling.
>   Snowdon, home
> of eagles, resting place of
> Merlin, core of Wales.
>
>   Light
> graces the mountainhead
> for a lifetime's look, before the mist
>   draws in again.

Levertov later comments that she was deeply impressed that it was 'the charged, legendary name, Eryri, not the common Snowdon that did spring atavistically to her [mother's] lips' giving Levertov a 'moment's glimpse not simply of a distant high mountain but of the world of Welsh legend'.[25] One can discern, particularly in this last poem, Levertov's unconscious 'constructing' of an image of Wales that is compounded in part of her mother's intimate, insider knowledge and, from her own non-native status, in part of a tendency to romance about her inheritance: 'Snowdon, home / of eagles, resting place of / Merlin, core of Wales.'

Indeed, Denise Levertov saw the very process of being taught by her mother to look properly, to observe until everything cohered, as something born of her mother's Welshness. In the interview with Wynn Thomas, Levertov pointed out that her mother:

> did have a tremendous influence on my life . . . She was the kind of person who pointed out beautiful things that she saw . . . She started me off really looking at things. And I think that her feeling for beauty in nature had something very *Welsh* about it, very Celtic one might say on a broader scale.[26]

Levertov commemorates her mother as the one:

> who taught me to look;
> to name the flowers when I was still close to the ground,
> my face level with theirs;
> or to watch the sublime metamorphoses
> unfold and unfold
> over the walled back garden of our street.
>
>   ('The 90th Year')[27]

An understanding of the depth of her mother's commitment to the landscape, language and culture of Wales is one of the elements that highlight for Denise Levertov, after twenty years' residence in the USA, her relative lack of a sense of home: 'Without a terrain in which, to which, I belong / language itself is my one home, my Jerusalem' ('From a Notebook, October '68 – May '69').[28] Further, it is in part a sense of what the Welsh historical experience of religion has been – mediated through her mother – that throws into relief for Levertov her own less committed position. She is deeply aware of how much her mother had been influenced by the Welsh religious revival of 1904–5, the profound conversion experience lasting her whole life: 'A singer . . . she loved Handel's *Messiah* aria "I know that my Redeemer liveth" and despised any performance of it which, though technically excellent, failed to give the emphasis of conviction to that word "know".'[29] Levertov comments, 'Such passionate knowledge, recurrent, intermittent, or in some cases, even sustained, is what I know I don't have.'[30] On the other hand, she sees in Welsh history 'too many centuries of somber nonconformism interven[ing] between the Wales of my mother's generation and that [legendary] heritage, cutting the people off from their ancient heroes far more sharply than the Irish country people seem ever to have been from theirs'.[31]

Yet, for the émigré, Denise Levertov, the myth of her more distant origins is something that clearly provides her with a sense of nurture and particular rootedness in the world. By the last decade of her life she finds that she has finally reached a point of acceptance of Christian belief and, in *Tesserae*, she becomes aware of how gradual that process of commitment has been. As early as 'Illustrious Ancestors' (1965), she celebrates a sense of uncanny appropriateness that at the same period in history, yet separated by thousands of miles, two of her forebears were bearing witness to similar perceptions of the grounding of their being in religious awareness.³² Schneour Zulman founded Habad Hasidism, and Angel Jones of Mold, the tailor, her great-great-grandfather, had apprentices come to learn biblical interpretation from him while cutting and stitching. She intends the poem to carry the sense that she had, and that was

> shared by my late sister, I believe, of having a definite and peculiar destiny which seemed signalized by our having had among our ancestors two men who, living at the same period (late 1700s, early 1800s) but in very different cultures, had preoccupations which gave them a basic kinship (had they known of one another and been able to cross the barriers of language and religious prejudice) a kinship that Olga and I felt must be recognized in heaven, or on earth would somehow be redeemed in us. . . . The presence in the imagination of such figures and their relation to oneself is a kind of personal mythology and can function as a source of confidence and as an inspiration for the artist.³³

This is a telling instance of Levertov's fascination with secret connections and coincidences. As is revealed here, the lived life of her forebears, 'thinking some line still taut between me and them',³⁴ had a discernible effect on the self she develops in a very different here and now. Many threads of connection with Welsh culture, history and landscape ran in the weave of Levertov's adult self. There was a substantial overlap between Levertov's own personal myth and the pool of collective myth on which Welsh people commonly draw.

II

In her prose autobiography, *Tesserae*, 'which has no pretensions to forming an entire mosaic',³⁵ Levertov's exploration of patterns of significant connection become more complex, swirling out over time, space and cultures, but Welsh stones in the design still draw the eye. For a full understanding of the richness and significance of *Tesserae* – a tessera being a small tile, made of glass or stone, used in mosaics – it is important to appreciate all that Levertov may have been signalling through such a title. From the standpoint of the achieved religious conviction of her final decade, she has fashioned her autobiography in the form of a vivid Byzantine mosaic in words. Her distinctive identity, with all the gifts bestowed on her by both nature and nurture, came into being through the chance meeting of two people in Constantinople: 'Thus Celt [Beatrice Spooner-Jones] and Jew [Paul Levertoff] met in Byzantium' (*Tesserae*, 11). A most important insight to bear in mind in reading *Tesserae* is Levertov's deep conviction, repeated on several occasions, that one of the important defining characteristics of human beings is that 'man is the animal that perceives analogies'.[36] My first reading of *Tesserae* will be to see it as a verbal equivalent of a sequence of Byzantine mosaics.

Although much Byzantine art was destroyed by the Iconoclasts, the still largely preserved Monreale cathedral in Sicily gives a full sense of achieved Byzantine mosaics.[37] In that cathedral, every wall is covered with mosaic scenes and, in its original design, there were sequences of 'precursor' scenes leading up to the life of Christ – Old Testament scenes, a series of depictions of the life of the Virgin Mary – before coming to the infancy of Christ, Christological scenes, the Miracles and Christian mysteries. Filling the whole bowl of the apse is an image of Christ enthroned in majesty. Narrower surfaces – piers, spandrels – bear single saints, prophets, angels. Evolution in Byzantine techniques had introduced gold tesserae, which were used to particularly marvellous effect on curved and uneven surfaces, where the play of light could give a sense of vibrant movement.

One of the strands of her life Levertov is exploring – delicately, unobtrusively – is how she came to recognize God's power in her life. A vivid telling of the seemingly predestined conversion of her Jewish father is clearly of 'precursor' relevance (*Tesserae*, 4–11). Other vignettes reveal her youthful noticing of religious power in other lives – 'The Voice' (101–2), 'The Two Ancients' (40) – culminating in Levertov's own creation of a Cathedral of Pearls in the final section, her Christ in Majesty equivalent (147–8). The 'Gypsies' (24–32) and the 'Oracles' (95–9) sections are analogues of the prophet mosaics, tracing both the exciting and bitter experiences which have convinced Levertov of the power of destiny and the ability of seers to prophesy it. An analogue of a mystery is Levertov's wondering questioning, on hearing the unearthly beauty of an enclosed nun's singing, that such a treasure should be kept hidden. Thirty years later, she comes to understand, in a dream, that praise is of deep importance to God (102). Much of her mosaic is of richly inhabited scenes – the Tonga section (114–35), 'Janus'

(52–6), 'What One Remembers' (138–46) – but there are pier and spandrel portraits of such individuals as the gardener (47–51) and the two Ancients (39–42). The delightful animal portraits of Jinny (72–3) and Mildred (136–7), her dream pig/dog, represent the animals which frequently adorn mosaic friezes. *Tesserae* is vividly visual, ranging from the total blackness of the London city-scene in wartime (86) to scenes where she makes full use of gold tesserae: the mysterious and transforming effect lamplight has on darkness at twilight (36–7); a glorious sunset (35); the epiphany of a magnolia in bloom (54); the Cathedral of Pearls (147–8); and the vivid description of the Balkan gypsies with great strings of silver and gold coins worn as necklaces (26).

The second analogy signalled by the title *Tesserae* and the experience of the text is that of a mosaic that has been eroded by the passage of time, where the detection of pattern is left, perforce, at times, to the construing mind of the beholder. In *Romanticism and the Forms of Ruin*, Thomas McFarland sees in the Romantics' fascination with fragments a deep understanding of a fragment's power to evoke imaginative worlds beyond itself. He writes:

> In every symbol the mind proceeds from the contemplation of a fragment of reality to the apprehension but not the comprehension (to use a distinction favoured by Coleridge and Kant before him) of a larger entity, which in direct proportion to the grandeur of its putative wholeness eludes all conceiving.[38]

In an autobiography that seeks to affirm its author's belief in barely understood connections, synchronicities, spiritual dimensions beyond rational understanding, fragments stimulate the very faculties necessary for apprehension. Each of the twenty-seven sections of *Tesserae* is a constellation of tesserae, often with symbolic resonance, and part of a larger picture that readers must discern for themselves.

Levertov's great poetic power of intuitively perceiving analogies makes the material world something of an emblem book, bodying forth deeper truths for her. As she delineates in a necessarily fragmentary way what she now perceives were childhood religious insights, her starting point chronologically in terms of her own religious awareness is the powerful family myth of her Jewish father's conversion to Christianity, explored in 'A Minor Role'

(*Tesserae*, 4–11). She evokes all the wonder she must have felt as a child hearing the story told: her good father as a daring Russian child playing an end-of-winter forbidden game – ice-floe-hopping in the thawing Dnieper river. Trudging home, he found on the ground a scrap of Hebrew text telling of a young boy in the temple expounding the scriptures to wise old rabbis. His father, a great respecter of the printed word, was inexplicably angry when shown this paper, tore it up and burned it: 'Secretly, he wished he had not given up the mysterious fragment' (*Tesserae*, 5). Many years later, as a student in Germany, realizing that what he had found as a child was a page from the Christian Gospels, Levertov's father decided to see what this mysterious forbidden text contained. In this way, in this fragmentary autobiography, Levertov reveals the active power a fragmentary text contained to stimulate the mind to discovery and revelation. As her father read these Gospels, he experienced 'a profound and shaking new conviction' (7) that Jesus of Nazareth was indeed the Messiah. The rest of his life was lived, at great cost, involving severance from his Jewish family, in the light of that unshakeable conviction. Such was the basic myth in Denise Levertov's awareness of her father, a foundation part of the answer to her question, 'Who are you and how did you become what you are?' She depicts individual selves as receptors of the numinous to very different degrees, her own lifelong journey towards faith seeming a much paler thing beside the glowing ardour of her own father's youthful act of faith.

The central idea of *Tesserae* is the importance of feeling and acknowledging connectedness and being aware of what a particular attachment consists of. Discerning the deep structure of *Tesserae* is left to the intuitive powers of the reader. The work stands as a beautifully realized gestalt, best understood in relation to her poem 'Web':

> Intricate and untraceable
> weaving and interweaving,
> dark strands with light:
>
> designed, beyond
> all spiderly contrivance,
> to link, not to entrap:

>   . . .
>   forever
>   forming,
>   transforming:
>   *all praise,*
>   *all praise to the*
>   *great web.* [39]

Levertov, sensitized by her mother from her earliest years to the beauty of the earth, nurtured herself by a cosmopolitan background, and in a nuclear age having come to understand the essential need for the transcendence of national frontiers by warm human interdependence, has argued forcibly elsewhere that we could be living on a planet in its death throes.[40] Tracing the web of her own human connectedness and feeling commitment to what she finds to be part of it reveals to herself and to the world the nature of her human identity.

Levertov has described elsewhere the need for 'rifts' in poetry, 'great gaps between perception and perception which must be leapt across if they are to be crossed at all';[41] in the early sections of *Tesserae*, too, the reader is invited to challenging engagement. The first chapters, while communicating a powerful sense of the family stories Levertov grew up with, explore, too, the different sorts of perceiving that Levertov came to trust in this unusual family environment. The first section describes her amazed coming to awareness after her father's death, on seeing one of Chagall's paintings, that both he and Marc Chagall, in their growing-up in Vitepsk, in Russia, had seemed to share a similar belief in a particular local pedlar's ability to fly – synchronicity indeed. In the second, 'Inheritance', she illustrates two important convictions in telling of her mother's visit, as a small child, to a Welsh great-uncle, who had been a drummer-boy at the Battle of Waterloo and had returned to pursuing the simple, meaningful life of a fisherman: his 'mode of life differed in few respects from that of some ancestors of his (and mine) long before the Norman Conquest' (*Tesserae*, 3). Not surprisingly, as an 'elective' American, in exile from her country of origin, and child of exiles from theirs, Levertov sets a high value on connections with traditional patterns of life. In 'Link', making a poetic interpretation of this visit, Levertov reveals how intimately a sense of history is, for her, bound up in people: 'our sense of history / has only such barelytouchings, uninterpreted / not-forgettings, to suffice / for its continuance'.[42] Further, her sense of wonder is considerable, given the speed of change in the twentieth century, that her mother had with her own eyes seen this Welsh relation who had himself beheld the campaign instigator, the commander of the French army, the Emperor, Napoleon himself, in person take responsibility for his defeat at Waterloo: 'So I, living in the age of jets and nukes, am separated only by the life span of one person, my mother, from looking into the eyes of a relative who had seen the Emperor at the moment of his defeat' (*Tesserae*, 3). Poetry that Levertov wrote in the same period as *Tesserae*, at the time of the first Gulf War, showed an appalled horror at the impersonality of hi-tech warfare, distancing, as it does, perpetrators from any awareness of the human cost of their actions.[43] We could learn again to be accountable in human terms, she seems to feel.

The third section of *Tesserae*, describing Levertov's father as a boy finding a scrap of Hebrew scripture, seems to posit a faith in personal destiny. The fourth describes Beatrice Levertoff, viewing an instant of a Budapest child's life in the one night she ever spent in Hungary. From her bird's-eye vantage point in a block of flats, Beatrice sees an airing pillow, left by a maid, fall from a high balcony to land at the feet of a surprised and delighted child who scampers off with it. With her privileged sight-line, only Beatrice is granted complete understanding of the meaning of the event, when of the two participants, one – the maid – is mystified and the other – the child – is perhaps prepared to believe in magic. For Levertov, this small incident in the material world seems to adumbrate the sort of understanding fleetingly achieved of the spiritual and numinous one. These early sections tentatively map glimmering perceptions of a network of affinities and analogies which help the finite human mind to live with mystery.

Tesserae identifies points of growth of the emerging personality. In this very writerly book, Levertov frequently offers the reader what seems to be a narrative anecdote: it is often left to the reader both to articulate what growth points are being implied and to connect such delicate germination with the later burgeoning of the poet, visionary and campaigner. For example, in an autobiographical essay, Levertov, by then a seasoned anti-war and anti-nuclear campaigner, writes, 'One is in despair . . . [at] the seemingly invincible power of rapacity'.[44] In 'At Tawstock' (*Tesserae*, 20–3), she re-creates a sense of her first awareness of such tendencies in living things when, as a four-year-old on a holiday walk, she hears the terrified cry of a rabbit caught by a stoat and dimly perceives nature red in tooth and claw. Later, she is terrified when she wanders into a room full of stuffed birds of prey.

In appalled contrast to her tracing the web of meaningful connections stands the Tonga chapter – 'Some Hours in the Late Seventies' (114–35) – quite the longest section in the book. Here Levertov is trying to interpret the world-view of mutually antagonistic or indifferent people and feels 'a sort of shudder, a sharp sensation – of dismay, is it? Or just a kind of amazement at how fragmented is the human species and how odd it is to hold in mind, in some kind of unity of perception, individuals so mutually unaware' (124).

Levertov cherished connection, yet commitment to deep and less-immediate human attachment sometimes, paradoxically, required her to stand in lonely isolation. She undertook public acts of great courage during her campaigning life, acts which set her beyond the social pale. She reveals in her poem 'The Day the Audience Walked Out on Me and Why' that she insisted in commemorating black deaths elsewhere, in a church memorial service for white students shot at Kent State University.[45] In 'The Last of Childhood – For Jean in This Life or the Next'(*Tesserae*, 59–64), she records an 'abiding grief' at her brutal severance of a friendship at the age of eleven with someone she owns was 'a kindred spirit'. Her friend, Jean, had refused, any longer, to take her shoes and socks off to paddle because 'now we were older it was *not ladylike* to mess about in the stream' (61). Levertov reacted so violently, it is strongly implied, because even at this age, she was refusing to accept the limitations on behaviour that class and gender would wish to impose. Although Levertov would always see cultural identification as central to any healthy sense of self, she often experienced social moulding as a cramping and deforming of the human spirit. As she implicitly traces the trajectory of her own ability to be a free-standing campaigner, less subject than most to the ways society has of moulding conformists, she sees powerful role-models in her courageous and principled parents who, while retaining important cultural norms of their early years, were able to cast off the shackles of much early conditioning: Levertov's father is portrayed as an eight-year-old boy engaged in ice-floe-hopping sometimes *against* the current (4) and her mother sets off for distant Constantinople with the words of the Welsh small-town washerwoman ringing in her ears: 'Miss Jones, I do admire your *bravety*' [sic] (12). Ultimately, Levertov sees herself as a world citizen, passionately committed to a visionary belief in the human family. As she sometimes traces, sometimes constructs, her origins in her poems, essays and autobiography, she reveals how strongly the threads of attachment that link her to the particular – to Wales and to Russian Jewry, for example – secure the web that stretches outward to connect her to a wider world.

Notes

[1] Denise Levertov, *Tesserae: Memories and Suppositions* (Newcastle upon Tyne: Bloodaxe, 1997). Further references are included in the text.
[2] Denise Levertov, 'Conversations 2: Denise Levertov Interviewed by M. Wynn Thomas', *Swansea Review*, 17 (1997), 11–15.
[3] Quoted in biographical preamble to *Tesserae*.
[4] Denise Levertov, 'Introductory Essay', *The Bloodaxe Book of Contemporary Women Poets: Eleven British Writers*, ed. Jeni Couzyn (Newcastle upon Tyne: Bloodaxe, 1985), pp. 75–9 (78).
[5] Linda Welshimer Wagner (ed.), *Denise Levertov: In Her Own Province* (New York: New Directions, 1979). Levertov entitles a biographical essay on her mother 'An American Poet with a Russian Name Tells about the Life of her 100% Welsh Mother'. In a later collection, Denise Levertov, *Light up the Cave* (New York: New Directions, 1981), she changes the title to 'Beatrice Levertoff'.
[6] Levertov, 'Introductory Essay', p. 78.
[7] John Bowlby, *Attachment and Loss 2: Separation: Anger and Anxiety*, 2/3 (Harmondsworth: Penguin, 1975), pp. 304–6.
[8] Denise Levertov, 'Beatrice Levertoff', pp. 238–43.
[9] Ibid., p. 241.
[10] Denise Levertov, *Breathing the Water* (New York: New Directions, 1987), p. 36.
[11] Levertov, 'Introductory Essay', p. 75.
[12] Ibid., p. 75.
[13] Levertov, 'Beatrice Levertoff', pp. 239–40.
[14] Levertov, 'Conversations 2', p. 13.
[15] Levertov, 'Beatrice Levertoff', p. 239.
[16] Denise Levertov, *A Door in the Hive/Evening Train* (Newcastle upon Tyne: Bloodaxe, 1993), p. 91.
[17] Denise Levertov, *Life in the Forest* (New York: New Directions, 1978), pp. 8–9.
[18] Michael S. Harper, 'Visit to Abercanaid', *The Anglo-Welsh Review*, 26, 58 (1977), 18–19. I am grateful to Daniel Williams for drawing my attention to the existence of this poem.
[19] Denise Levertov, *Candles in Babylon* (New York: New Directions, 1982), p. 43.
[20] Ibid., p. 75.

21 Denise Levertov, *Sands of the Well* (Newcastle upon Tyne: Bloodaxe, 1998).
22 Levertov, *A Door in the Hive/Evening Train*, p. 158.
23 Denise Levertov, *Selected Poems* (Newcastle upon Tyne: Bloodaxe, 1986), p. 19.
24 In fact 'Eryri', meaning 'home of eagles', is the whole area of Snowdonia. 'Yr Wyddfa' refers to Snowdon itself.
25 Denise Levertov, 'The Sense of Pilgrimage', *The Poet in the World* (New York: New Directions, 1973), pp. 62–86 (69–70).
26 Levertov, 'Conversations 2', p. 13.
27 Levertov, *Life in the Forest*, p. 24.
28 Denise Levertov, *Relearning the Alphabet* (New York: New Directions, 1970), p. 97.
29 Denise Levertov, 'Work That Enfaiths', *New and Selected Essays* (New York: New Directions, 1992), pp. 247–57 (247).
30 Ibid.
31 Levertov, 'The Sense of Pilgrimage', p. 69.
32 Denise Levertov, *The Jacob's Ladder* (New York: New Directions, 1961), p. 87.
33 Levertov, 'The Sense of Pilgrimage', p. 70.
34 Levertov, *The Jacob's Ladder*, p. 87.
35 Author's note in *Tesserae*.
36 Levertov, 'The Sense of Pilgrimage', p. 84.
37 An account of a fully achieved Byzantine mosaic which seems to illuminate Levertov's intentions in *Tesserae* is given in the entry on 'Monreale Cathedral' in the *Dictionary of Art*, vol. 21, ed. J. Turner (New York: Grove, 1996), pp. 897–901.
38 Thomas McFarland, *Romanticism and the Forms of Ruin: Wordsworth, Coleridge and Modalities of Fragmentation* (Princeton: Princeton University Press, 1981), p. 27.
39 Levertov, *A Door in the Hive/Evening Train*, p. 76.
40 Denise Levertov, 'Address to the Commission on the Environment and Energy at the World Peace Parliament, Sofia, Bulgaria. September 24, 1980', *Light up the Cave*, p. 179.
41 Denise Levertov, 'Some Notes on Organic Form', *New and Selected Essays*, pp. 67–73.
42 Levertov, *A Door in the Hive/Evening Train*, p. 158.
43 See, for example 'The Certainty', ibid., p. 175.
44 Levertov, 'Introductory Essay', p. 79.
45 Levertov, *Selected Poems*, pp. 100–1.

12

'For Old Tom read Uncle Tom': Emlyn Williams and Ralph Ellison

DANIEL WILLIAMS

In a typically trenchant reading of Emlyn Williams's *The Corn is Green* (1938) M. Wynn Thomas argues that the play offers a 'ringing affirmation of Britishness'.[1] Williams's play is a reworking of the Pygmalion story, in which Miss Moffat, an 'admirable member of the eccentric, philanthropic, programme of the English middle class', educates the bright miner, Morgan Evans, out of the squalor and limitations of his Welsh life and prepares him to take up a place at Oxford University.[2] Thomas argues that a 'sophisticated people's culture is never hinted at in *The Corn is Green*', and thus 'the transition from one culture to another' is made to seem 'relatively troublefree and completely desirable'.[3] This reading is reinforced by the fact that the Welsh speakers in the play, especially as embodied in the figure of Old Tom, are a backward people speaking a limited local patois.

> MISS RONBERRY [*nervously*] Is there anything you would like to know, Mr Tom?
> OLD TOM Where iss Shakespeare?
> MISS RONBERRY Where? . . . Shakespeare, Mr Tom, was a very great writer.
> OLD TOM Writer? Like the Bible?
> MISS RONBERRY Like the Bible.
> OLD TOM [*looking at her doubtfully*] Dear me, and me thinkin' the man was a place. [*following the others, muttering sadly*] If I iss been born fifty years later, I iss been top of the class.[4]

Wynn Thomas concludes his discussion of this passage by suggesting that 'for Old Tom read Uncle Tom, perhaps'.⁵ To compare 'Old Tom' with 'Uncle Tom' is to bring African-American sources to bear on the study of Welsh literature, and my intention in this chapter is to explore some of the implications of Wynn Thomas's intriguing suggestion.

In his introduction to the 1981 reprint of *Invisible Man* – described as 'the veritable *Moby Dick* of the racial crisis' upon its first appearance in 1952⁶ – the African-American novelist Ralph Ellison recounted the gestation of his novel as follows:

> I had published a story in which a young Afro-American seaman, ashore in Swansea, South Wales, was forced to grapple with the troublesome 'American' aspects of his identity after white Americans had blacked his eye during a wartime blackout on the Swansea street called Straight (no, his name was not Saul, nor did he become a Paul). But here the pressure toward self-scrutiny came from a group of Welshmen who rescued him and surprised him by greeting him as a 'Black Yank' and inviting him to a private club, and then sang the American National Anthem in his honor. The story was published in 1944, but now in 1945 on a Vermont farm, the theme of a young Negro's quest for identity was reasserting itself in a far more bewildering form.⁷

Ellison described *Invisible Man* as having 'erupted out of what had been conceived as a war novel'.⁸ His wartime experiences as a Merchant Marine aboard the *SS Sun Yat Sen* had brought him to Swansea, and in addition to the story referred to in his introduction, Ellison had been working on two others based on his experiences in Wales. In a hitherto unpublished short story entitled 'The Red Cross at Morriston, Swansea, S.W.' the narrator describes his journey through the city to a Red Cross club 'held in Lebannon Church Hall' where he comments on the palpable familiarity of what the sociologist Alfred Zimmern had famously described in 1921 as 'American Wales':⁹

> Hayes . . . was saying that his club was housed in a structure erected in the early eighteenth century . . . Hayes' reference to a church hall completely disarmed me for the loud Count Basie recording I heard as we reached the building. Suddenly it was like coming home . . . But for the accent – incidentally they do speak the way you heard in 'The Corn is Green' – I might have been in Harlem, on Broadway, or for that matter, in Brooklyn.¹⁰

If Wales seems curiously familiar, there are some notable cultural differences:

> Straight ahead, a stage, the kind you find in high school auditoriums faced the room. And to our right, men and girls lounged in groups of upholstered chairs, conversing somehow over the blare of the phonograph. I asked Hayes why the stage and learned that Welsh drama had developed out of the Nonconformist religious movement, which instituted amateur dramatics; thus the stage; thus, at long range, such contemporary Welsh dramatists as Emlyn Williams and Richard Llewellyn.[11]

Richard Llewellyn would have been familiar to Ellison as John Ford's Hollywood version of *How Green Was My Valley* had won the best picture Oscar in 1941, thus creating a hugely influential exportable version of Welshness.[12] The references to *The Corn is Green* and Emlyn Williams are more intriguing. In stating that 'they do speak the way you heard in "The Corn is Green"', Ellison is clearly assuming that his readers are aware of Williams's play. Ellison had composed his story before the successful Hollywood version of *The Corn is Green* was released in 1945. A version of the play had opened in New York, with Ethel Barrymore as Miss Moffat, in November 1940, however, and went on to win the New York Drama Critics' Circle award for the 'best play of foreign authorship presented in New York during the season 1940–41'.[13] Ellison was living in New York and moving in literary circles during the early forties, and his references to Williams suggest that the play had some impact upon him.

In the penultimate paragraph of *Invisible Man* the narrator meditates upon his own invisibility and comments cryptically that:

> In going underground, I whipped it all except the mind, the mind. And the mind that has conceived a plan of living must never lose sight of the chaos against which the pattern was conceived. That goes for societies as well as for individuals . . . And there's still a conflict within me: With Louis Armstrong one half of me says, 'Open the window and let the foul air out', while the other says, 'It was good green corn before the harvest'.[14]

Jazz trumpeter Louis Armstrong has the ability to transform the 'bad breath' of city life into art, and while the narrator seeks to achieve something similar, he is also drawn back to the folk traditions (the 'good green corn') of the rural South. The title of

Williams's *The Corn is Green* comes from a similarly structured passage written by the promising miner Morgan Evans. He wishes to replace the 'carbon monoxide' in the mine for a 'smell . . . like fresh flowers lying about' and imagines a surreal scene where he walks 'through the . . . shaft, in the dark' and 'can touch with my hands the leaves on the trees, and underneath where the corn is green'.[15] To speak of an 'influence' operating between writers is invariably problematic, but Ellison's reference to the 'good green corn' is particularly intriguing, given his earlier references to Emlyn Williams and his play. The connections are too tenuous for any firm links to be made, but a 'contrapuntal' reading of Ellison and Williams may prove to be illuminating.[16] The characters in the opening section of *Invisible Man*, for instance, bear a suggestive resemblance to the characters in *The Corn is Green*, and Williams's play – read by Wynn Thomas as embodying a colonialist mindset – looks rather different when read in the light cast by Ellison's writings specifically, and by African-American cultural criticism more generally.[17]

Both *The Corn is Green* and the opening section of *Invisible Man* are centrally concerned with the process of social and racial uplift through education. The figures of the educationalists Miss Moffat and Miss Ronberry in *The Corn is Green* are paralleled in the figures of the African-American educationalist Bledsoe and the white philanthropist Mr Norton in Ellison's *Invisible Man*. Where Morgan Evans is presented as someone who may become 'a great statesman of our country' in *The Corn is Green*, the 'Invisible Man' is believed to be 'a potential Booker T. Washington'.[18] The rustic, virtually Welsh-monoglot Old Tom, who is often 'carried away by the music', finds his equivalent in the figure of Jim Trueblood, the performer of the 'primitive spirituals' that embarrass the narrator of *Invisible Man* with their 'earthly harmonies'.[19] In encountering Trueblood, the educated narrator gives voice to his prejudices: 'How all of us at the college hated the black-belt people, the 'peasants', during those days! We were trying to lift them up and they, like Trueblood, did everything it seemed to pull us down.'[20] As the narrative develops, the Invisible Man comes to shed his earlier prejudices and to consider Trueblood an embodiment of a distinctive African-American consciousness. Morgan Evans never comes to realize the alienating effects of his education in *The Corn is Green*, but there are suggestions throughout the play that the results of Miss Moffat's philanthropic efforts are not wholly positive. Morgan, for instance, laments the fact that he is increasingly regarded by his fellow miners as '[c]i bach yr ysgol! The schoolmistress's little dog!'[21] and the play does not end with a final and triumphal farewell as Morgan leaves for Oxford. His departure takes place offstage, while the audience sees Miss Moffat holding Morgan and Bessie's illegitimate child and noting that 'you musn't be clumsy this time'.[22] It seems that the Welsh future lies in English hands.

Wynn Thomas's proposal, 'for Old Tom read Uncle Tom', may be suggestively related to the structure of Williams's play, where a predominant Britishness is occasionally undermined by voices critical of linguistic and cultural domination. Whilst the image of 'Uncle Tom' invokes the unthreatening and submissive African-American type of Harriet Beecher Stowe's abolitionist novel, Houston A. Baker has traced some of the ways in which African-American spokesmen were able to use that minstrel mask in order to promote their political programmes within the white world.[23] Ellison foregrounds the use of such strategies in *Invisible Man*, most notably when the narrator recalls his grandfather's death:

> On his deathbed he called my father to him and said, 'Son, after I'm gone I want you to keep up the good fight. I never told you, but our life is a war and I have been a traitor all my born days, a spy in the enemy's country ever since I gave up my gun back in the Reconstruction. Live with your head in the lion's mouth. I want you to overcome 'em with yeses, undermine 'em with grins, agree 'em to death and destruction, let 'em swoller you till they vomit or bust wide open'.[24]

In keeping with Baker's theory, the minstrel mask is used to hide a submerged hatred and desire for revenge. The challenge for African-American spokespersons, argues Baker, was to transform 'the mask and its sounds into a negligible discursive currency'.[25] It may be illuminating to consider Emlyn Williams in such terms – as a playwright whose works are characterized by the 'self-conscious adoption of minstrel tones and types to keep his audience tuned in'.[26]

That *The Corn is Green* may be more than a work of 'Anglocentric conservatism'[27] is suggested by a fascinating dialogue between Williams and the Monmouthshire anthropologist Lord

Raglan in the pages of the journal *Wales* in 1958. In an article entitled 'I Take My Stand' Raglan cast his anthropologist's eye over Wales. His title invokes the highly reactionary manifesto of the Southern Agrarians in the 1930s, and while Allen Tate, John Crowe Ransom and others had vented their dislike of industrialism, urbanization, immigration and the American left in defending the values of the old South, Raglan, defining himself as 'a Monmouthshire man', mounted an attack on the Welsh language:

> Most of the speakers of Welsh are, as I have said, illiterate or semi-literate, but there are a few thousand people who have learnt to speak the literary language, and who make a regular cult of it . . . The Welsh language . . . is used for at least three undesirable purposes, to conceal the results of scholarship, to try to lower the standards of official competence, and, worst of all, to create enmity where none existed.[28]

Emlyn Williams responded in the next issue of *Wales* in an ironic mode, signalled by his title: 'A Dyma Fi, Druan o Gymro, Yn Sefyll' ('And Here am I, a Poor Welshman, Standing').

> My blood has never boiled – perhaps it doesn't belong to the right group – but when I finished reading Lord Raglan's article 'I Take My Stand', in my October *Wales*, I was conscious of a low but steady simmer; I can still hear it. It's getting louder.
> I am a Welshman who spoke no colloquial English till I was eight; but since I was 21 I have lived mainly in London, working in English, which has naturally, through the years, become for me a sharper instrument than my native and cherished Welsh. I am not a Welsh Nationalist, Oxford and London have been very good to me, I have not even any strong feelings that a Welsh child brought up outside Wales in a completely English social milieu should be made to speak Welsh. So I am presumably fairly impartial. Yet when I see, in print, a dictum that when Welsh ceases to be spoken 'it will be a happy day for Wales', I don't feel impartial at all . . . I must be fair to my mother – she can't have been quite hopeless – nor can my father, for they acquired a smattering of English, and in no time were making sprightly use of it, particularly my father. But I must make a clean breast of Taid and Nain, on both sides: all four grandparents can only have spoken English of the most broken (not to say estropié) kind, and the whole job-lot qualify, straight away as pretty well 100 per cent illiterates. My maternal grandfather could recite most mellifluously from the Song of Solomon,

and from poems by Ceiriog as sweetly elegiac as 'Lycidas'; but, alas, he did it in Welsh.[29]

Here we witness a Welsh equivalent of what Baker describes as the deliberate adoption of 'minstrel tones'. Behind a veneer of Britishness – 'Oxford and London have been very good to me' – lies a robust defence of Welsh-language culture in the face of Raglan's bigotry. It is an example of a dominant society's language being used against itself. Writing in 1950, the critic F. W. Bateson noted the 'bogus slickness' and 'peculiar lucidity' that characterized the 'second-rate writers on the linguistic fringe – Anglo-Jews like Guedalla, Anglo-Scots like Compton Mackenzie, Anglo-Welshmen like Emlyn Williams'.[30] The possibility of subversive intent may account for Bateson's description of these peripheral writers' '*peculiar* lucidity', and may also account for his excessive dismissiveness. 'Slick' and 'lucid' may be appropriate adjectives to describe the mode and manner of Williams's style, but there are times when his mastery of English forms is used to critical effect. Both the tone and content of Williams's response to Raglan, for instance, are captured in John Goronwy Jones's ironically charged words in *The Corn is Green*:

> It is terrible, isn't it, the people on these green fields and flowery hillsides bein' turned out of Heaven because they cannot answer Saint Peter when he asks them who they are in English? It is wicked, isn't it, the Welsh children not bein' born knowing English, isn't it? [*In a crescendo of ironic mimicry*] Good heavens, God bless my soul, by Jove, this that and the other!derlineerville[31]

Whilst these words are uttered by a minor character in the play of 1938, the tone is very similar to that adopted by Williams in his exchange with Lord Raglan twenty years later.

Lord Raglan is a particularly interesting figure in the context of this present discussion, for if his wartime experiences in Wales were one source for *Invisible Man*, Ralph Ellison also noted that he was 'much concerned with findings such as Lord Raglan's as a literary matter' when composing the novel.[32]

> I was reading Lord Raglan's *The Hero*, which has to do with tradition, myth and drama. As you will recall, Lord Raglan was concerned with

the manner in which myth became involved with the histories of living persons, became incorporated into their personal legends. [33]

Ellison's biographer, Lawrence Jackson, traces the influences of Raglan's *The Hero: A Study in Tradition, Myth and Drama* (1936) on the young novelist's thought, and notes that the structure of Ellison's Welsh-based short story, 'In a Strange Country', derives from the 'dramatic situation that developed heroism: the stranger making his way into the village'.[34] The story begins with the main protagonist, Parker, sitting in a Welsh pub recalling events that have happened earlier that evening:

> Coming ashore from the ship he had felt the excited expectancy of entering a strange land. Moving along the road in the dark he had planned to stay ashore all night, and in the morning he would see the country with fresh eyes . . . Someone had cried 'Jesus H. Christ', and he had thought, He's from home, and grinned and apologized into the light they flashed in his eyes. He had felt the blow coming when they yelled, 'It's a goddamn nigger', but it struck him anyway. He was having a time of it when some of Mr Catti's countrymen stepped in and Mr Catti had guided him into the pub . . . At first he had included them in his blind rage. But they had seemed so genuinely and uncondescendingly polite that he was disarmed. Now the anger and resentment had slowly ebbed, and he felt only a smouldering sense of self-hate and ineffectiveness. Why should he blame them when they had helped him? *He* had been the one so glad to hear an American voice. You can't take it out on them, they're a different breed; even from the English.[35]

The passage traces a shift in Parker's perception of the Welsh, from initially including them in his 'blind rage' to his increasing awareness of their ethnic difference. Parker has a black eye following his encounter with the white GIs, and issues of sight and perception play a central role throughout a tale primarily concerned with the meaning and constitution of the African-American self – the black 'I'.

This Emersonian play between 'eye' and 'I' is prevalent in *Invisible Man*. The 'invisibility to which I refer', states the narrator of the novel's 'Prologue',

> occurs because of a peculiar disposition of the eyes of those with whom I come in contact. A matter of the construction of their inner eyes, those

eyes with which they look through their physical eyes upon reality. I am not complaining, nor am I protesting either. It is sometimes advantageous to be unseen, although it is most often rather wearing on the nerves. Then too, you're constantly being bumped against those of poor vision. Or again, you often doubt if you really exist.[36]

In the earlier story it is under the gaze of the Welsh that Parker begins to perceive the possibility of uniting his own divided consciousness as a 'Negro' and an 'American':

> 'Are there many like me in Wales?'
> 'Oh yes! Yanks all over the place. Black Yanks and white.'
> 'Black *Yanks*?' He wanted to smile.[37]

Upon entering the club with his Welsh hosts the light strikes Parker's 'injured eye, it was as though it were being peeled by an invisible hand', and the story proceeds to explore the layers of identity that constitute the African-American self.[38]

If Ellison's encounter with Wales led to fictional explorations of the inherent duality of African-American identity, Williams's *The Corn is Green* also offers a plural vision of 'Welshness', ranging from the 'bespectacled, gloomy and intense' Mr John Goronwy Jones to the 'big, slow' Robbart Robbatch, from the 'quick and impudent' Morgan Evans to the self-deprecating Old Tom.[39] If figures such as the comical Squire and philanthropic Miss Moffat suggest that *The Corn is Green* offers an affirmation of Britishness, there is evidence of other motivations at work. Whilst Old Tom is made to seem foolish, he is also described as 'an elderly, distinguished-looking, grey-bearded peasant'.[40] Russell Stephens has noted Williams's extensive use of Welsh, often untranslated, 'which in places gives the play a bilingual quality' thus testifying to the presence and strength of an indigenous culture.[41] Indeed, the play may be read in light of the Raglan–Williams exchange, for while the 'punctiliously pukka' style of Williams's response, like the play's familiar Pygmalion narrative, is clearly appealing to an English audience, behind the 'peculiar lucidity' of the prose, as beneath the play's melodramatic surface, lies a submerged critique of cultural imperialist assumptions.[42]

That this critique should not be immediately apparent is in accordance with Houston A. Baker's account of the uses made of the 'Uncle Tom' figure. Whilst the adoption of minstrel tones allows the African-American spokesperson to keep the audience tuned in while engaging in 'crafty political analyses', it is of the essence of strategic minstrelsy that 'there can be no worry that the Negro is getting "out of hand"'.[43] In the context of 1930s Wales *The Corn is Green* can certainly be seen to play an essentially placatory role. Wales was of course in the grip of a severe economic depression throughout the 1930s, and the radical working-class politics spawned by that context caused considerable alarm in middle-class circles. The late 1930s also saw a less widespread but widely observed growth in Welsh national consciousness, particularly following the burning of an RAF bombing school in Penyberth, in the Welsh-speaking heartland of the Llŷn peninsula, in 1936 by three leading Welsh Nationalists. The story of Morgan Evans's rise from the mine to Oxford, and from Wales to England, through education, forms a link between classes and nations, and suggests that a common set of values exists which transcend the divisions of class and nationhood. The play is also set in the late nineteenth century, thus allowing Williams to detach his work from the radicalized politics of south Wales in the 1930s, and from the challenge posed by an emergent Welsh nationalism.

If questions of class and nationhood are suppressed, whether consciously or otherwise, in *The Corn is Green*, it is interesting to note that five years later these issues were foregrounded in Ralph Ellison's Welsh short stories. This is particularly the case in the final scene of 'In a Strange Country', which takes place in a club where a male-voice choir rehearsal is taking place:

> When the opening bars were struck, he saw the others pushing back their chairs and standing, and he stood, understanding even as Mr Catti whispered, 'Our national anthem'.
> There was something in the music and in the way they held their heads that was strangely moving. He hummed beneath his breath. When it was over he would ask for the words.
> But even while he heard the final triumphal chord still sounding, the piano struck up 'God Save the King'. It was not nearly so stirring. Then swiftly modulating they swept into the 'Internationale', to words about an international army. He was carried back to when he was a small boy marching in the streets behind the bands that came to his southern town
> . . .
> Mr Catti had nudged him. He looked up, seeing the conductor looking straight at him, smiling. They were all looking at him. Why, was

it his eye? Were they playing a joke? And suddenly he recognized the
melody and felt that his knees would give way. It was as though he had
been pushed into the horrible foreboding country of dreams and they
were enticing him into some unwilled and degrading act, from which
only his failure to remember the words would save him. Only now the
melody seemed charged with some vast new meaning which that part of
him that wanted to sing could not fit with the old familiar words. And
beyond the music he kept hearing the soldiers' voices, yelling as they had
when the light struck his eye. He saw the singers still staring, and as
though to betray him he heard his own voice singing out like a suddenly
amplified radio:

> '... Gave proof through the night
> That our flag was still there ...'

It was like the voice of another over whom he had no control. His eye
throbbed. A wave of guilt shook him, followed by a burst of relief. For
the first time in your whole life, he thought with dreamlike wonder, the
words are not ironic. He stood in confusion as the song ended, staring
into the men's Welsh faces, not knowing whether to curse them or to
return their good-natured smiles.[44]

Dai Smith is the only Welsh critic to have discussed this story, and he
quotes selectively from this conclusion to suggest that 'the story is a
sentimental but forceful expression of what south Wales, by the
1940s, had come to stand for in the estimation of others'.[45] Writing
from an American perspective, John F. Callahan suggests that the
'strange country' of the title stands 'less for Wales than for America,
and like many Americans, Parker discovers his Americanness
overseas'.[46] I am not inclined to disagree with either of these
readings, but neither pays attention to the anthems being sung or to
the different reactions that they elicit. Barbara Foley argues persuasively that 'In a Strange Country' is embedded in the discourse of
the American Communist Party (CPUSA), and that the figure of
Paul Robeson – the CPUSA's 'most prominent antifascist publicist' –
informs the story.[47] Whilst Ellison offers a searing critique of the
Communists in *Invisible Man*, he was closely involved with the
political and cultural Left during the 1930s and '40s.[48] As the story
develops, various lines from Othello come to Parker's mind; 'Put out
that light, Othello – or do you enjoy being hit with one?'[49] Robeson
was particularly famous for playing the role of Othello, in Britain
and the United States, and the play's final soliloquy was a standard

item in his concert performances. Surprisingly, Foley does not refer to Robeson's close connections with Wales, which ranged from marching with the miners in the late 1920s to his appearance as the genial giant David Goliath in a film depicting an African-American's experiences in a Welsh mining community, *Proud Valley* (1940).[50] The final scene of 'In a Strange Country' could have been lifted from that film, although Parker's comments on the particular significance of the individual anthems give the sentimental scene a broader political significance.

Parker notes that the Welsh anthem and the 'Internationale' are sung with greater passion than 'God Save the King'. This observation reinforces a connection made earlier in the story between Wales and Russia, for a Welsh song evokes an image of 'a Russian peasant kneeling to kiss the earth and rising wet-eyed to enter into battle with cries of fierce exultation' in Parker's mind.[51] In the final scene the 'Internationale' leads somewhat curiously to images of 'the bands that came to his southern town'. It seems that Ellison is making connections between folk cultures, and the fact that the 'Internationale' functions as a link between the Welsh and American anthems evokes the internationalism promoted by the Popular Front politics of the period; a reading reinforced by the hovering presence of Robeson behind the narrative. Perhaps most significant, however, is the fact that the songs represent a range of identities that are being embraced simultaneously by the Welsh. In wartime Wales, Parker encounters a people, like his own, who retain a sense of their own distinctiveness whilst also identifying and contributing to the war effort of a larger nation-state. The plurality of identities expressed by the Welsh creates a space where Parker can, for the first time it seems, identify with the 'Star-Spangled Banner'. The story thus traces the formation of a 'Black Yank' in a strange country.

The series of anthems performed by the choir at the conclusion of 'In a Strange Country' is reflective of a period in Wales where a dominant Britishness was being challenged by internationalist and nationalist conceptions of being and belonging. Whilst Emlyn Williams sought to suppress the class and national elements within his play, Ellison foregrounds the fact that behind a British identity lay elements of other residual and potentially emergent structures of feeling that were active within the culture. The diversity of identities embraced by the Welsh spoke directly to Ellison's own experience. It becomes particularly clear in his remarkable essays on jazz and literature that, for Ellison, American identity is something that is always trying to be achieved, an identity that is in a process of continual emergence. Ellison never denies the specificities and distinctiveness of African-American culture, but at the heart of his fiction and criticism lies a belief in a common – not homogeneous – democratic culture. In reviewing LeRoi Jones's nationalist history of African-American music, *Blues People*, Ellison argued that

> Taken as a theory of American Negro culture it can only contribute to more confusion than clarity. For Jones has stumbled over that ironic obstacle which lies in the path of any who would fashion a theory of American Negro culture while ignoring the intricate network of connections which binds Negroes to the larger society. To do so is to attempt a delicate brain surgery with a switch-blade. And it is possible that any viable theory of Negro American culture obligates us to fashion a more adequate theory of American culture as a whole. The heel bone is, after all, connected to the head bone.[52]

In this discussion of Emlyn Williams and Ralph Ellison I hope to have suggested that an engagement with African-American cultural criticism may obligate us to fashion more adequate theories of Welsh culture and the 'intricate network of connections' which binds it to the 'larger society'. It strikes me that many Anglophone Welsh writers could be read in terms of the ways in which they adopted the 'minstrel tones' expected of them in a British context in order to turn the language of the dominant culture against itself. There's more work to be done on the ways in which we may 'for [the Welsh] Old Tom read [the African-American] Uncle Tom'.

Notes

[1] M. Wynn Thomas, *Internal Difference: Literature in Twentieth-Century Wales* (Cardiff: University of Wales Press, 1992), p. 71.
[2] Ibid., p. 71.
[3] Ibid., p. 72.
[4] Emlyn Williams, *The Corn is Green, with Two Other Plays* (London: Pan Books, 1950), p. 44.
[5] Thomas, *Internal Difference*, p. 73.
[6] F. W. Dupee, 'On *Invisible Man*', *Washington Post* (26 September, 1965), p. 4.

[7] Ralph Ellison, 'Introduction', *Invisible Man* ([1952] New York: Vintage, 1995), p. xiv.
[8] Ellison, 'Introduction', p. vii.
[9] On Zimmern see Dai Smith, *Aneurin Bevan and the World of South Wales* (Cardiff: University of Wales Press, 1993), p. i.
[10] 'At the Red Cross in Morriston, S.W.', Ralph Ellison Papers, Library of Congress, Washington DC. Box 165. No page numbers.
[11] Dylan Thomas and Alun Lewis are included in earlier drafts of this story, but omitted, presumably because they were not dramatists.
[12] See David Berry, *Wales and the Cinema: The First Hundred Years* (Cardiff: University of Wales Press, 1994), pp. 166–72.
[13] Russell Stephens, *Emlyn Williams: The Making of a Dramatist* (Bridgend: Seren, 2000), p. 191.
[14] Ellison, *Invisible Man*, p. 486.
[15] Williams, *The Corn is Green*, p. 37.
[16] The term is Dai Smith's, in *Aneurin Bevan*, p. 12.
[17] Russell Stephens also argues that 'Williams's best-known and finest play is also his most colonialist', *Emlyn Williams*, p. 187.
[18] Williams, *The Corn is Green*, p. 94; Ellison, *Invisible Man*, p. 15.
[19] Williams, *The Corn is Green*, p. 42; Ellison, *Invisible Man*, p. 43.
[20] Ibid., p. 43.
[21] Williams, *The Corn is Green*, p. 62.
[22] Ibid., p. 96.
[23] Houston A. Baker Jr., *Modernism and the Harlem Renaissance* (Chicago: Chicago University Press, 1987).
[24] Ellison, *Invisible Man*, p. 17.
[25] Baker, *Modernism*, p. 24.
[26] Ibid., p. 30.
[27] This is how Stephen Knight describes the play in ' "A New Enormous Music": Industrial Fictions in Wales', in M. Wynn Thomas (ed.), *Welsh Writing in English: A Guide to Welsh Literature* (Cardiff: University of Wales Press, 2003), p. 48. Wynn Thomas discusses the Williams–Raglan debate in *Internal Difference*, pp. 73–5.
[28] Lord Raglan, 'I Take My Stand', *Wales* (October 1958), 17.
[29] Emlyn Williams, 'A Dyma Fi, Druan o Gymro, Yn Sefyll (I Take My Stand)', *Wales* (November 1958), 16, 18.
[30] F. W. Bateson, *English Poetry: A Critical Introduction* (London: Longmans, Green & Co., 1950), p. 93.
[31] Williams, *The Corn is Green*, p. 13.
[32] Ralph Ellison, 'On Initiation Rites and Power', *Going to the Territory* (New York: Vintage, 1987), p. 44.
[33] Ibid., p. 43.
[34] Lawrence Jackson, *Ralph Ellison: Emergence of Genius* (New York: John Wiley and Sons, 2002), pp. 297, 320.
[35] Ellison, 'In a Strange Country', *Flying Home and Other Stories* (London: Penguin, 1998), p. 138.
[36] Ellison, *Invisible Man*, pp. 3–4.
[37] Ellison, 'In a Strange Country', p. 139.
[38] Ibid., p. 140.
[39] Williams, *The Corn is Green*, pp. 12, 25.
[40] Ibid., p. 42.

[41] Stephens, *Emlyn Williams*, p. 182.
[42] Thomas, *Internal Difference*, p. 74
[43] Baker, *Modernism*, p. 30.
[44] Ellison, 'In a Strange Country', pp. 145–6.
[45] Dai Smith, *Aneurin Bevan*, p. 10.
[46] John F. Callahan, 'Introduction', Ralph Ellison, *Flying Home and Other Stories*, p. xxxvi.
[47] Barbara Foley, 'Reading Redness', *Journal of Narrative Theory*, 29, 3 (1999), 332, 334.
[48] See Jackson, *Ralph Ellison*, pp. 198–253.
[49] Ellison, 'In a Strange Country', p. 144.
[50] On *Proud Valley* see Berry, *Wales and the Cinema*, pp. 166–72.
[51] Ellison, 'In a Strange Country', p. 142.
[52] Ralph Ellison, 'Blues People', *Shadow and Act* ([1953] New York: Quality Paperback, 1994), p. 253.

IV
TRANSLATIONS

TONY CONRAN

CIVILIZATION IN WAITING?

(Catullus Variations)

for Wynn Thomas at sixty

QUOI DONO LEPIDUM NOVUM LIBELLUM?

> *To whom shall I donate this sprightly sequence*
> *New and just polished with dry pumice?*
> *To you, Cornelius: you always counted*
> *My trifles worth consideration – even*
> *At a time you, alone of Italians,*
> *In three tomes, magisterial and erudite*
> *(By God!) dared explicate all Ages.*
> *So take my pages now, for what they're worth –*
> *And this Age, may the muses make 'em last!*
>
> Catullus, Carmina, 1

1

It is rare that the registers
Of a first green come down to us –
Matter-of-fact yet grateful
Of a new start. Civilization, is it,
In a scholar or two, alone of
The Cymry, daring what's impossible?

That's a requisite, certainly. But
The trifles, Wynn, *nugae*, knicknacks
Of a changed heart, personal as a lovers'
Tiff – that's what you've got to watch!

Glacier's in retreat, the rock's
Yellowly sterile in a dry April
Yet already a seed communicates.
The croziers of a sporeling uncurl.

2

> *'Dear heart, how like you this?'*
> Sir Thomas Wyatt

A moment then. Sometimes no more than that.
Scholars have toiled, *cyfarwyddiaid*
Instructed our mabinogi. Translators
Have pleaded, and a brief ripeness is all.
By the waters of Po and Trwyeryn and Taff
We've sung hymns in tabernas. Now, prosperity
Empowers our solitude. Verona
Or Uplands, a Cornwall-facing door . . .

For Catullus, Cornelius in Verona was
News. So today: Anglo-Welsh scholarship
Laboriously erudite, must be
A compendium of Ages, a tribal melt.

Civilization can only begin
When the agenda is Everything.

3

Civilizations have unlikely gates.

A mishmash of devolved powers,
Associate cities, authorities
Like maggots, crawling on the benevolence
(Such as it is) of the Central Directive . . .

Yet out of such garbage endlessly rotting
A boy crept from his house at harvest moon,
Bare-foot, along the winnowing sea
And in remembering a bird, a widower
That all the summer cried, his civilization
Opened to a common sorrow.

America
('These States') in that ragged vision
Judges itself. Nothing – intolerance,
Fear, race-hatred – deflects that cry.

4

. . . the baronets wake from dreams of commerce
                                        Idris Davies

Many-tribed Cardiff sniffs the wind.
Silures, Chinese, Yemeni
Sound past. Prancing yuppy girls
From furthest Ordovicia
Tinkle in Welsh. Anglo-Japanese,
– A dialect on walking streets
Beyond the jazz, the feathered drum –
Is still snap-happy, but's seen better days.

Assembly, Arts Council, University Press –
These successor states to Wales,
Visigoth kingdoms, last after the loot
A decade or two, till the next bacillus
Takes like a vaccination – a scar
On Cardiff's thigh all that's left.

5

Is this the City State we dream of?
Like the good fairies that shade into
The out-of-focus of a christening
The Regrets whisper solicitude.
It is always so. Birth happens,
An acropolis finds its god, the world
Won't be the same. Regrets veil
Their faces, the grey keepers,
The well-wishing Eumenides!

To endorse the matricide
Of an innocent past, Regrets
Must be invited. And in Cardiff

Shall they be finders, in the groves
Of Cathays, or the Norwegian Church?

6

The voice of one crying in the wilderness –
– That's me, boy! –
Crawls like a cough over the fences.
The dust has it. Red phlegm
In the tin bucket quivers. The sound
Of the wind's still kitching in odd corners,
Like a fox on tiptoe, snuffles in bins.

Wynn, you know these Valleys. All of them
To be exalted, wave in the world-wide web
Like a floppy-fingered glove? The crooked
Straight? Black slack levelled green? e-mail
It is, lays the bare mountains low.
The aloneness of suburbs, shiftless,
Reaching to Rhydaman, Aberdare.

7

Diflannodd yr Wtopia oddi ar gopa Gellionnen
                                    Gwenallt
   (Utopia vanished from the top of Gellionnen)

That summer in the Pontardawe folk do
Where we met your Karen in a clattering marquee
Twelve o'clock at night, clutching the last dregs
Of coffee, while a girl's voice reconstituted
For the wan five of us, a Gaelic world –

I stayed in Allt-wen that summer, in a respectable
Terrace circling the slope. My eye, buzzard-like,
Orbited the black-hole Utopia
Vanished from Gellionnen. Irish fiddlers
Lazed with tall tales. Welsh wannabes strummed.

I was that wizened fellow, lag turned scholar of pain,
Watching the lights of my enquiry
– Family, neighbourhood, sacrifice, anguish –
Twirl to the nothing world, a dark weight of time.

8

An enormous pinpoint sits like the god Pan
Whistling up stars from the dust.
Some clatter into it and vanish. Others
Though keeping safe distance, are pulled
In billion-lightyear orbits about the
Incredible weight of the hole.

Thus, the Milky Way, Christ's blood,
Streams in the firmament.

           And this
Utopia, lost as its emptied suns –
Can you hear it? Can you feel
The cloven goat's foot tap time
To its scrannel pipe, jigging

A galaxy together? Is this *us*
Crowding our orbits through the wide space of Wales?

Notes

Of the so-called New Poets of the last years of the Roman Republic, Catullus is the only one whose poems have survived. He was from Verona and probably of Celtic origin. The New Poets seem to have been largely a north Italian movement, from Cis-Alpine Gaul, a kind of well-heeled 'Anglo-Welsh'. Translation and adaptation were a highway of inspiration for Latin poets (in their case, from Greek) as they have been for modern Anglo-Irish and Anglo-Welsh. It is one of the ways these latter have differed from poets of contemporary England, who tend to translate simply to widen their experience, not to find roots.

In the poem here translated as a template, Cornelius is Cornelius Nepos, the historian, probably a fellow Veronese.

cyfarwyddiaid (plural of *cyfarwydd*) – the medieval storytellers who orally narrated the Welsh myths written down in the *Mabinogion*.

Uplands – the district of Swansea where Dylan Thomas lived as a boy.

Cornwall-facing door – see the Second Branch of the *Mabinogion*, where the wounded Brân tells his surviving followers to cut off his head and take it back to Gwales, an island off Pembroke. There they will live in perfect joy and the head will talk and carouse with them, until one of them opens the door that looks towards Cornwall. Then all their sorrow will return, the head will die and Gwales be uninhabitable. They must go to London with the head and bury it, to preserve Britain from danger. See also my *Castles* (Llandysul: Gomer, 1993), Variations 31–4.

A boy crept from his house – see Walt Whitman, 'Sea Drift'.

Silures – the Celtic tribe inhabiting south-east Wales.

Ordovicia – the territory of the Ordovicii, a tribe inhabiting most of North Wales.

Cathays – Cardiff's civic centre.

the Norwegian Church – a church built for Norwegian sailors in the Cardiff dockland, now an arts centre.

that wizened fellow – D. Gwenallt Jones the poet. He took his name from Allt-wen, where he was brought up. Gellionnen is the slope opposite. Gwenallt went to prison as a conscientious objector in the First World War.

An enormous pinpoint – Galaxies are said to be formed in the perturbation caused by hugely powerful primordial 'black holes', sucking particles and dust towards them as they travel through space.

14
Early Translations of Dafydd ap Gwilym

DAFYDD JOHNSTON

Dafydd ap Gwilym is by far the most frequently translated of all Welsh poets, and the enormous linguistic and thematic complexity of his poetry makes it a very rewarding topic in the study of literary translation in Wales. Most of the translations have been based on modern scholarly editions, particularly Thomas Parry's *Gwaith Dafydd ap Gwilym*, published in 1952, but there was also a brief spate of pioneering translation, stimulated by the publication in 1789 of the first collected edition, *Barddoniaeth Dafydd ab Gwilym*.[1] These early translations have remained largely unknown, but systematic study of them is now possible with the aid of the on-line bibliography of literary translations from Welsh into English, BWLET, established in 2002 as a result of an AHRB-funded research project led by Professor M. Wynn Thomas.[2]

Barddoniaeth Dafydd ab Gwilym could be said to be an edition awaiting translation of the poems, since the Introduction by William Owen Pughe is almost entirely in English, a clear indication that for its London-Welsh editors this poetry was primarily an object of antiquarian study. Pughe himself quotes some extracts in translation, but appropriately enough the first to publish translations of complete poems was the extraordinary literary mimic Iolo Morganwg (Edward Williams), who, as will be seen, had himself made a creative contribution to the 1789 edition. Iolo included striking English versions of two of Dafydd's poems in his *Poems, Lyric and Pastoral* of 1794, one of which will be discussed below. For some years translations continued to appear in piecemeal fashion, scattered here and there in journals and anthologies. William Owen Pughe quoted another extract in the first issue of his *Cambrian Register* (1795), but it was not until the third issue, in 1818, that he published a complete translation of Dafydd's conversation with the Grey Friar. Edward Jones (Bardd y Brenin) included translations of three poems in his *Bardic Museum* of 1802, and a certain 'F. S.' was responsible for a translation of one in *The Cambrian* in 1808. T. J. Llywelyn Prichard's anthology *The Cambrian Wreath* (1828) included six of Dafydd's poems, reprinting the two translations by Iolo Morganwg, one by Pughe, two anonymous and one attributed to Rhydychenwr ('An Oxford Man'). This self-effacing tendency (perhaps because of the rather risqué nature of the poems being translated) is also apparent in the use of the eisteddfodic name Maelog by a translator who published a total of eight poems in *The Cambrian Quarterly Magazine*, between 1829 and 1833. Maelog subsequently added to these to produce the first collected volume, containing forty-seven poems, entitled *Translations into English Verse from the Poems of Davyth ap Gwilym* (London, 1834). This was the only collection of Dafydd ap Gwilym's poems in English published in the nineteenth century, and seems to mark the end of the first wave of translation. Seven of Maelog's translations were included in the second edition of *Barddoniaeth Dafydd ab Gwilym* in 1873.

Maelog is known to have been the nom de plume of Arthur James Johnes (1809–71), a lawyer and later judge from Garthmyl in Montgomeryshire.[3] Johnes studied at the newly established University College, London, and under the influence of the London-Welsh Cymmrodorion Society he mastered the Welsh language there.[4] He was awarded the Cymmrodorion Royal Medal in 1831 for his *Essay on the Causes which have produced Dissent from the Established Church in the Principality of Wales* (reprinted in 1834 and 1870), an influential work which argued that it was the Anglican Church's neglect of the Welsh language which was mainly responsible for the dramatic rise of Nonconformism over the previous century. Church reform was one of a number of radical causes that Johnes supported, but Marian Henry Jones rightly disputes Gwenallt's extravagant claim, on the basis of his sympathy for the Hungarian nationalist Kossuth, that Johnes was the father of the nationalist movement in the first half of the century.[5] As his correspondence shows, he belonged to a wide circle of Welsh Anglican antiquarians and cultural nationalists, including William Owen Pughe in his old age (to whom he dedicated his translations of Dafydd ap Gwilym), Gwallter Mechain, Carnhuanawc (one of the founders of *The Cambrian Quarterly Magazine*) and Lady Augusta Hall of Llanover.[6] The earliest reference to the work of translating Dafydd ap Gwilym in Johnes's correspondence is in a letter about the *Cambrian Quarterly* from Angharad Llwyd, in September 1829, which shows the demand for translation at that time:

> In an octavo volume of Poems entitled 'Beauties of British Poetry' selected by Sidney Melmoth printed in 1801 at Huddersfield . . . you may find a beautiful specimen of Dd: ab Gwylym's Awen in Cowydd of the 'Fair Pilgrim' which is *very little known*, and extremely suitable to *your work* . . .[7]

Angharad Llwyd was an industrious collector of Welsh poetry from manuscripts, and well qualified to judge the quality of a translation. Lady Augusta Hall, on the other hand, had very little Welsh, and her enthusiastic response to Johnes's translations in a letter of 1852 was based on their quality as English poetry, an attitude which actually led her to oppose indiscriminate publication of translations:

> You will be pleased to hear that in spite of your long silence, & the non-arrival of your long-promised books, that Miss Williams has had quite a *fight* with me because I would not let her send your translation of the Ode to Summer by D. ap G. to the 'Star of Gwent'. She considers it one of the most beautiful poems that ever appeared in the English language, nor do I dispute that it is so; but as you are the *only* person with whom I ever was acquainted who rendered Welsh verse into English verse *without* disgracing the original, I would *not* allow any versified translation of Welsh Poetry to appear in the Star of Gwent, being sure that if a fashion was commenced, every English Rhymer who had a smattering of Welsh would think himself an Arthur Johnes, & we should have most ludicrous versions declared to be literal transcripts of the writings of the Welsh Bards![8]

Johnes's other major work was a treatise entitled *Philological Proofs of the Original Unity and Recent Origin of the Human Race. Derived from a Comparison of the Languages of Asia,*

Europe, Africa, and America (London, 1846), which originated as an unsuccessful entry to the Abergavenny Eisteddfod of 1842. Although an idealistic theory, this work does nevertheless recognize the substantial differences between neighbouring languages, such as Welsh and English, and is clearly relevant to Johnes's experience as a translator, in terms of the difficulty of the enterprise on the one hand, but also in its faith in the possibility of successful translation.

The essay on the causes of dissent has a more specific relevance to Johnes's translations of Dafydd ap Gwilym. The Anglican Church at that time was in danger of being marginalized in Welsh culture, associated with Englishness and aristocratic privilege, and the work of the literary antiquarians can be seen as a nostalgic return to a lost cultural unity. Johnes despised the gloomy censoriousness of the Nonconformists,[9] and Dafydd ap Gwilym's poetry represented for him an innocent joy in the pleasures of this world, belonging to what Prys Morgan has referred to as 'Merrie Wales'.[10] He was able to identify in particular with Dafydd's attacks on the mendicant friars, whom Johnes saw as medieval Nonconformists threatening the unity of the established church. But the matter is further complicated by the prevailing anti-Catholic prejudice, which was common to both Anglicans and Nonconformists in nineteenth-century Britain. Like previous commentators, Johnes's answer to this problem was to regard Dafydd as a kind of proto-Protestant, somehow detached from the superstition of his age. William Owen Pughe had already offered such an interpretation in his Introduction to the 1789 edition:

> Though Dafydd ab Gwilym lived in an age deeply immersed in ignorance, yet it is obvious from his works that he was little affected with the superstition of the times. He had very little veneration for the monks; nor would he bend the least to the authority of the priesthood in general, in those points that were derogatory to an enlightened mind.[11]

A key poem in this respect is Dafydd's conversation with the Grey Friar, which Pughe similarly interpreted as an attack on 'the Roman priesthood' in his introductory note to his translation in *The Cambrian Register* in 1818 (reproduced in *The Cambrian Wreath* in 1828). Johnes was undoubtedly influenced by this interpretation, but he does not make the mistake of lumping together priests, friars and monks. His opposition to contemporary Nonconformists led him to distinguish, quite rightly, between friars and parish priests, and this distinction seems to have been even more important to him than the anti-Catholicism which governed Pughe's interpretation:

> The fondness displayed by Davyth ap Gwilym for the embellishments of the church forms a singular contrast with the acrimony with which he so often assails her priesthood. In the one instance we see the taste of the poet, in the other we recognize the feelings of the man. It is highly interesting to observe that the bard's fiercest invectives are directed against the eleemosynary clergy – the Franciscan and Dominican friars – who are also the object of Chaucer's bitterest satire; and in a poem previously quoted it is observable that he appears to insinuate against these orders the same charges that are advanced by his contemporary – an abject devotion to the Romish see – and hypocritical professions of religion combined with the servile arts and low frauds of the common mendicant.[12]

The confident distinction between the taste of the poet and the feelings of the man will seem dubious to the modern reader; I would suggest that Johnes is in fact adopting a strategy of projecting on to the original author an ambiguity in his own attitude towards medieval religion. His orthodox Protestant prejudice, combined with British chauvinism, made it difficult for him to admit to the aesthetic attraction of the ceremonies of the Roman Catholic Church, which would have been all the more appealing in contrast to the puritanism of the Nonconformist chapels. That attraction is apparent in his translation of the poem now known as 'Offeren y Llwyn' ('The Woodland Mass'), the only prose translation in his collection, which he prefaces with the following note: 'This poem contains many beautiful and fanciful allusions to the ceremonies of the Roman Catholic Church. I have translated it into prose, and almost literally, as the best means of conveying the spirit of the original.'[13] On the whole the translation is indeed a faithful rendering of the elaborate imagery depicting the thrush as a priest celebrating mass, but at a crucial point there is a departure from the literal sense, which is indicative of the difficulty posed by the fusion of religion and sexuality. These are the concluding lines:

> He raised for us on the hills there
> The sacred wafer made of a fair leaf:

And the beautiful nightingale, slender and tall,
From the corner of the glen near him,
Priest of the dingle! sang to a thousand;
And the bells of the mass continually did ring,
And raised the host
To the sky, above the thicket,
And sang stanzas to our Lord and Creator,
With sylvan ecstasy and love!
I am enraptured with the song
Which was matured in the birchen grove of the woods.[14]

In rendering the line 'A charegl nwyf a chariad' as 'With sylvan ecstasy and love' Johnes changes the sense in three significant ways. Firstly, the metaphor of the chalice contained in the word *caregl* is omitted altogether. The raising of the communion cup represented the climax of the ceremony of Mass, and it is only at this point in the poem that the religious imagery is specifically associated with sexual love. Otherwise it is possible to read the metaphorical ceremony as nature's worship of God (but it should be borne in mind that the thrush has been sent by the poet's lover Morfudd). Such a reading lies behind the second change which Johnes made to the line, which is the introduction of the adjective 'sylvan', a neo-classical locution typical of the pastoral tradition. Finally, any threat of promiscuous sexuality in the line is completely defused by rendering *nwyf* as 'ecstasy', with reference to the songbird rather than the lovers.

This last point might be regarded as more debatable since 'ecstasy' has been used here by three later translators, including the highly respected Dafydd ap Gwilym scholar Rachel Bromwich.[15] But such congruence is no proof of accuracy, and can be explained either as an instance of the influence of the earliest translators on their successors (Johnes's translation was available in the 1873 edition of *Barddoniaeth Dafydd ab Gwilym*), or, more likely, as the result of a common tendency to spiritualize the intense sexuality of Dafydd ap Gwilym's poetry. Thomas Parry, Dafydd ap Gwilym's most recent editor, was not free from this tendency, and the meanings he gives for *nwyf*, 'llawenydd, gorfoledd' (joy), could be taken to support the translation 'ecstasy'. Nevertheless, the primary meaning of *nwyf* is physical vigour (used, for instance, of spirited horses), encompassing sexual desire, and the word is always used by Dafydd ap Gwilym in sexual contexts.[16] In opting for 'ecstasy' translators have continued the religious theme of the poem, whereas in fact the confines of the extended metaphor of bird as priest are broken at this very point by switching to the human lovers. The idea of love as a drink to be shared from a cup is a particularly potent one (bringing to mind the story of Tristan and Isolde), and the potential blasphemy of the image was clearly too much for Johnes.

The theme of ecstasy is anticipated in Johnes's rendering of 'lle digrif' (literally 'a delightful place') in the first line of the poem as 'a place of ecstasy', the experience thus becoming a function of the place, not the girl who sent the bird.[17] And the state of mind of the poet-subject is heightened by rendering *bodlon* (literally 'content') in the penultimate line as 'enraptured'. This is the Romantic response to nature, grounded in a very strong sense of place. There may well be a specific influence here from Wordsworth's 'Lines Composed a Few Miles above Tintern Abbey' of 1798, where the 'sylvan Wye' inspires 'wild ecstasies' and 'dizzy raptures'.[18]

The decision to translate 'Offeren y Llwyn' into prose certainly indicates Johnes's intention to convey the sense more closely than usual, since all the other translations in his collection are into rhyming couplets, in which some of the original sense is inevitably sacrificed for the sake of the metre. Johnes does allow himself a certain freedom in terms of line-length, which varies from poem to poem, sometimes approximating closely to the *cywydd* line at seven or, more often, eight syllables, sometimes longer at ten, eleven or even twelve, and also in terms of rhyme scheme, occasionally varying the couplet rhyme by adopting schemes such as *abab* or *abba*. But the greatest liberty which he takes in these verse translations is that of omitting lines altogether, sometimes summarizing their content in a prose commentary, but more often making no acknowledgement of the omission.

Selective translation is one of the strategies Johnes adopts in order to defuse the sexuality of Dafydd ap Gwilym's poetry. In the first place, the act of selection of less than one-fifth of the 262 poems in *Barddoniaeth Dafydd ab Gwilym* enabled him to avoid what he refers to as 'allusions repugnant to the decorous moral feeling of the present day'.[19] Thus, for instance, he did not include what is for modern readers perhaps the definitive Dafydd ap Gwilym poem, 'Trafferth mewn Tafarn' ('Trouble in a Tavern'), or various others in which it is clear that the poet's sole aim is to have casual sex.[20] Unacceptable passages in the poems selected are either simply not translated or else glossed over by euphemism, after the manner of Bowdler's treatment of Shakespeare in his expurgated edition of 1818. For instance, in a poem about Morfudd's marriage Dafydd speaks of her going under another man to be made pregnant, a remarkably bitter and degrading reference to marital intercourse which was clearly unacceptable to Johnes, who translates as follows:

> These proofs of love I hoped might bind
> My Morvyth to be ever true:
> Alas! to deep despair consign'd,
> My bosom's blighted hopes I rue,
> And the base craft that gave her charms,
> Oh, anguish! to another's arms![21]

A particular problem posed by this passage was its depiction of the woman as an active partner in the sexual act, since female sexuality was the most problematic aspect of this awkward subject for Victorians.[22] One of the most memorable aspects of Dafydd ap Gwilym's poetry, on the other hand, is the portrait of his lover Morfudd as a passionate, wayward individual, and it is interesting to observe how Johnes tones down this portrait to make it conform to Victorian ideals of docile femininity. The key terms are those in the second of these two lines: 'The girl of clear and brilliant cheek, / And gestures modest, kind, and meek'.[23] The idea of modesty is indeed present in the original text in the word *gwyl*, which did also convey the associated concepts of meekness and kindness. Ideals of femininity had not changed so radically since the Middle Ages as to render the terms untranslatable, but what is telling here is the expansion of one term into three, which outweigh the dominant emphasis on physical beauty in the original. Another term which induces the formula 'kind and meek' is *mwyn*, 'gentle'.[24] In fact *mwyn* is most often used in Middle Welsh in the sense of 'noble', and it has undergone exactly the same semantic shift as 'gentle', a shift which is no doubt related to the modification of the ideal here observed.

The medieval ideal of female beauty is remarkable for its emphasis on whiteness of skin, an appearance which would strike us today as quite unhealthy. Aristocratic girls were still to be admired for their paleness of skin in the Victorian era, but a crucial difference was that by then the pale hue had acquired a moral significance, symbolic of virginal purity. Johnes therefore tends to add moral qualifiers in translating such descriptions, as for instance in his rendering of 'Yr Wylan' ('The Seagull'), where the girl is 'of virgin hue' and 'a maid so pure and bright'.[25]

It might well be asked why Johnes should have chosen to translate the poem about Morfudd's marriage, given the need to expurgate it to conform with these ideals. One answer might be that very few of Dafydd ab Gwilym's poems would be acceptable to Victorian sensibilities without some form of censorship. But that particular poem demanded inclusion because one of the governing principles of the selection was the need to construct a life of the poet in order to give meaning to the texts ascribed to him. The random incidents of fabliaux poems, such as 'Trafferth mewn Tafarn', could be easily omitted, but pivotal events in the life of the subject, such as the marriage of his lover, were essential. Of course, in this Johnes was simply following the lead of William Owen Pughe, who first set out the poet's life in his Introduction to *Barddoniaeth Dafydd ab Gwilym* and organized the edition to reflect that life, beginning with the poems to the principal patron, Ifor Hael of Glamorgan. Dafydd's friendship with Ifor gives dignity to a life which might otherwise appear to be devoted entirely to the vain pursuit of sexual gratification.

There was a problem with the original collection, in that it lacked any poems to Ifor at the end of the life, but this deficiency was made good by some of the sixteen poems provided by Iolo Morganwg, just before publication, which form an Appendix (Ychwanegiad). It was not until 1922 that eleven of these were shown to have been composed by Iolo himself.[26] They are extremely skilful forgeries, and there was of course no reason why Johnes should have doubted their authenticity any more than the original editors did. Johnes translated six poems from the Appendix, and not surprisingly these proved to be much more amenable to translation than their medieval counterparts. The three poems in which Dafydd bids farewell to Morfudd and to Ifor give a fitting sense of sentimental closure to the poet's life, and they are the most faithful of all Johnes's translations. It is ironic, but again not surprising, that these were selected in preference to genuine poems, which look back on lost bliss with much more complex feeling and imagination than the Romantic nostalgia of Iolo Morganwg's compositions.[27] Johnes's appreciative introductory note to 'The Summer' shows why these appealed so much to him:

> This fine poem was evidently composed after the death of his early patron, Ivor. The melancholy and affecting allusion to the lost friend of his youth, with which the poet concludes his gorgeous description of the summer landscape of South Wales, forms a transition of great beauty and pathos.[28]

In contrast to the two genuine Dafydd ap Gwilym poems on the subject of summer, this one has a specific location in Glamorgan, a pastoral idyll set off by the contrast with 'the land of wild, wild Gwyneth'.[29] Glamorgan itself could provide a wild Romantic setting, as in 'The Dream', a translation of another of Iolo Morganwg's compositions, where the dreamer is swept away by streams like 'Taf's o'erflooded river'.[30] It was in the eighteenth century that the mountainous landscapes of Wales took on a sublime significance;[31] for Dafydd ap Gwilym and his contemporaries they were a mere inconvenience, as seen in poems such as 'The Peat Pool' and 'The Echo Rock'. In the latter translation Johnes clearly revels in the Gothic mood:

> Yon old bald rock and rugged stones,
> That peer and totter o'er the dell,
> And murmur forth unearthly tones
> Like some base witch that casts a spell,
> Babble more wildly after rain
> Than seven-locked Merddin the insane![32]

Dafydd ap Gwilym's complaint about the mist is located in the woodland where he had arranged to meet a girl; the translation expands the scene to take in all the variety of Wales's landscape:

> The swarth excretion of the night
> Veil'd path and heath, and mountain height,
> With many a dark and mantling wave,
> Till heav'n was rayless as a cave.
> Hung o'er the rocks a scowling tent,

> It wrapped heav'n's dawning battlement:
> The woods, the hills, the shore, the sea,
> The birchen shrubs, were lost to me.³³

Wild Gothic landscapes dominate the handful of original poems at the end of Johnes's collection, such as 'To an Echo in Snowdon', and were no doubt calculated to stir the imagination of the tourist to 'wild Wales'. But the taste for Romantic tourism is indulged most extravagantly in the one translation by Iolo Morganwg included in Johnes's collection, entitled 'Morvyth's Pilgrimage', which recounts an unnamed girl's pilgrimage from Anglesey to St David's to do penance for having caused the death of her lover.³⁴ This is considerably longer than any other poem in the collection, for the simple reason that Iolo Morganwg saw fit to add descriptions of the various landscapes along the girl's journey, expanding on brief references to the rivers she must cross. This passage on Snowdonia has no basis whatsoever in the original:

> O! could I guard thy lovely form
> Safe through yon desert of the storm,
> Where fiercely rage encountering gales,
> And whirlwinds rend th'affrighted vales:
> Sons of the tempest, cease to blow,
> Sleep in your cavern'd glens below;
> Ye streams that, with terrific sound,
> Pour from your thousand hills around,
> Cease with rude clamours to dismay
> A gentle pilgrim on her way!³⁵

Like the mountains, rivers were nothing more than a hindrance for the medieval poet, whereas for the Romantic translator they have become the very essence of the poetry.

Another type of poem which figures quite prominently in Johnes's selection is the satirical complaint or curse, like that to the mirror which reflected the love-stricken poet's ravaged features, and several to Morfudd's jealous husband. These contain some of Johnes's most successful passages of translation, unfettered by prudishness and unencumbered by notions of sublimity and the neoclassical diction which accompanied them. This is part of the poet's abusive address to his own shadow:

Bard

Whence then art thou, giant's child?
Shape of darkness, huge and wild;
Bald of brow as aged bear,
Bloated uncouth form of air;
More like images that scud
Through our dreams, than flesh and blood;
Shaped like stork on frozen pool,
Thin as palmer (wand'ring fool!)
Long-shanked as a crane that feeds
Greedily among the reeds;
Like a black and shaven monk
Is thy dark and spectral trunk,
Or a corpse in winding-sheet. –

Shadow

I have followed sure and fleet
On thy steps – were I to tell
But one half – thou knowest well . . .[36]

Passages such as this reflect the taste for the bizarre and macabre seen in Gothic novels, which were at the height of their popularity in the early years of the nineteenth century. They form a counterbalance to the celebration of love and nature, and in this respect Johnes makes an interesting comparison with Robert Burns in order to sum up Dafydd ap Gwilym's genius:

> As before observed, Davyth ap Gwilym has been compared to Petrarch; and no doubt his personal history bears in one respect a strong and interesting resemblance to that of the Italian poet. But in all the peculiarities of his genius, our bard approaches more nearly to Burns than to any poet, whether of his own or other countries. He has the same originality, the same intense sympathy with nature, and, above all, the same magic transitions from satire and raillery to wild sublimity and deep pathos.[37]

There may well be a valid historical basis to the comparison, in that Burns was heir to a Scots tradition of 'flyting' which was related to the medieval Welsh practice of *dychan*, satire, on which Dafydd ap Gwilym drew for comic effect in these poems. But the real point of the comparison is essentially ahistorical. In giving Burns precedence over Petrarch, Johnes is rejecting a European medievalism and placing Dafydd ap Gwilym in a British cultural tradition which is somehow free of historical context. In actual fact, a much more substantial comparison could be made between Burns and Iolo Morganwg, two who combined native poetic traditions with skilled mimicry of English literary discourse. Given that just over one in eight of the poems in Johnes's collection are actually the work of Iolo Morganwg, and that those contain the highest concentration of 'wild sublimity and deep pathos', the similarity which Johnes sees between Dafydd ap Gwilym and Burns is all the more understandable.

Translation was an integral part of the process, begun by the 1789 edition, of transforming Dafydd ap Gwilym from an author in the medieval sense, one whose name acted as a magnet for a variety of love and nature poetry in manuscripts,[38] into an author in the modern sense, one with a life informing a coherent literary oeuvre. The canon was still unstable and hybrid, unbeknown to the translator, and indeed the creative additions to it were crucial in enabling him to produce a version of Dafydd ap Gwilym which was acceptable and meaningful to a nineteenth-century readership.

Notes

[1] Thomas Parry (ed.), *Gwaith Dafydd ap Gwilym* (Cardiff: Gwasg Prifysgol Cymru, 1952); hereafter referred to as GDG; Owain Myfyr and William Owen Pughe (eds), *Barddoniaeth Dafydd ab Gwilym* (London, 1789); hereafter referred to as BDG.

[2] *www.bwlet.net*. For a useful introduction to this field of study see M. Wynn Thomas, 'The Good Thieves? Translating Welsh Literature into English', *Corresponding Cultures: The Two Literatures of Wales* (Cardiff: University of Wales Press, 1999), pp. 111–55.

[3] See Meic Stephens (ed.), *The New Companion to the Literature of Wales* (Cardiff: University of Wales Press, 1998), p. 366; and Marian Henry Jones, 'The Letters of Arthur James Johnes, 1809–71', *National Library of Wales Journal*, X (1957–8), 233–64, 329–64.

[4] A letter from Gwallter Mechain (one of the very few in Johnes's correspondence written in Welsh) in 1824 recommends a Welsh tutor in London (Jones, 'Letters', 240).

[5] Jones, 'Letters', 233; D. Gwenallt Jones (ed.), *Detholiad o Ryddiaith Gymraeg R. J. Derfel* (Dinbych: Y Clwb Llyfrau Cymraeg, 1945), pp. 18–20.

[6] On this circle, known in Welsh as *yr Hen Bersoniaid Llengar*, see Prys Morgan, *The Eighteenth Century Renaissance* (Llandybïe: Christopher Davies, 1981), pp. 137–41.

⁷ Jones, 'Letters', 241; the translation referred to is presumably that by Iolo Morganwg discussed below (although this publication is not listed in the BWLET bibliography). In 1832 Johnes was invited by the Cymmrodorion (Jones, 'Letters', 250–1) to translate the poems of Lewis Glyn Cothi (eventually to be published by Ioan Tegid and Gwallter Mechain in 1837–9), but nothing seems to have come of this, not surprisingly, since praise poetry of that sort would hardly have appealed to Johnes's Romantic tastes.

⁸ Jones, 'Letters', 349; see the editorial footnote on that page referring to Carnhuanawc's opposition to the translation of bardic poetry on similar grounds in 1830. Johnes's translations are recommended as 'elegant and faithful' by Robert Williams in his entry on Dafydd ap Gwilym in *A Biographical Dictionary of Eminent Welshmen* (Llandovery: W. Rees, 1852), p. 115.

⁹ In a passage comparing the mendicant friars to modern Nonconformists, Johnes states that 'this disposition to dwell on judgements, rather than on mercies, is the peculiarity which, more than any positive difference of doctrine, distinguishes the Methodist minister of the present day from the clergy of the Church of England'; Arthur James Johnes, *An Essay on the Causes which have produced Dissent from the Established Church, in the Principality of Wales* (London: Henry Hooper, 1835), p. 111. See also subsequent editions.

¹⁰ Morgan, *The Eighteenth Century Renaissance*, pp. 13–39.

¹¹ BDG, p. xix.

¹² Maelog [Arthur James Johnes], *Translations into English Verse from the Poems of Davyth ap Gwilym* (London: Henry Hooper, 1834), p. xxxvi; hereafter referred to as *Translations*. Most of Johnes's introduction is acknowledged to have been taken with only minor changes from John Humffreys Parry's life of Dafydd ap Gwilym in *The Cambrian Plutarch* (London: W. Simpkin and R. Marshall, 1824), which in turn is derived from Pughe's Introduction to BDG; however, the final pages from xxxiii onwards are stated to be 'for the most part' Johnes's own work. The poem referred to in this passage is number CCXVII in BDG, a satire on a Dominican friar which is actually now believed to be the work of Dafydd ap Gwilym's contemporary Madog Benfras. For a recent translation see Helen Fulton, *Selections from the Dafydd ap Gwilym Apocrypha* (Llandysul: Gomer, 1996), p. 10.

¹³ Maelog, *Translations*, p. 31.

¹⁴ Ibid., p. 32 (see GDG, poem 122; BDG, poem XLV).

¹⁵ H. Idris and David Bell, *Dafydd ap Gwilym: Fifty Poems* (London: The Honourable Society of Cymmrodorion, 1942), p. 265; Gwyn Williams, *The Burning Tree* (London: Faber & Faber, 1956), p. 89; Rachel Bromwich, *Dafydd ap Gwilym: A Selection of Poems*, 2nd edn (Harmondsworth: Penguin, 1985), p. 80. Joseph Clancy, *Medieval Welsh Lyrics* (London: Macmillan; New York; St. Martin's Press, 1965), p. 50, has the similar word 'bliss'. Gwyn Thomas, *Dafydd ap Gwilym: His Poems* (Cardiff: University of Wales Press, 2001), p. 237, has 'passion'.

¹⁶ See *Geiriadur Prifysgol Cymru / A Dictionary of the Welsh Language* (Cardiff: University of Wales Press, 1950–2002), p. 2600.

¹⁷ The phrase 'place of ecstasy' renders 'lle nwyf' again in a description of the lovers' bower; Maelog, *Translations*, p. 14.

¹⁸ On the Welsh dimension of the Romantic movement see Damian Walford Davies, *Presences that Disturb: Models of Romantic Identity in the Literature and Culture of the 1790s* (Cardiff: University of Wales Press, 2003).

¹⁹ Maelog, *Translations*, p. xl.

²⁰ GDG, poem 124.

21 Maelog, *Translations*, p. 45; this is GDG, poem 85, ll. 25–32 (Johnes's source-text in BDG is not substantially different in this passage). James Hardiman also censored his material by selective translation in his *Irish Minstrelsy* (1831); see Michael Cronin, *Translating Ireland* (Cork: Cork University Press, 1996), pp. 111–12.

22 The moral attitudes associated with that term clearly predated Victoria's coronation in 1837.

23 Maelog, *Translations* (see GDG, poem 81, ll. 1–2).

24 Ibid., p. 95 (BDG, poem CCXXVI, l. 35; note that GDG, poem 105, l. 35 does not have the word *mwyn*).

25 Ibid., p. 12 (GDG, poem 118, ll. 14 and 24).

26 G. J. Williams, *Iolo Morganwg a Chywyddau'r Ychwanegiad* (London: Cymdeithas yr Eisteddfod Genedlaethol, 1926).

27 *Marwnad Ifor a Nest* (GDG, poem 11), *Morfudd yn Hen* (GDG, poem 139), and *Yr Adfail* (GDG, poem 144).

28 Maelog, *Translations*, p. 96. This is the poem appreciated so enthusiastically by Lady Llanover and her companion (see note 8 above).

29 The idiosyncratic spelling of the place-name Gwynedd is not a play on a girl's name, but rather Johnes's effort to convey the sound of the Welsh *dd* to English readers, as in *Davyth*.

30 Maelog, *Translations*, p. 48; a genuine Dafydd ap Gwilym dream poem (GDG, poem 39) is set in an idealized forest landscape.

31 See Morgan, *The Eighteenth Century Renaissance*, pp. 101–6.

32 Maelog, *Translations*, p. 58 (GDG, poem 130).

33 Ibid., p. 21 (GDG, poem 68).

34 Ibid., pp. 35–41 (GDG, poem 99, BDG, poem XXXIII); this was originally published in Iolo's *Poems, Lyric and Pastoral* under the title 'The Fair Pilgrim' (and apparently reprinted in a collection of 1801, see note 7 above).

35 Maelog, *Translations*, pp. 38–9.

36 Ibid., pp. 29–30 (GDG, poem 141, BDG, poem CLXXI); the introductory note to the poem states that it contains 'many sarcastic allusions to the religious orders'.

37 Ibid., p. xli.

38 See Helen Fulton, 'Awdurdod ac Awduriaeth: Golygu'r Cywyddwyr', *Cyfoeth y Testun: Ysgrifau ar Lenyddiaeth Gymraeg yr Oesoedd Canol*, eds Iestyn Daniel et al. (Cardiff: University of Wales Press, 2003), pp. 50–76.

15

Uncle Tom's Welsh Dress: Ethnicity, Authority and Translation

MELINDA GRAY

When Harriet Beecher Stowe's novel *Uncle Tom's Cabin; Or, Life Among the Lowly* was published in two volumes by John P. Jewett and Co. of Boston, Massachusetts, in March 1852, following its first publication in serial weekly instalments in the anti-slavery newspaper *The National Era*, it met with immediate commercial success. There was no precedent in the publishing world for the number of copies sold in the first year.[1] The American press was alive with letters and reviews that voiced a full range of responses from readers of every ilk: abolitionists and plantation-owners, freed slaves, established writers, politicians, women and men. These early readers of the novel were drawn into heated argument over whether Stowe had correctly represented the southern way of life, and whether American slavery was a moral or an immoral institution. They opened the first national conversation about race by analysing Uncle Tom and the novel's other 'Negro' characters. They discussed what to do with freed slaves; should they be returned to Africa, or might they have a place in American society? They took sides over the question of whether Stowe's book imparted truth or lies; and whether it was good literature, or a document whose value resided mainly in its provocations. Of all the many stories that survive about the novel's fascination for these early readers, the most celebrated is the greeting Abraham Lincoln was supposed to have given Stowe when she visited the White House in 1862: 'So you're the little woman who wrote the book that started this great war!'[2] By re-reading the stories and debates around the novel, we can appreciate that it carried a rich load of local significance for its early readers. It provoked a passionate debate over American slavery that took place on a national scale at a time when the emerging identity of the American nation was fragile.

Even in this early period, the discussions of *Uncle Tom's Cabin* were not limited to its American readership; nor were they contained by the English language. Over the course of the nineteenth century, the novel was translated more often than any other text into an ever-expanding array of languages and cultural forms. Uncle Tom, Little Eva and others of Stowe's characters soon turned up in stage plays, songs and film; it was a phenomenon of electric dissemination remarked on by American poet and philosopher Ralph Waldo Emerson, who wrote that Stowe's novel 'encircled the globe'.[3] Stowe's family was known to have assembled a collection of the translations, as Florine Thayer McCray, an early biographer, attests:

> Many foreign publishers and translators sent their reproductions to the author and in the library of Mrs Stowe's house in Hartford, the writer has seen many most interesting and curious editions. At intervals since the publication of 'Uncle Tom's Cabin' the author has received editions of her own work from the most unexpected sources, and the more interesting ones have been preserved, though with that characteristic lack of appreciation of her own greatness, and the carelessness which familiarity and close associations with a famous author, seem to make possible, neither Mrs Stowe nor her children, appear to have invested them with high value, and when asked for by the present writer, a few of them were found after some search on the shelves in the back of a closet, scattered about and in imperfect preservation. Among them were specimens of several of the French editions, by various translators, and a few of the German issues. There were numerous Italian editions, Spanish and Cuban, Dutch, Swedish and Danish. One from Abertawy, India, in the provincial dialect; one in Polish; . . . There was one which seemed to be all consonants, chiefly L's, W's, Y's in the Welsh. This was illustrated by George Cruikshank in his most peculiar style.[4]

The illustrations by the celebrated Cruikshank identify this Welsh translation as being by Hugh Williams, published in 1853 by John Cassell of Ludgate Hill, London.[5] Williams's Welsh translation tops off McCray's catalogue of 'interesting and curious' editions, neglected by the author but valued by the biographer, who views them as a testament to Stowe's far-reaching influence and 'greatness'.

Very little has been written about the early translations of Stowe's novel, other than these nineteenth-century accounts that view them as a sign of the writer's brilliance and the book's unparalleled success. Reverence for an authentic, original text and for its author was common among Victorian writers, who typically believed that a translation should bring the reader as close as possible to the experience of reading the original text in its language of composition.[6] Today, interest in the broader transmission of *Uncle Tom's Cabin* leads to important questions about how to understand the translations in relation to the idea of the novel's 'original timeliness'.[7] What were the effects of translating Stowe's novel from English into other languages? To what extent do the early rewritings, recastings, adaptations and translations variously shift or unmoor the novel from its immediate local significance? If the exigencies of time and place powerfully affected this novel's first readings, might it then be especially vulnerable to violent displacement through translation? Did translation disengage this novel from the very representations and the pressured discourses (of, for instance, race and slavery, gender and domesticity) that gave it such broad influence and drew so many readers in the first place? E. G. Millward goes to the heart of the matter with his observation of the danger, for translators of this novel into Welsh, that it would be read for entertainment and nothing more: as the fairy-tale of a dark-skinned man in a faraway land, in which good ultimately triumphs over evil.[8] As Millward also suggests, this danger is one William Rees almost certainly considered and worked against in 1853 as he designed and wrote his unorthodox version of the novel for Welsh readers.[9]

More recent scholars have argued that the broader transmission of Stowe's novel had tremendous productive value for American culture. Rather than reading the texts engendered by *Uncle Tom's Cabin* as displacements or betrayals of the original and its immediate readership, Philip Fisher argues that they represent 'a radical capture of imaginative space' aimed at actively transforming the historical moment in which they were composed and broadcast. According to Fisher, 'the international popularity of Stowe's book, the plays and recitations, illustrations and cultural clichés derived from it, installed the slave system in the public realm', helping to make intimately familiar what had been unspeakable. In the process of making slaves and slavery imaginable, the story's original form was necessarily discarded and even forgotten. Fisher's metaphor for Stowe's novel is 'a window that becomes, in time, itself visible', but which was once alluringly transparent: 'initially, it was easy to look through this opening into a world that had been both concealed and unstructured'.[10] As the window became visible, people stopped reading Stowe's novel. It was an artefact of the nineteenth century, still referenced in popular culture but considered by many critics to be an example of ante-bellum writing at its sentimental and even racist worst.

In returning to the novel today, and to the Welsh translations that were published in the 1850s, we observe the window, lean forward and peer through it, but we keep our hands on the frame, for it is now impossible not to recognize that it is there and part of the scene we are viewing. In so doing, we discover that Stowe's novel was open to transformation and made itself uniquely available for adaptation and translation. Because of its artful employment of the dominant nineteenth-century discourses of religion, race and domesticity, it served as the raw material for countless other texts. The patterns of discourse in the novel proved to be extremely affecting, and yet they were easily unravelled and manipulated in the service of many different kinds of cultural projects. If translations can be said always to occupy a position 'in-between', the Welsh translations of this novel that circulated in the United States make a spectacular illustration of this view.[11] They were taking part in the crucial piece of cultural work by which, in Fisher's words, 'the unimaginable becomes, finally, the obvious'.[12] Yet these translations can also be understood to have performed a series of other tasks for their readers, who were in the 1850s negotiating their own relation to both Welsh and American societies through language.

Shortly after the publication of *Uncle Tom's Cabin*, the novel and the debates about it crossed the Atlantic to engulf British and Continental readers as well. In the words of one Welsh journalist,

> Mae y llyfr hwn yn cael rhediad digyffelyb yn Lloegr – tu hwnt hyd yn nod i weithiau Dickens, a phawb ereill; y mae bron yn nwylaw pawb, meistr a gwas; ceir ef yn nwylaw y feistres yn y parlwr a'r forwyn yn y

gegin; y mae cannoedd o filoedd o gopïau ohono wedi eu gwerthu eisioes; y mae hefyd yn cael ei ddwyn i'r chwareufwrdd, ac y mae rhyw benboethyn wedi ysgrifennu dilyniad iddo, yn mha un y mae yn dwyn Uncle Tom yn fyw i Loegr.

(This book has had an unparalleled run in England – beyond even what Dickens has had, or anyone else; it's in the hands of almost everyone, master and servant; in the hands of the mistress in the parlour and the maid in the kitchen; hundreds of thousands of copies of it have already sold; it has also been taken to the stage, and some hothead has written a sequel to it, in which Uncle Tom comes to live in England.)[13]

In Britain, readers purchased 150,000 copies of the book in its first year, and additionally there were newspaper serializations, reprints and the translations.[14] A letter from a London publisher offers a vivid picture of the publishing frenzy. In England, he writes,

the discovery was soon made that anyone was at liberty to reprint the book, and the initiative was thus given to a new era in cheap literature, founded on American reprints. . . . Within twelve months of its first appearance eighteen different London publishing houses were engaged in supplying the great demand that had set in, the total number of editions being forty, varying from fine art-illustrated editions at 15s., 10s. and 7s. 6d. to the cheap popular editions of 1s., 9d. and 6d.

At the end of a year, he estimates, 'the aggregate number of copies circulating in Great Britain and the colonies exceeds one and a half millions'.[15]

The first full Welsh translation was published in London by John Cassell, who had already circulated an English-language edition to British readers. Cassell's translation was rapidly followed by others. In March 1853, one of the Welsh-American journals, *Y Cyfaill* (*The Companion*), reported the following:

Y mae yn ffaith fod tri gwahanol argraffiadau yn dyfod allan yn Gymraeg: un gan yr enwog John Cassel, o Lundain (ond bydd y pris hwn yn uchel); un arall o gyfieithiad y Parch. Wm. Rees, Liverpool; ac hefyd, yr un rhataf gan Rosser, Abertawy, o gyfieithad y Lefiad, gyda rhagymadrodd gan olygydd campus y *Cylchgrawn*.

(In fact, three different editions are coming out in Welsh: one by the famous John Cassell of London (but the price of this will be high); another one, a translation by the Rev. Wm. Rees of Liverpool; and also the least expensive one, by Rosser of Swansea, translated by 'Y Lefiad', with an introduction by the famous editor of the *Cylchgrawn* (the *Magazine*).)[16]

In Welsh, too, the novel was made available to readers of varying means. Peppered with 'Uncle Tom' trivia, the American newspapers also took note of the Welsh translations and marvelled at the novel's ever-expanding readership. On 31 December 1852, Frederick Douglass's abolitionist newspaper advertised that *'Uncle Tom's Cabin* has been translated into Welsh, and bears the title of 'Caban F'Ewythr Tum'.[17] A year later, the following announcement appeared in *The Independent*, a New York journal:

> With the consent of Mrs Stowe, Rev. Robert Everett . . . is about to translate and publish this death-blow on slavery for the benefit of the 100,000 Welsh emigrants scattered over this country. Mr E. is a fine scholar, and a warm friend of the oppressed, and we have no doubt that 'Uncle Tom' in his Welsh dress, strong and beautiful, will make a fine appearance and gain thousands of friends among the descendants of Prince Llywelyn and Owain Glyndŵr.[18]

The metaphor of 'dress' or costume for translation was a common one, suggesting a confidence that what mattered in the novel would survive translation essentially unchanged – and, indeed, the two translations associated with Robert Everett strove for accuracy and faithfulness to the original.

Stowe's stamp of approval for the translation was advertised not only in *The Independent*, but also in *Y Cenhadwr Americanaidd* (The *American Messenger*), the journal of the Welsh Congregationalists in the United States, which Everett himself edited.[19] Of the Welsh translators, Everett seems to have been the only one to have received Stowe's permission to publish a translation of the novel. In her lifetime, Stowe gave permission for a number of translations from English and even wrote a new preface for an authorized French edition.[20] Many more translations, however, appeared without her authorization. In 1853, she filed suit against a German publisher who had translated, printed and sold her novel without her permission and without giving her royalties. The case was decided against her, for copyright law at mid-century viewed the content of a published book as public property.[21] Everett reiterates Stowe's permission in prefaces to both of the translations issued under his name, suggesting a close tie between his own work and hers.

The first of the two translations linked to Everett appeared in instalments from January 1853 in *Y Cenhadwr* under the title 'Bwthyn F'Ewythr Tom; Neu Fywyd yn Mhlith yr Iselradd' ('Uncle Tom's Cabin; Or Life Among the Lowly').[22] The editorial preface to this translation notes that it had appeared in print before, recently, in the Welsh newspaper *Yr Amserau (The Times)*. Everett was evidently not the translator in this case. Though neither journal published the translator's name, E. G. Millward speculates that he was William Rees, recently retired from the editorship of *Yr Amserau*.[23] A second Welsh-American journal, *Y Cyfaill (O'r Hen Wlad) (The Friend (From the Old Country))*, ran the first instalment of a translation in the very same month as did *Y Cenhadwr*; the title of this was 'Caban 'N Ewythr Twm; Neu, Fywyd Negroaidd yn Nhalaethau Caethwasawl America' ('Uncle Tom's Cabin; or, Negro Life in the Slave States of America').[24] While the first instalments of the two seem to be identical, there were noticeable differences between the second instalments. In *Y Cyfaill*'s February instalment, for instance, the text was accompanied by footnotes in which the translator explained 'Quadroon and mulatto women' and gave them Welsh equivalents ('y melyniad' and 'merched melynddu').[25] At the end of a third instalment, in May, this translation is finally attributed to 'Y Lefiad' (Thomas Levi).[26] The magazines and journals that published these early translations of Stowe's novel were a veritable jungle of translators, editors and authors in which the identity of the translator is often invisible, and the authority of the translation did not hinge on a single name.

A second translation that came out under Everett's name in 1854 bore the title *Caban F'Ewythr Twm*. This single illustrated volume was the only full Welsh translation to be published as a book in the United States. Once again, the text was not wholly Everett's work, but an edition of Hugh Williams's translation for John Cassell in London. As Everett claims on the title-page, he had taken pains to amend and improve Cassell's edition ('adolygwyd a diwygiwyd'). And in his own introduction, which he substituted for Stowe's,

Everett writes that his aim in making the changes to Williams's translation was to give as true, or 'natural', a translation as he could for an audience of Welsh Americans:

> Edrychasom yn fanwl a gofalus dros y Cyfieithiad i'r Gymraeg, gan amcanu ac ymdrechu ei gael yn gyfieithiad naturiol a chywir. Yr ydym yn awr yn ei gyflwyno yn bryderus i Gymry America gan obeithio y rhoddir iddo dderbyniad cynnes a chyffredinol, ac y gwna y lledaeniad ohono yn ein hiaith dan ddwyfol fendith lawer o ddaioni.
>
> (I have looked closely and carefully through the Welsh translation, aiming and striving to get it natural and correct. Now I present it anxiously to the Welsh of America, hoping that it will be given a warm and general acceptance, and that the circulation of it in our language with God's blessing will do much good.)[27]

What 'good' did Everett have in mind, one wonders? Robert Everett was a fairly well-known abolitionist whose views on slavery earned him both applause and scorn from Welsh Americans. One hope, clearly, was that his translation would fortify his readers' abolitionist views and persuade others to come over to the abolitionist camp. In this sense, there was more at stake in this Welsh translation than in those that circulated in Wales; for Everett's readers were Americans. He makes this clear elsewhere in the introduction when he writes of slavery as 'y camwri mawr hwn, sydd yn nod mor waradwyddus arnom fel gwlad' ('this great injury, which is such a shameful mark on us as a nation').[28] The position his readers took with respect to slavery could make a difference to the future of the United States.

In another sense, Revd Everett's *gwlad* indicated the people of God. In this, too, his translation was true to Stowe's novel, whose religion most Welsh readers would have easily comprehended. It can hardly be a coincidence that three of the four early translators were ministers.

In yet a third sense, the translation may have been intended to 'do something' for the Welsh language, appearing as it did at a time when the Welsh-American periodicals published scores of poems in praise of the Welsh language, as well as letters and articles discussing the best way to preserve the Welsh language in the United States. One example of this literature are the verses that appear in the January 1853 issue of *Y Cyfaill* under the heading

'Gwarth Y Cymro Sydd Yn Gwadu Iaith ei Wlad' ('Disgrace of the Welshman Who Disowns the Language of his Country'). 'Mr Editor', writes the correspondent:

> Dichon y gall fod rhai o hiliogaeth Dic Shon Dafydd (coffa da amdano), wedi cyrhaedd yna i'r Gorllewin, pa rai ydynt yn ceisio perswadio eu hunain mai gwell iddynt 'sisial iaith y Saeson', a chefnu yn llwyr, ac am byth, ar yr hen 'Gymraeg, lwysaeg, lon'. Ond cyn iddynt ddyfod i'r cyfryw benderfyniad, annogwch hwy i ddarllen yr englynion rhagorol a ganlyn.

(Perhaps it is that some descendants of Dic Shon Dafydd (remember him kindly), having arrived there in the West, are trying to persuade themselves that it is better they 'whisper the Englishman's language' and forsake the old 'Welsh, fair and merry'. But before they come to such a conclusion, encourage them to read the excellent englynion that follow.)[29]

Of the ten *englynion*, the following two are characteristic:

> Bradu hen Gymru werddgain – yw gwadu
> Ei gwiwdeg iaith gywrain;
> 'Boed i Gymro seinio'i sain
> Llawndeg yn nghanol Llundain.
> . . .
> Pechod yw gwrthod a gwerthu – unol
> Ac enwog iaith Cymru,
> Am sothach, gan ymsythu;
> O, waeled gwr i'w wlad gu!

> (Treason against fair Wales it is, to disown
> Her fit, fine, vigorous tongue;
> Let the Welshman pronounce its resonant sounds
> In the very heart of London.
> . . .
> A sin it is to sell out, to reject this
> Famous, unifying language of Wales;
> And for rubbish! With a swagger!
> Oh, such a villain, to his beloved country.)

In these verses and elsewhere in the Welsh-American journals at mid-century, the Welsh language was viewed as an article that might be carelessly cast off in favour of English, and at the cost of a valued feeling of Welsh identity across the diaspora.

Uncle Tom's Cabin was often praised by readers as an instrument of education, not only for disseminating information to its readers about slavery and life in the south, but also for its great variety of language. In her biography of Stowe, for instance, Florine McCray transcribes a letter to Calvin Stowe, Harriet Beecher's husband, from the librarian at the British Library, who was creating a collection of editions and translations of *Uncle Tom's Cabin*:

> The possession . . . of such a book as *Uncle Tom's Cabin* is very different from such a book as 'Thomas à Kempis' in the information it affords to the student of a language. There is every variety of style, from that of animated narration and passionate wailing to that of the most familiar dialogue, and dialogue not only of the upper classes but of the lowest. The student who once mastered 'Uncle Tom' in Welsh or Wallachian is not likely to meet any further difficulties in his progress through Welsh or Wallachian prose. Thus it appears that this book was destined to stand pre-eminent as an educator, not only morally but technically.[30]

In the March 1853 issue of *Y Cyfaill*, one journalist made a similar argument. Of the multiple Welsh translations of Stowe's novel, he writes that each would have something to offer:

> Diau y bydd pob un yn dda yn ei ffordd. Felly bydd digon o ewythroedd, o bosibl; pa le y mae y modrybau ar eu gyfer? Byddai 'Uncle Tom' yn llyfr ysgol rhagorol, trwy rhoddi y rhai sydd yn dysgy gramadeg i ddiwygio y gwallau sydd ynddo, y rhai a adawyd o bwrpas gan yr awdyres enwog; bydd hyny hefyd yn tueddu yr ieuengctyd i gasau caethfasnach.

> (Presumably each translation will be good in its own way. It is quite possible that there will be plenty of uncles; where are the aunts to stand by their sides? *Uncle Tom* will be an exceptional school text, for it will help those who are learning grammar to correct the mistakes in it, those which were intentionally placed there by the famous authoress; this will also incline the youth to hate slavery.)[31]

The translations would be a useful tool for teaching Welsh to schoolchildren, who would absorb a healthy dislike of slavery together with their grammar lesson. An interesting implication is that the intentional 'mistakes' – presumably the dialect writing and colloquialisms – were to be kept out of the Welsh language. The curious association of missing 'aunts' and education reflects an idea that surfaced repeatedly in the journals of mid-century, that the transmission and preservation of the Welsh language in the United States would be best carried out by women and particularly by mothers. In the words of Reverend J. P. Harris,

> Ei gorchwyl hi yw planu anwyldeb at yr iaith yn y meddwl ieuangaidd, tra eto nas gall y plentyn lefaru; ie iddi hi y perthyna feithrin ynddo hoffed o'r iaith tra yn ei fagu, fel y sugno o'i hysbryd gyda llaeth y fron . . . Fel hyn yr ysgrifenir yr iaith gan fys y fam ar lech y galon, ac y bydd yn gymlethedig a bodoliaeth y dyn.
>
> ([The mother's] task is to plant affection for the language in the youngest mind, while the child yet cannot speak. Indeed, she is the one to nurture his affection for the language while she raises him, as though he were sucking its spirit with her breast-milk . . . In this way, the mother's finger will inscribe the language on the heart's slate, and it will be entangled with the man's very being.)[32]

According to preservationist writings, the mother inscribed her own language on to the heart of her child, who would in turn grow up to be a patriot and a poet. That the author of *Uncle Tom's Cabin* was a woman and a mother gives a further resonance to the notion that this novel would have substantial power and influence over its Welsh-language readers.

If *Uncle Tom's Cabin* inscribed a vision that has been described as 'unifying and millennial', evangelistic and regenerative, the Welsh-language translations circulated in the United States at mid-century were striving for the same.[33] By readers of the translations, the Welsh language would not have been viewed as an impediment to the fulfilment of such a vision; instead, it was perceived to be a tool for reaching into the hearts of readers, for tapping their deepest allegiances, and for bringing them to full consciousness as citizen-actors in the American Union. As *The Independent* suggests in its advertisement for Robert Everett's book, Welsh readers of *Uncle Tom's Cabin* in the United States were the 'descendants of Prince Llywelyn and Owain Glyndŵr' and therefore actors with parts to play in an unfolding pageant of ethnic and national identity.

Notes

[1] The novel sold 10,000 copies in a week and by the end of a year, 300,000 copies had sold in the United States. See Thomas F. Gossett, *Uncle Tom's Cabin and American Culture* (Dallas, TX: Southern Methodist University Press, 1985), p. 164.

[2] Ibid., p. 314. Gossett also suggests that Lincoln may not have read the novel (see pp. 314–15).

[3] Emerson is quoted in Gossett, *American Culture*, p. 165. Emerson, 'Success', *The Complete Works of Ralph Waldo Emerson*, ed. Edward Waldo Emerson, 12 vols (Boston: Houghton Mifflin Co., 1903–4), 7, 286.

[4] Florine Thayer McCray, *The Life-Work of the Author of Uncle Tom's Cabin* (New York: Funk and Wagnalls, 1889), p. 114.

[5] Neither was Williams's the only Welsh translation of *Uncle Tom's Cabin* in Stowe's possession. In the Schlesinger Library's collection of the Harriet Beecher Stowe family papers is a red leather-bound copy of *Crynodeb o Gaban 'Newyrth Tom; Neu, Fywyd Negroaidd yn America*, published by J. Rosser of Swansea, Wales. The overleaf of this copy bears an inscription handwritten in English by the translator: 'Uncle Tom's Cabin in Welsh; translated by Thomos Levi (Y Lefiad) and humbly presented to the Authoress, Mrs H. B. Stowe as a token of esteem and love. Ystradgynlais, N Swansea, South Wales, June 9, 1853.'

[6] See Susan Bassnett, *Translation Studies* ([1980]; London, New York: Routledge, 1991), pp. 71–5.

[7] As Susan Belasco has written, this novel 'is deeply embedded and implicated in the context in which it was written. To consider the novel's original timeliness and then to think about how it speaks to us today represent important steps in understanding the way literature is shaped by both the writer's and the reader's expectations and experiences'; Susan Belasco, 'The Writing, Reception, and Reputation of Uncle Tom's Cabin', *Approaches to Teaching Stowe's Uncle Tom's Cabin*, eds Elizabeth Ammons and Susan Belasco (New York: Modern Language Association of America, 2000), pp. 21–36 (35–6).

[8] E. G. Millward, *Cenedl o Bobl Ddewrion: Agweddau ar Lenyddiaeth Oes Victoria* (Llandysul: Gomer, 1991). 'Perygl unrhyw gyfieithiad i'r Gymraeg oedd y câi ei ddarllen fel stori antur ddifyr, foesol, a dim mwy: hanes rhyw ddyn du mewn gwlad bell a'r stori'n dangos, bid siŵr, fod y da'n trechu'r drwg yn y pen draw' (p. 93).

[9] Millward, *Cenedl o Bobl Ddewrion*, pp. 93–4; William Rees, *Aelwyd F'Ewythr Robert: Neu, Hanes Caban F'Ewythr Tomos* (Dinbych: Thomas Gee, 1853). When he wrote his version of Stowe's novel, William Rees, also known as Gwilym Hiraethog, was a minister in Liverpool and a well-known writer, poet and editor. In Rees's brilliant and creative translation, a young man reads *Uncle Tom's Cabin* aloud to old Uncle Robert, his wife, their two servants and others, and so relates the ideas in Stowe's novel to life in contemporary Wales. See also Ioan Williams, 'Gwilym Hiraethog (William Rees, 1802–83)', *A Guide to Welsh Literature c. 1800–1900*, ed. Hywel Teifi Edwards (Cardiff: University of Wales Press, 2000), pp. 61–4.

[10] Philip Fisher, *Hard Facts: Setting and Form in the American Novel* (New York, Oxford: Oxford University Press, 1987), pp. 6, 8.

[11] Susan Bassnett directed my attention to Homi Bhabha's metaphorical use of translation: 'We should remember that it is the "inter" – the cutting edge of translation and renegotiation, the *in-between* space – that carries the burden of the

meaning of culture'; Homi Bhabha, *The Location of Culture* (New York, London: Routledge, 1994), p. 38; cited in Bassnett, *Translation Studies*, p. 6.

[12] Fisher, *Hard Facts*, p. 8.

[13] 'Uncle Tom's Cabin', *Y Cyfaill (o'r Hen Wlad)*, XV, 179 (Tachwedd 1852), 354.

[14] See Belasco, 'Writing, Reception, and Reputation', p. 31; and Mason I. Lowance, Jr. et al. (eds), *The Stowe Debate: Rhetorical Structures in Uncle Tom's Cabin* (Amherst, MA: University of Massachusetts Press, 1994), p. 2.

[15] Charles Edward Stowe, *Life of Harriet Beecher Stowe: Compiled from her Letters and Journals* (Boston, New York: Houghton, Mifflin & Co., 1889), p. 190.

[16] *Y Cyfaill*, XVI, 183 (Mawrth 1853), 123.

[17] *Frederick Douglass' Paper* (31 December 1852).

[18] *The Independent* (16 December 1852).

[19] *Y Cenhadwr*, XIV, 1 (Ionawr 1853), 14; 'A gyhoeddir trwy hawlfraint oddiwrth yr Awdures'.

[20] For this 'Preface to the European Edition', see Stowe, *Life*, pp. 192–5.

[21] Lowance et al., *Stowe Debate*, p. 10. For a fascinating reading of Justice Robert Grier's ruling on this case, see also Meredith L. McGill, *American Literature and the Culture of Reprinting, 1834–1853* (Philadelphia: University of Pennsylvania Press, 2003), pp. 272–5.

[22] *Y Cenhadwr*, XIV, 1 (Ionawr 1853), 14–18. The translation in *Y Cenhadwr* is notable as the only one of the Welsh translations that gives 'cabin' as anything other than *caban*. According to *Geiriadur Prifysgol Cymru*, the Welsh *caban* is used as early as the mid-sixteenth century to mean a ship's cabin; in the nineteenth century it was also being used in the north Wales quarries to mean a shelter for use during blasting ('caban ymochel') or an eating shed ('caban bwyta'). Everett would presumably have been familiar with the word, as he had emigrated to New York from Denbigh in 1823; however, *bwthyn* must have seemed to him a more accurate translation for the humble dwelling where Uncle Tom resides at the beginning of Stowe's novel.

[23] Millward, *Cenedl o Bobl Ddewrion*, p. 90. See my note 9, above.

[24] *Y Cyfaill*, XVI, 181 (Ionawr 1853), 17–22.

[25] Ibid., XVI, 182 (Chwefror 1853), 56.

[26] Ibid., XVI (Mai 1853), 183.

[27] *Caban F'Ewythr Twm; Neu, Fywyd yn mhlith yr Iselradd. Gan Harriet Beecher Stowe. O argraffiad Llundain wedi ei ddiwigio gan Robert Everett* (Remsen, NY: John R. Everett, Swyddfa y 'Cenhadwr', 1854). Everett finally settled on *caban*, presumably because Stowe's title was by then common currency.

[28] Everett, *Caban F'Ewythr Twm*.

[29] *Y Cyfaill*, XVI, 181 (Ionawr 1853), 25.

[30] McCray, *Life-Work*, pp. 116–17.

[31] *Y Cyfaill*, XVI, 183 (Mawrth 1853), 123.

[32] Y Parch. J. P. Harris (Carnhuanawc), 'Traethawd ar y Cyfryngau Gorau i Amddiffyn a Chadw'r Iaith Gymraeg (An Essay on the Best Methods for Defending and Keeping the Welsh Language)', *Y Cylchgrawn Cenedlaethol* (Awst 1855), 298.

[33] Harold K. Bush, Jr., 'The Declaration of Independence and Uncle Tom's Cabin: A Rhetorical Criticism Approach', *Approaches to Teaching Stowe's Uncle Tom's Cabin*, eds Ammons and Belasco, pp. 172–83 (172). Bush argues that *Uncle Tom's Cabin* strives rhetorically to bring speaker and listener together in what he understands 'to be Stowe's primary aim in writing her novel: to engender a unifying and millennial vision by which the Union might be saved'.

16
Global Questions and Local Visions: A Microcosmopolitan Perspective

MICHAEL CRONIN

The Irish-language translator and writer Seosamh Mac Grianna is on his way to Algeria when he changes his mind. The thought strikes him in London that instead of going to north Africa he should go instead to a country that is much nearer, but in a sense equally foreign: Wales. He explains his decision in terms of his own singular destiny as traveller and writer:

> Dar liom, goidé is fiú dom an ród mór leathan a shiúlas achan duine a leanstan? Ní hé mo bhealach é. Chan ar bhealach na gcarr agus na gcabhlach a gheobhas mise mo chinniúint. Bheadh leisc ar ainbhíosan a aidhmheáil go raibh sé riamh sa Bhreatain Bhig. In ainm Dé, siúil na háiteacha nach siúlann daoine eile, mura mbíodh le feiceáil agat ach tithe cearc.[1]

(I think what's the point of walking the big, wide road that everybody else follows? It is not my way. I will not find my destiny where cars and navies go. An ignoramus would be reluctant to admit that he was ever in Wales. For God's sake, walk in places where nobody else walks, even if you see nothing but hen-houses.)

Mac Grianna took his own advice and travelled to Wales, an experience that would lead him to write a separate work on the country entitled simply *An Bhreatain Bheag*.[2] However, not many Irish writers and intellectuals have followed the path trodden by Mac Grianna, and as recently as 2000 M. Wynn Thomas, in his prefatory remarks to a collection of essays on the literatures of

Scotland, Wales and Ireland, noted that, '[a]lthough there is ample evidence here of several of the cultures of the Anglo-Celtic archipelago speaking to each other, there is next to no evidence of them speaking empathically for each other – what is noticeable is that very few of the contributors have felt sufficiently confident in their knowledge of a neighbouring culture to venture to draw parallels, or at least to make comparisons, between that culture and their own'.[3] What this chapter proposes to do is to suggest a conceptual framework for a way of thinking about the cultures of countries like Wales and Ireland that is potentially of interest not just to those who wander off the beaten track of international travel but to those who throng the *ród mór leathan*, the big wide road of contemporary globalization theory.

Cosmopolitanism

It is commonly claimed that it was the Greek philosopher Diogenes who, in the fourth century, first defined himself as a citizen of the world. Later, Aristippus, in a more evocative image expressed a similar idea by claiming that the road to Hades was the same distance from any point in the world. In 1552 Erasmus refused the citizenship of the city of Zurich, offered by Zwingli, declaring that, 'I want to be a citizen not of one single city but of the whole world'.[4] The ideal of humanity as a collection of free and equal beings, possessing the same basic rights and where notions of hospitality, openness to others and freedom of movement are primordial, underlies much thinking about cultural contact and the intercultural, from antiquity to our own times. Peter Coulmas, in his *Weltbürger: Geschichte einer Menschheitssehnsucht* (1990) offers the reader a historical overview of the vicissitudes of cosmopolitan thought down through the centuries and openly states his preference for a world-view which he believes to be the only one capable of ensuring lasting peace and friendship between the different peoples on the planet. For Coulmas, a decline in cosmopolitanism is always synonymous with the rise of particularism and the birth of nationalism. When he goes on to describe important moments in the history of cosmopolitanism, it is almost invariably in the context of great empires of yesteryear, the Greek, the Roman, the Byzantine, the Carolingian, the French, the Spanish, the Austro-

Hungarian and the British.⁵ This approach is not particularly quixotic and it has become a historical commonplace to underline the multi-ethnic and multilingual character of empires, even if the focus is not as resolutely centred on the west as is the case with Coulmas.⁶ The version of cosmopolitanism made explicit by Coulmas is what we might term *macrocosmopolitanism*, namely, a tendency to locate the cosmopolitan moment in the construction of empires, in the development of large nation-states (France, Great Britain, Germany) or more recently, in the creation of supranational organizations (European Union, United Nations, World Health Organization).

For the macrocosmopolitan, it is only large political units which are capable of allowing the development of a progressive and inclusive vision of humanity, even if occasional hegemonic overreaching cannot be ruled out. Small nations, ethnic groups concerned with the protection or preservation of cultural identity, and former colonies which still subscribe to an ideology of national liberation are dangerously suspect in this macroscopic conception of cosmopolitanism. Bloody conflicts in the Balkans and in Northern Ireland seem to provide more recent justification for the distrust, in Pascalian terms, of the infinitely great for the infinitely small.

Coulmas evokes the popularity of the motto, 'small is beautiful', associating it with a fashionable interest in local costumes, dances and languages. His verdict is clear: 'this nostalgic looking back is clearly opposed to the onward march of history towards larger political entities'. Worse still, he declares, '[t]he small state is praised'.⁷ These small states have a function which is clearly described in a chapter on the great metropolises of history. The latter benefit from the arrival of immigrants from less important states, 'by means of this brain-drain, many brilliant minds escape their country of origin, particularly, small countries offering few possibilities'.⁸ In *Culture* Raymond Williams offers a similar description of the role of the metropolis, with his notion that those who participated in the many avant-garde artistic groups were, frequently, 'immigrants to such a metropolis, not only from outlying regions but from other and smaller national cultures, now seen as culturally provincial in relation to the metropolis'.⁹ Indeed, for Matthew Arnold in an earlier period it was precisely the centripetal pull of the centre that made the notion of separate nationhood for the Irish or the Welsh or the Bretons a dangerous illusion:

> Small nationalities inevitably gravitate towards the larger nationalities in their immediate neighbourhood. Their ultimate fusion is so natural and irresistible that even the sentiment of the absorbed race, ceases, with time, to struggle against it; the Cornishman and the Breton become, at last, in feeling as well as in political fact, an Englishman and a Frenchman.[10]

The nineteenth-century Swiss writer Rodolphe Töpffer noted, with mordant cynicism, that consecration from the macrocosmopolitan viewpoint could come only through the metropolis, whose judgements were then internalized by those on the metropolitan edge:

> Il faut donc de toute nécessité que cet homme, s'il tient à être illustre, transporte dans la capitale sa pacotille de talent, que là il la déballe devant les experts parisiens, qu'il paie l'expertise, et alors on lui confectionne une renommée qui de la capitale est expédiée dans les provinces où elle est acceptée avec empressement.

> (It is absolutely necessary that if this man wishes to be famous he must bring his trashy talent to the capital, that there he must lay it out before the Parisian experts, pay for their valuation, and then a reputation is concocted for him which goes from the capital into the provinces where it is accepted with enthusiasm.)[11]

The existence of small countries is justified by their being a kind of pre-cosmopolitan nursery, a warehouse of the mind where cognitive raw materials await the necessary processing and polish of the present and former capitals of empires. If Coulmas is cited at length it is because he offers in summary form a number of the basic theses of macrocosmopolitanism, in particular, an abiding hostility to political entities that are seen to be primarily defined by notions of national sovereignty or cultural particularism.

Microcosmopolitanism

What I would like to propose in this chapter is a notion of *microcosmopolitanism* which will be opposed to that of macrocosmopolitanism. Microcosmopolitan thought shares a number of macrocosmopolitan core ideals (freedom/openness/tolerance/ respect for the other), but it is distinctly different in foregrounding other perspectives, other areas of work and research and, above all, in freeing cosmopolitanism from a historical vision and a set of ideological presuppositions that threaten both its survival as a necessary element of human self-understanding and its ability to speak meaningfully to many different political situations, including that of Wales. Why do we need a microcosmopolitan perspective, and of what does it consist? I will begin with the necessity for such a perspective.

There are now more nation-states than at any other time in the world's history. Currently, none of these nations seem particularly keen on abandoning their independence and, in the case of countries like Tibet and Chechnya, the struggle for national independence still goes on. In this context, it is unlikely that small or new nations, who have, often with great difficulty, freed themselves from a former colonial presence, will be particularly impressed by being told that the notion of nation is outdated and reactionary and that clinging to such a notion automatically disqualifies them from belonging to the cosmopolitan community. A dangerous and fatal consequence of this approach is to set up a progressive cosmopolitanism, in opposition to a bigoted, essentialist nationalism, where the latter has no place for the former. In other words, the inhabitants of smaller political units find themselves subject to the 'double bind' famously described by Gregory Bateson.[12] Either you abandon any form of national identification associated with the worst forms of irredentist prejudice and embrace the cosmopolitan credo, or you persist with a claim of national specificity and place yourself outside the cosmopolitan pale, being by definition incapable of openness to the other. The effects of this particular double bind are particularly damaging and, in intellectual life, bring about the paralysis that Bateson noted so clearly in our emotional lives. Extreme nationalists of all hues take refuge in virulent denunciations of anything construed to represent the cosmopolitan (as has been demonstrated in such a tragic fashion in European history by the history of anti-Semitism) while the proponents of macrocosmopolitanism, for their part, are trenchantly hostile to any movement of thought that might appear to harbour sympathy for nationalist ideology.

Another version of this unhelpful dualism is to be found in certain analyses of the phenomenon of globalization. Globalization is typically presented by its opponents as a process of wholesale standardization,[13] dominated by large multinational corporations and international organizations, such as the World Bank and the International Monetary Fund, acting at the behest of the political and economic interests of the world's remaining super power, the United States.[14] This thesis has been challenged by a number of thinkers, such as Roland Robertson, Jonathan Friedman and Manuel Castells, who view globalization as being as much a fragmentary and centrifugal process as a unifying and centripetal one.[15] Their analyses, which would appear to challenge the hegemony of the powerful, do not in fact offer smaller nations a particularly promising role as, once again, they are cast in the position of *Fidei Defensor*, as the touchy and scrupulous guardians of national difference. Once again, there is the trap of the essentialist conception of national identity, the identity logic criticized by Alain Finkielkraut in his *La Défaite de la pensée*, where political and cultural differences are reduced to a simplistic and homogeneous version of particularism, usually to favour the material and social interests of local elites.[16] For a national of a smaller nation who has been interested in Ireland's relationship with elsewhere and who has lived on an island that has seen over 3,000 people die in a conflict around issues of identity, the binarism of macrocosmopolitan thinking, which also underlines Samuel Huntington's thesis on the clash of civilizations or Benjamin Barber's vision of 'Jihad vs. McWorld', is hardly persuasive and deeply disabling, intellectually and politically. Writers and intellectuals from nations such as Ireland, Scotland and Wales should not have to be condemned to the facile dualism of macro perspectives.[17]

Microcosmopolitan thinking is not an approach which involves the opposition of smaller political units to larger political units (national or transnational), but one which in the general context of the cosmopolitan ideals mentioned earlier seeks to diversify or complexify the smaller unit. In other words, it is a cosmopolitanism not from above but from below. Guy Scarpetta, in his *Éloge du cosmopolitisme*, is deeply critical of any 'defence of difference', which he believes leads inevitably to the 'affirmation of a biological inequality between nations'.[18] The defence of difference is always problematic if the notion is understood in a essentialist and unitary sense, but what I wish to advance here is a defence of difference, not beyond, but within the national political unit. If I may modify an idea first put forward in *Across the Lines*, microcosmopolitanism is linked to what I have called fractal differentialism.[19] This term expresses the notion of a cultural complexity which remains constant from the micro to the macro scale. That is to say, the same degree of diversity is to be found at the level of entities judged to be small or insignificant as at the level of large entities. Its origin lies in a paper published in 1977 by the French mathematician, Benoît Mandelbrot. Mandelbrot asked the following question: 'How long is the coast of Britain?' His answer was that at one level the coast was infinitely long. An observer from a satellite would make one guess, which would be shorter than, say, that of a Paul Theroux negotiating every inlet, bay and cove on the coast, and Theroux's guess would be shorter than that of a tiny insect having to negotiate every pebble.[20] As James Gleick pointed out, 'Mandelbrot found that as the scale of measurement becomes smaller, the measured length of a coastline rises without limit, bays and peninsulas revealing ever smaller sub-bays and sub-peninsulas at least down to atomic scales.'[21] Mandelbrot's discovery was that the coastline had a characteristic degree of roughness or irregularity, and that this degree remained constant across different scales. Mandelbrot called the new geometry that he had originated 'fractal' geometry. The shapes or fractals in this new geometry allowed infinite length to be contained in finite space. The experience of the traveller bears out the discovery of the mathematician. The traveller on foot becomes aware of the immeasurable complexity of short distances in a way that is invisible to the traveller behind the windscreen or looking down from the air.

A particularly striking example of the phenomenon is offered in the work of the English mathematician and cartographer, Tim Robinson. In his *Stones of Aran: Labyrinth*, he offers a detailed exploration of the 14,000 fields that go to make up the island of Inismore off the west coast of Ireland.[22] The French historian, Emmanuel Leroy Ladurie, many years earlier offered a similarly fine-grained history of a small village in southern France in *Montaillou*.[23] What Robinson clearly demonstrates, as he goes through field after field on this small island, is not only the remarkable richness of these reduced spaces but also the omnipresence of the traces of foreignness, of other languages and cultures, in a place that through the work of John Millington Synge and others was closely identified with Irish language and culture and Irish cultural nationalism. The local is honoured in Robinson's work, but it is a local that is informed by diversity and difference. In a sense, it is the fractal travelling of the intercultural researcher, of researchers like the scholar and critic Wynn Thomas, whom this work rightly honours, that allows for the elaboration of a theory of the microcosmopolitan.

Microcosmopolitanism helps thinkers from smaller nations to circumvent the terminal paralysis of identity logic, not through a programmatic condemnation of elites ruling from above, but through a patient undermining of conventional thinking from below. A microcosmopolitan perspective also avoids the ready assimilation of cosmopolitanism to economic and social privilege, which is apparent not only in the tirades of the European Far Right but also in the analyses of progressive thinkers, who are sceptical about the uses to which cosmopolitanism is put by transnational capital. Timothy Brennan, for example, launches a trenchant attack against cosmopolitan thinking in *At Home in the World: Cosmopolitanism Now*, where he denounces the current vogue for cosmopolitanism as simply the well-meaning version of American imperialism which, under cover of cultural pluralism, wishes to ensure the continued dominance of its political, economic, military and cultural interests.[24] Danilo Zolo, in *Cosmopolis: Prospects for World Government*, is similarly hostile:

> What western cosmopolitans call 'global civil society' in fact goes no further than a network of connections and functional interdependencies which have developed within certain important sectors of the 'global market', above all finance, technology, automation, manufacturing industry and the service sector. Nor, moreover, does it go much beyond the optimistic expectation of affluent westerners to be able to feel universally recognized as citizens of the world – citizens of a welcoming, peaceful, ordered and democratic 'global village' – without for a moment or in any way ceasing to be 'themselves', i.e. western citizens.[25]

The microcosmopolitan movement, by situating diversity, difference and exchange at the micro-levels of society, challenges the monopoly (real or imaginary) of a deracinated elite on cosmopolitan ideals by attempting to show that elsewhere is next door, in one's immediate environment.

City and country

If there is a place that would seem to offer itself quite readily to the microcosmopolitan approach, it would appear to be the city. Lewis Mumford in 1961 was already claiming that the 'global city is the world writ small, within its walls can be found every social class, every people, every language'.[26] The cities that have been classed as the great world cities of the past have included Athens, Alexandria, Rome, Constantinople, Paris, Vienna, London and New York, but now they include cities such as Karachi, Toyko, São Paolo, Mexico City and Montreal, to give some more recent examples. For certain thinkers, such as Manuel Castells, Saskia Sassen and Gerard Delanty, cities, and in particular the large international metropolises, are going to become more and more important at the expense of nation-states.[27] These global metropolises, key nodes in international communications networks, by bringing together a plethora of different cultures, languages and identities, are seen as an inexhaustible reservoir for the renewal of the cosmopolitan spirit. Cities are indeed striking examples of the potential of a microcosmopolitan approach. The work of a scholar of hybridity, Sherry Simon, on the Mile End district in Montreal, shows that much indeed can be learned from exploring the intercultural spaces of cities.[28] The fact that by the end of the twenty-first century more than 80 per cent of the planet's population will be living in urban centres would seem to be yet another reason for favouring an exclusively urban focus in research.

The danger, however, is that we end up once again giving new life to a jaded binary opposition: town or country, progress or reaction. In this view, cosmopolitanism is the proper business of cities and the role of the rural population is to act as guarantors for the authenticity of the land. It has become a critical commonplace, for example, to show how the city of Dublin was marginalized in Irish writing for many years after independence because in the nationalist imaginary the city was a foreign presence, an alien substance in the Irish body politic (Dublin – city of the Vikings, seat of British colonial power).[29] The countryside alone was deemed worthy of interest by many of the post-independence short-story writers (the genre that found particular favour with Irish writers for many decades after the establishment of the Free State), because it was the countryside that was seen to be the incarnation of much that was deemed to be specific to Ireland. Needless to say, in Ireland, it was mainly urban intellectuals – Yeats, Synge, Standish O'Grady, George Moore – who contributed to the Romantic deification of the land in cultural nationalism.[30] If the more extreme forms of nationalism see the city as the polluted well of the cosmopolitan destroying the manly vigour of the nation, the ready and too-facile identification of the city with cosmopolitanism in the work of many thinkers on cosmopolitanism itself tends ironically to give succour to the most retrograde forms of nationalism.

One could argue that instead of arguing by implication and by default for a patriotism of the land, it is more enabling to argue for a cosmopolitanism of the land, in other words, to define specificity through and not against multiplicity. Casual observers of Irish setdancing in a pub in rural Clare might properly feel that they are witnessing a practice which is deeply rooted in a locality, but they are also seeing the fruit of the influence of French dancing-masters who came to Ireland at the end of the eighteenth century, finding themselves unemployed due to the exile or untimely demise of their aristocratic patrons.[31] More recently, *Riverdance*, for all its egregious excesses and Celticist parody, is a striking synthesis of Irish figure-dancing and Hollywood musicals. To stress hybridity in nonurban settings is not to devalue but to revalue. That is to say, to emphasize the multiple origins of a cultural practice, the intercultural dynamic in a microcosmopolitanism of the land, is not to give in to a moralizing condemnation of particularisms on the grounds that traditions are always bogus, that the supposedly authentic is an elaborate historical trick and that we all know why the Scots were encouraged to wear kilts. The withering scepticism noticeable in the work of Benedict Anderson and Eric Hobsbawm, and amplified ad nauseam in the commentary of media pundits, is damaging to a genuine openness of cultures and engenders a counter-reaction to a current of cosmopolitan thinking seen as destructive, condescending and hegemonic.[32] A key element of the microcosmopolitan argument being advanced here is that diversity enriches a country, a people, a community, but that diversity should not be opposed to identity from the point of view of a dismissive, macrocosmopolitan moralism.

If I have insisted on the necessity of considering cosmopolitanism as a phenomenon that is not the unique preserve of the urban, the underlying concerns are partly ecological. It is unlikely that rampant urbanization of both our societies and our planet is the best way for humanity to proceed. The accelerated drift from the countryside in these islands and throughout Europe is a factor that detracts from, rather than enhances, cultural diversity and that represents a significant threat to linguistic diversity, to name but one component of cultural specificity. It has become something of a critical commonplace in recent years for commentators on the literatures of the smaller nations of the 'Anglo-Celtic archipelago' to resist the *rurification* of these literatures. In other words, there has been an understandable hostility to the depiction of Irish, Welsh or Scottish writing as providing accounts of picturesque, non-urban experiences for the jaded intellects of the metropolitan centres; non-metropolitan writing acting as a cultural alibi for the consuming passions of tourism. The insistence on the importance of the urban voice in contemporary Irish writing, of a tradition of describing town and city experience in Welsh-language poetry and prose and of the avatars of the urban sensibility in Scottish fiction are perfectly necessary correctives to the platitudes of the postcard. However, it is important that we do not lose sight of the considerable body of writing in English, Welsh, Irish Gaelic, Scots Gaelic and Scots which highlights the microcosmopolitan complexity of places and cultures which are outside the critical purview of the urban metropolis. In this way, in the investigation of the links between culture, place and language from the perspective of the fractal differentialism mentioned earlier it will be possible to develop a reading of, for example, Irish and Welsh rural experience, which is not condemned to a wistful *passéisme* but is forward-looking, in its restoration of political complexity and cultural dynamism to areas of Irish and Welsh territory and memory. Such a move, an integral part of the microcosmopolitan project, would both revitalize enquiry into a substantial body of our respective literatures and also have important implications for the development of a progressive literary and cultural criticism in dealing with rural communities throughout the world.

A transnational history of translation

Gerard Delanty, in his conclusion to *Citizenship in a Global Age*, offers his own definition of the cosmopolitan moment:

> The cosmopolitan moment occurs when context-bound cultures encounter each other and undergo transformation as a result. Only in this way can the twin pitfalls of the false universalism of liberalism's universalistic morality and the communitarian retreat into the particular be avoided.[33]

The classic double bind is to be forced to choose between the false universality of a world culture promised by more hegemonic varieties of globalization and the romanticism of the particular. For Delanty, what is indispensable for the emergence of a genuine cosmopolitanism is the encounter, the interaction between the local and the transnational, hence his interest in a strategic alliance between cities and regions that bypasses the nation-state. By way of illustration of the necessary link between the microcosmopolitan and the transnational, I will mention briefly an area which has been of interest to Wynn Thomas in his writings, namely the history of translation, but in this instance I will be looking at Ireland rather than Wales. Contrary to earlier practice in the field of translation studies, it is no longer possible to limit histories of translation to literary phenomena within the territorial boundaries of the nation-state, but account must be taken of the multiple translation activities of a country's diaspora. It is in this sense that any history of translation must be a 'transnational' history rather than a 'national' history. In the Irish case, it is possible to identify at least three moments in this transnational translation history. The first moment, dating back to the early medieval period, sees the involvement of the Irish in the reconstruction of the Carlongian educational system and, in particular, in the revival of instruction in Latin. The Irish, as speakers of a Celtic language, markedly different from Latin, found that they were teaching Latin as a genuinely foreign language. Not only was Latin a foreign language for the Irish teachers, but it had also become a foreign language for many of their Continental pupils, as a result of the depredations of the invasions by nomadic tribes and the collapse of the Roman Empire. The geographical spread of their activities, abetted by the marked nomadism of the Irish monks, meant that their cultural influence was experienced far from their home-base in Ireland. Not surprisingly, this religious and pedagogic expansionism has translation consequences. The ninth century sees the emergence of a group of Irish translators – Johannes Scotus Eriugena, Sedulius Scotus and Martinus Hiberniensis – whose Greek–Latin translations are to make a significant contribution to the Carolingian renaissance and the revival of Neoplatonism in Europe.[34] What is particularly striking in tracing translation activity is the constant traffic in texts, ideas and literary models between Irish monasteries, local powerhouses in a strongly decentralized country, and Irish monastic foundations in Britain and on the European continent.

The second moment in this transnational history occurs in the seventeenth century, when the religious and political persecution of Irish Catholics leads to the establishment of a series of Irish colleges on the European continent. Irish-language translations are produced in Rome, Prague and Salamanca, but it is Saint Anthony's College in Louvain, established in 1603, that is to become the most important site of translation activity. The acquisition of a printing press in 1611 to publish texts in Irish gives an added importance to the translation activity in Louvain, as translations were hitherto largely produced and circulated in manuscript form, which greatly increased the cost and limited the possibilities of distribution. The translations themselves not only demonstrate the engagement of scholars formed by native intellectual traditions with the ideological ferment of the Counter-Reformation but, in their very language, will ultimately influence the linguistic development of modern Irish.[35]

A third moment in this diasporic history of Irish translation emerges in the twentieth century and is principally the work of Irish modernists in exile, such as James Joyce, Samuel Beckett, Denis Devlin, Brian Coffey and Thomas McGreevy, who will make translation an integral part of their specific transnational poetics.[36] Another dimension of this diasporic experience, although much less studied, is the presence of the Irish as missionaries, pedagogues and linguists in colonial and post-colonial West Africa. Irish modernism would be, properly speaking, inconceivable without continued contact with the European continent, but similarly the most remote village on the island had a contact either with North America or England/ Scotland/Wales through emigration, or with

Latin America and western/southern Africa through the activity of the Church. Literature in the Irish and English languages bears ample witness to the nature and extent of these contacts, and it is generally accepted that a territorially exclusivist nationalist historiography has often tended to disregard or minimize the importance of the diasporic. However, what a microcosmopolitan transnationalism is arguing for is not that place or identity be dissolved into a rootless geography of free-floating diasporic fragments, but rather that we take transnational phenomena like translation in smaller nations, such as Ireland and Wales, to reinvest place with the full complexity of their microcosmopolitan connectedness. In this sense, the words of the Scottish academic and activist, Alastair McIntosh, have a particular resonance: 'If any of us dig deep enough where we stand, we will find ourselves connected to all parts of the world.'[37] It is in the context of Wynn Thomas's lifelong concern with a specific place, Wales, and with the microcosmopolitan commitment to the complexity of the local that it is important that we look afresh at the connection between particularism and universality. Particularism is easily parodied. A concern with specific places or peoples or cultures can appear more limiting, or indeed, narcissistic than a more universal, abstract compassion for all of nature, or all of humanity. The philosopher Val Plumwood argues, however, that care for or empathy with specific aspects of nature rather than with nature as an abstraction is vital if there is to be any substance or commitment to our concern. As she observes, '[c]are and responsibility for particular animals, trees and rivers that are well known, loved, and appropriately connected to the self are an important basis for acquiring a wider, more generalized concern'.[38] The major drawback with finding particular attachments to be ethically suspect and advocating instead a genuine, 'impartial' identification with nature or with the good, however defined, is that one can end up favouring an indiscriminate identification which subverts the basis for the initial concern, that is the desire to preserve difference. Plumwood comments:

> this 'transpersonal' identification is so indiscriminate and intent on denying particular meanings, it cannot allow for the deep and highly particularistic attachment to place that has motivated both the passion of many modern conservationists and the love of many indigenous peoples for their land.[39]

If we transfer our attention from biodiversity to cultural ecology it is possible to measure the particular importance of scholarship that is focused on a specific place, such as Wales, but which is equally alert to the news from elsewhere. In a sense, what Plumwood intimates and Wynn Thomas demonstrates so persuasively in his writing and academic activities is that it is the microcosmopolitanism of the margin rather than the macrocosmopolitanism of the centre that allows for a cultural politics which is crucially re-centred but not, ultimately, self-centred.

Notes

[1] Seosamh Mac Grianna, *Mo Bhealach Féin* (Baile Átha Cliath: Oifig an tSoláthair, 1940), pp. 83–4.

[2] Seosamh Mac Grianna, *An Bhreatain Bheag* (Baile Átha Cliath: Oifig an tSoláthair, 1937). *An Bhreatain Bheag* (lit. Little Britain) is 'Wales' in Irish.

[3] M. Wynn Thomas, 'Introduction', *Nations and Relations: Writing Across the British Isles*, eds Tony Brown and Russell Stephens (Cardiff: New Welsh Review, 2000), p. iv.

[4] Cited in Johann Huizinga, 'Erasmus über Vaterland und Nationen', *Gedenkschrift zum 400. Todestag des Erasmus von Rotterdam* (Bâle, 1936), p. 34. My translation.

[5] Peter Coulmas, *Weltbürger: Geschichte einer Menschheitssehnsucht* (Reinbek: Rowohlt, 1990), pp. 9–13.

[6] A typical example of this approach is the ambitious historical survey contained in Felipe Fernández Armesto, *Millennium: A History of Our Last Thousand Years* (London: Black Swan, 1996).

[7] Coulmas, *Weltbürger*, p. 303. My translation.

[8] Ibid., p. 272. My translation.

[9] Raymond Williams, *Culture* (London: Fontana, 1981), p. 84.

[10] Matthew Arnold, 'England and the Italian Question' [1859], *The Complete Prose Works*, ed. R. H. Super, vol. 1 (Ann Arbor: University of Michigan Press, 1961), p. 71. For a fuller discussion of Arnold's thinking on nationality see Daniel Williams's excellent essay, 'Pan-Celticism and the Limits of Post-Colonialism: W. B. Yeats, Ernest Rhys and William Sharp in the 1890s', *Nations and Relations: Writing Across the British Isles*, eds Tony Brown and Russell Stephens (Cardiff: New Welsh Review, 2000), pp. 1–29.

[11] Cited by Jérôme Meizoz, *Ramuz, un passager clandestin des lettres françaises* (Geneva: Zoé, 1997), p. 168.

[12] Gregory Bateson, 'Double Bind', *Steps to an Ecology of Mind* (London: Paladin, 1973), pp. 242–9.

[13] George Ritzer, *The McDonaldization of Society* (Thousand Oaks, CA: Pine Forge Press, 1993).

[14] Naomi Klein, *Fences and Windows: Dispatches from the Front Line of the Globalization Debate* (London: Flamingo, 2002).

[15] Jonathan Friedman, *Cultural Identity and Global Process* (London: Sage, 1994); Roland Robertson, *Globalization: Social Theory and Global Culture*

(London: Sage, 1992); Manuel Castells, *The Power of Identity* (Oxford: Blackwell, 1997).

[16] Alain Finkielkraut, *La Défaite de la pensée* (Paris: Gallimard, 1987), pp. 65–106. Translated as *The Undoing of Thought*, tr. Dennis O'Keeffe (London: Claridge, 1988).

[17] Samuel Huntington, 'The Clash of Civilizations', *Foreign Affairs*, 72, 3 (1993), 22–50; Benjamin Barber, *Jihad vs. McWorld* (New York: Ballantine Press, 1996).

[18] Guy Scarpetta, *Éloge du cosmopolitisme* (Paris: Grasset, 1981), p. 19.

[19] Michael Cronin, *Across the Lines: Travel, Language, Translation* (Cork: Cork University Press, 2000), pp. 16–21.

[20] Benoît Mandelbrot, *The Fractal Geometry of Nature* (New York: Freeman, 1977).

[21] James Gleick, *Chaos: Making a New Science* (London: Cardinal, 1987), p. 96.

[22] Tim Robinson, *Stones of Aran: Labyrinth* (Dublin: Lilliput Press, 1995).

[23] Emmanuel Leroy Ladurie, *Montaillou, village occitan de 1294 à 1324* (Paris: Gallimard, 1976).

[24] Timothy Brennan, *At Home in the World: Cosmopolitanism Now* (Cambridge, MA: Harvard University Press, 1994).

[25] Danilo Zolo, *Cosmopolis: Prospects for World Government*, tr. David McKie (Cambridge: Polity Press, 1997), p. 137.

[26] Lewis Mumford, *The City in History* (London: Penguin, 1991), p. 620.

[27] Manuel Castells, *The Rise of the Network Society* (Oxford: Blackwell, 1997), pp. 376–428; Saskia Sassen, *The Global City: New York, London, Tokyo* (Princeton, NJ: Princeton University Press, 1991); Saskia Sassen, 'The State and the Global City', *Globalization and Its Discontents* (New York: The New Press, 1998), pp. 195–218; Gerard Delanty, *Citizenship in a Global Age* (Buckingham: Open University Press, 2000), pp. 99–102.

[28] Sherry Simon, *L'Hybridité culturelle* (Montréal: L'île de la tortue, 1999).

[29] The classic statement of this position is Fintan O'Toole, 'Going West: The Country versus the City in Irish Writing', *The Crane Bag*, 9, 2, 111–16.

[30] John Hutchinson, *The Dynamics of Cultural Nationalism and the Creation of the Irish Nation State* (London: Allen and Unwin, 1987).

[31] Pat Murphy, *Toss the Feathers: Irish Set Dancing* (Cork: Mercier Press, 1995).

[32] Eric Hobsbawm, *Myths and Nationalism since 1780: Programme, Myth, Reality* (Cambridge: Cambridge University Press, 1990); Benedict Anderson, *Imagined Communities: Reflections on the Origin and Spread of Nationalism* (London: Verso, 1991).

[33] Delanty, *Citizenship*, p. 145.

[34] Dorothy Whitelock, Rosamond McKitterick and David Dumville, *Ireland in Early Medieval Europe* (Cambridge: Cambridge University Press, 1982); James P. Mackey (ed.), *The Cultures of Europe: The Irish Contribution* (Belfast: The Institute of Irish Studies, 1994); William J. Shiels and Diana Wood (eds), *The Churches, Ireland and the Irish* (Oxford: Oxford University Press, 1989); Michael Cronin, *Translating Ireland: Translation, Languages, Cultures* (Cork: Cork University Press, 1996), pp. 12–15.

[35] Tomás Ó Cléirigh, *Aodh Mac Aingil agus an Scoil Nua-Ghaeilge i Lobháin* (Dublin: An Gúm, 1985).

[36] Kathleen Shields, *Language, Poetry and Identity in Twentieth-Century Ireland* (Bern: Peter Lang, 2000).

[37] Alastair McIntosh, *Soul and Soil: People versus Corporate Power* (London: Aurum, 2001), p. 7.

[38] Val Plumwood, 'Nature, Self, and Gender: Feminism, Environmental Philosophy and the Critique of Rationalism', *Reflections on Nature: Readings in Environmental Philosophy*, eds L. Gruen and D. Jamieson (Oxford: Oxford University Press, 1994), pp. 145–6.
[39] Ibid., 152.

V
WELSH CORRESPONDENCES

GRAHAME DAVIES

Cyfannu
(I M. Wynn Thomas)

Mae gan bob un ei stori, am wn i,
dalennau gloyw rhwng dau ddifancoll mawr,
ychydig ofod i groniclo cri
cyn cau am byth o'u golau rhwng dau glawr.
A hwyrach na fedr rhamant hanes un
gydsynio â gwyddoniaeth lem y llall,
na delfryd awdur a abertha'i hun
gytuno â rhyw bropagandydd dall.
Ond hwn a fynnodd weld y gweithiau oll
mewn trem synoptig ar y silffoedd llawn
heb fod y geiryn lleiaf iddo ar goll,
heb fod un sillaf nas adnabu'i ddawn,
gan ganfod undod mewn amrywiaeth pur
yng nghymod y cyfrolau ar y mur.

Making whole

Each person has their story, I suppose,
bright pages open in an endless night,
a little space before the covers close
to chronicle their longing for the light.
And maybe one's romantic turn of phrase
dismays another's scientific mind,
and maybe one who sacrificed his days
would never love the propaganda-blind.
But this one saw the corpus as a whole
in one synoptic glance along the shelf,
each word a cell of our collective soul,
each syllable essential in itself,
and found the common thread uniting all
the volumes reconciled along the wall.

Translated by the author, Grahame Davies

18
Poetic Lands and Borderlands: Henry Vaughan to Robert Frost

JEREMY HOOKER

I

A border, such as the Marches of Wales, may be a political division fraught with historical conflicts or tensions. At the same time, 'border' is a word rich in metaphorical possibilities, which may be used to explore contrary or complementary states, such as time and eternity, innocence and experience, belonging and not belonging. Thus, David Jones describes 'man' as 'a "borderer", he is the sole inhabitant of a tract of country where matter marches with spirit'.[1] The aim of this chapter is to work round and about this poetic location. It examines writings by two seventeenth-century poets, Henry Vaughan and Thomas Traherne,[2] and by two modern poets, Edward Thomas and Robert Frost, with special reference to their construction of poetic 'borderlands' which both express tensions and enable their partial or complete resolution.

Henry Vaughan's 'The Retreat' is about the contrary states of innocence and experience:

> Happy those early days! when I
> Shined in my Angel-infancy.
> Before I understood this place
> Appointed for my second race,
> Or taught my soul to fancy aught
> But a white, celestial thought,
> When yet I had not walked above
> A mile, or two, from my first love,

> And looking back (at that short space,)
> Could see a glimpse of his bright face;
> When on some *gilded cloud*, or *flower*
> My gazing soul would dwell an hour,
> And in those weaker glories spy
> Some shadows of eternity;
> Before I taught my tongue to wound
> My conscience with a sinful sound,
> Or had the black art to dispense
> A several sin to every sense,
> But felt through all this fleshly dress
> Bright *shoots* of everlastingness.
> O how I long to travel back
> And tread again that ancient track!
> That I might once more reach that plain,
> Where first I left my glorious train,
> From whence the enlightened spirit sees
> That shady city of palm trees;
> But (ah!) my soul with too much stay
> Is drunk, and staggers in the way.
> Some men a forward motion love,
> But I by backward steps would move,
> And when this dust falls to the urn
> In that state I came return.[3]

The poem incorporates temporal and spatial distance: before and after; the place of 'my first love' and here, 'this place / Appointed for my second race'. Imagery of light counters the double movement with a sense of presence (here/always) – 'shined', 'white, celestial thought', 'bright face', 'Bright *shoots* of everlastingness', 'enlightened spirit'.

It is tempting to focus exclusively upon the visionary quality of the poem, in which imagery of light, connecting 'Angel-infancy' and 'everlastingness', establishes the presence of eternity. But we should not overlook the poem's more mundane context. Its title has several meanings, one of which surely refers to Henry Vaughan's actual situation in the 1650s: that of a defeated Royalist and an Anglican whose Church the victorious Puritans had closed. Vaughan had literally retreated to his home in Wales, where he occupied himself with writing sacred poetry, which for him must have provided a substitute for the Anglican Church and its rituals and ceremonies. In this retreat he took upon himself the title

'Silurist', invoking the Celtic tribe which successfully defied the Romans for some twenty-five years in south-east Wales. For the first time, a Welsh poet using the English language was proclaiming himself a voice of resistance. The resistance had deep roots, for, as M. Wynn Thomas has argued, Vaughan's belief in 'the Church of England [as] the reincarnation of the ancient pre-Catholic British Church' underlies 'the unique power of Vaughan's invocation of his native landscape'.[4]

The two-part *Silex Scintillans* may be seen as, among other things, a largely implicit riposte to Puritan triumphalism. Together and individually, the poems construct a poetic landscape which embodies religious continuity and thus stands firm against, and survives, the Puritan fragmentation of the tradition which Vaughan passionately espoused. The cosmic order represented in the Church survives for Vaughan in the only places where it can during the Commonwealth, in his heart and mind and in his native landscape. But this is not to say he was not a poet of personal brokenness – his sacred poems spring from his sense of Christian mortification and renewal – or a man brought close to despair by the Puritan victory.

It is easy to understand why, on political grounds alone, Vaughan should be a poet of longing. In 'The Retreat', for example, longing is at once explicit subject and emotional charge: 'O how I long to travel back / And tread again that ancient track!' Towards the end of the poem he assimilates the goal of his yearning to Moses's view of 'the valley of Jericho, the city of palm-trees' (Deuteronomy 34: 3). But personal feeling vibrates throughout the poem.

'Some men a forward motion love, / But I by backward steps would move.' Is this impulse in Vaughan a form of *hiraeth*, that Welsh nostalgia for childhood, or 'yearning for an ideal spiritual state',[5] that some ascribe to the Welsh historical experience of military and political defeat? Or is Vaughan in 'The Retreat' invoking Platonic anamnesis, or a Christianized idea of original innocence before the Fall? Stevie Davies describes nostalgia as 'the compulsive force which drives [Henry Vaughan's] poems'.[6] But, in words that apply to Thomas Traherne too, she also writes as follows of Vaughan's poems about childhood:

> 'Verily I say unto you, Whosoever shall not receive the kingdom of God as a little child, he shall not enter therein' (Mark 10: 15): Vaughan takes Christ at his word. It is as hard for literary critics as for learned

theologians to squeeze through the eye of that needle, if their trade is polysyllables and their minds are swollen with ratiocination.⁷

It is necessary to remember these words when discussing Vaughan's and Traherne's treatment of childhood, not least because they were at once devout Christians and highly intelligent men, well versed in scripture and theology.

There is something else we should not forget, too. While we cannot be sure of the age of the Vaughan or Traherne child, we can be certain that for them the child represents primary vision, which precedes language, or occurs at a very early stage of language acquisition. As Stevie Davies reminds us, 'infancy' derives from the Latin for 'languageless'.⁸ In 'The Retreat' the speaker invokes a state before he knew anything but 'a white, celestial thought'. Here we may pause to consider that if this 'thought' were what the poem was about, there would be no poem. It is movement that makes 'The Retreat' – emotion, above all the emotion of longing and *active* light (shining/shooting), time and physical movement; to use a word Vaughan favours, the poem is *quick*.

Here, perhaps, we encounter the principal problem for mystical poetry, if by mysticism we understand a condition of complete union, or perfect innocence. It has been said of childhood, for instance, that we can remember the state only 'through the divided consciousness of adult sensibility and memory'.⁹ How can anyone articulate a condition before the acquisition of language? Whether this is understood in religious or psychological terms, as original innocence or oneness with the mother, it may be described as the condition of complete belonging. And that is what no one can express. An isolated 'white, celestial thought' says nothing; in order to 'speak' it needs the context of the poem, including its contrary, 'the black art'. Vaughan identifies sin with speech: 'I taught my tongue to wound / My conscience with a sinful sound'. What this goes to show is that we know innocence by sin and the languageless state by language. 'The Retreat' also demonstrates that we cannot know anything about a condition of ultimate belonging except by longing.

A new word for longing entered the language in the seventeenth century. Johannes Hofer, a Swiss doctor, coined *nostalgia* (from Greek *nostos*, return home, and *algia*, longing), to describe a curable disease, which afflicted Swiss soldiers serving abroad, among others. From being regarded as a curable disease by some doctors, even into the twentieth century, some commentators now regard nostalgia as 'the incurable modern condition'.[10] In this spirit, Georg Lukacs, in 1916, identified modern experience itself as 'transcendental homelessness'.[11] Svetlana Boym, in *The Future of Nostalgia*, writes:

> Modern nostalgia is a mourning for the impossibility of mythical return, for the loss of an enchanted world with clear borders and values; it could be a secular expression of a spiritual longing, a nostalgia for an absolute, a home that is both physical and spiritual, the edenic unity of time and space before entry into history. The nostalgic is looking for a spiritual addressee.[12]

Of course, longing for the past did not originate in the seventeenth century. The myth of a Golden Age at the beginning of time goes back millennia and may be, in one form or another, worldwide. It is evident, however, that nostalgia intensified in the seventeenth century; and in Britain, with religious conflict and civil war, desire quickened for a more innocent, more whole, condition. It is ironic in this context that modern writers have projected their own nostalgia for a less fragmented, more integrated world on to the seventeenth century. Chief among these, T. S. Eliot, in 'The Metaphysical Poets' (1921), described John Donne and his contemporary poets as in possession of an undissociated sensibility.[13]

With the idea of nostalgia in mind, it is instructive to reflect upon Traherne's treatment of contraries. Traherne was a man of Herefordshire, which his biographer Gladys I. Wade describes as 'a sort of transition county, half English, half Welsh'.[14] As a boy and a man, he would have heard Welsh spoken. A. M. Allchin writes:

> He was born and brought up on the frontier of a people in whose tradition, whether he knew it or not, the work of the poet is understood above all else as the work of praise, praise of God in and through a transfigured world. That was evidently how he understood his calling.[15]

This is suggestive, but properly tentative; and we have to add that Traherne, in common with other metaphysical poets, identified with the Psalmist and drew upon the language and spirit of his thanksgivings. Nor can we prove that Traherne's longing for edenic vision owed anything to *hiraeth*; we cannot demonstrate the influence of Wales and Welshness upon him, although it is clear that he was a 'borderer' in David Jones's sense and lived in 'the march-lands of matter and spirit, time and not-time'.[16] As Julia Smith reminds us, 'during the last few years, it has become increasingly clear that we know even less about Traherne's life than we thought we did'.[17] At the same time it has become clearer to us, not least through Traherne's *Select Meditations* and Julia Smith's scholarly work, that he was a man concerned in, and deeply affected by, the political issues of his time. It could scarcely have been otherwise for one who grew up during the Civil War, and who either was, or adopted the role of, a Puritan under the Commonwealth and who emerged as a devout Anglican following the Restoration. And this, above all, was a man who was a thinker of such complexity that twentieth-century critics could not agree upon his inheritance or what he made of it.[18] Their differences of opinion may call to mind, as a remote echo, Ted Hughes's idea of the Puritan spirit and the old Catholic spirit as the 'two savage competitors for the English soul'.[19] Hughes's view may be extreme, but it serves to remind us that men were killing and dying over religious differences in Traherne's lifetime. It may also remind us that, if we have no grounds for inferring an internalized civil war in Traherne, we have to acknowledge the tension of contraries in his writings.

If we fail to do so, we will misread him, including the most famous passage in his writings, from the *Centuries of Meditations*:

> The Corn was Orient and Immortal Wheat, which never should be reaped, nor was ever sown. I thought it had stood from Everlasting to Everlasting. The Dust and Stones of the Street were as Precious as GOLD. The Gates were at first the End of the World, The Green Trees when I saw them first through one of the Gates Transported and Ravished me; their Sweetnes and unusual Beauty made my Heart to leap, and almost mad with Extasie, they were such strange and Wonderful Thing[s]: The Men! O what Venerable and Revernd Creatures did the Aged seem! Immortal Cherubims! And yong Men Glittering and Sparkling Angels and Maids strange Seraphick Pieces of Life and Beauty! Boys and Girles Tumbling in the Street, and Playing, were moving Jewels. I knew not that they were Born or should Die. But all things abided Eternaly as they were in their Proper Places. Eternity was Manifest in the Light of the Day, and som thing infinit Behind evry thing appeared . . .[20]

Gladys Wade describes the passage as 'pure magic'; which it is.[21] But it is also effective poetic and religious writing, because it holds different elements in tension. What prevents the ecstasy from being mere effusiveness is concreteness – 'the Dust and Stones', 'the Green Trees', 'Boys and Girles Tumbling in the Street' – and the work of sceptical intelligence. The latter can be seen in, for example (emphases added): 'I *Thought* it had stood'; 'O what Venerable and Revernd Creatures did the Aged *seem*'; 'I *knew* not that they were Born or should Die'. Traherne goes on to say: 'The Citie *seemed* to stand in Eden'; and 'I *knew* no Churlish Proprieties, nor Bounds, nor Divisions'. Experience tempers innocent ecstasy, or ecstatic innocence, before Traherne writes: 'So that with much adoe I was corrupted; and made to learn the Dirty Devices of this World. Which now I unlearn, and becom as it were a little Child again, that I may enter into the Kingdom of GOD.' Here, 'as it were' is of a piece with the tension Traherne creates between innocence and ignorance, child's vision and adult seeing, then and now, angelic and human, ecstasy and sceptical intelligence. One contrary does not negate the other, but completes it. Experience validates innocence. The man is writing about a period when, as a child, he could not write; he is writing with knowledge of corruption, and in the process of 'unlearning', which parallels that in which the learned Vaughan recalls 'a white, celestial thought'.

The passage persuades us as adults because in depicting innocence it embodies the perspective of experience. This is generally true of Traherne's treatment of original innocence. Further evidence for this may be gained by considering a passage which might be thought the opposite of the vision at the city gates. The following describes a crisis which the young Traherne underwent:

> Another time, in a Lowering and sad Evening, being alone in the field, when all things were dead and quiet, a certain Want and Horror fell upon me, beyond imagination. The unprofitableness and Silence of the Place dissatisfied me, its Wideness terrified me, from the utmost Ends of the Earth fears surrounded me. How did I know but Dangers might suddainly arise from the East, and invade me from the unknown Regions beyond the Seas? I was a Weak and little child, and had forgotten there was a man alive in the Earth. Yet som thing also of Hope and Expectation comforted me from every Border. This taught me that I was concernd in all the World . . . [22]

How different a being 'a Weak and little child', who 'had forgotten there was a man alive in the Earth', is from the child at the Gates of Hereford. There, 'all the World was mine, and I the only Spectator and Enjoyer of it'; but the vision included other people and the apparent possessiveness did not contradict Traherne's 'social mysticism', as Edward Thomas calls it;[23] the child Traherne is 'the sole Heir of the whole World', among his co-heirs. It would fit the subject of Traherne's Welshness if we could identify the 'Border' with the Welsh Marches and 'Dangers [which] might suddainly arise from the East' with England, historically the direction from which dangers come for the Welsh. However, we have no warrant for this, though we may feel the actuality of 'the field' locates it in an isolated situation outside Hereford. Traherne experienced there what at the end of the section he calls 'the Wideness and Emptiness of the Universe'. In modern psychological terms, we might speak of solipsism and agrophobia; we might also invoke 'transcendental homelessness' and longing to belong.

The vision at the Gates of Hereford is the contrary to the experience of 'being alone in the field'. At the Gates, 'som thing infinit Behind evry thing appeared', the invisible substantiating the visible; all was in place, because 'all things abided Eternaly as they were in their Proper Places'. As space is grounded upon infinity, time receives its meaning from eternity – but one cannot be known apart from the other. Traherne is the poet of 'Felicity', because he knows emptiness; he is the poet of belonging to the universe, because he knows want or longing.

He is not a poet of place in the sense that Henry Vaughan is; the poet of a country that is at once biblical and the landscape of Brycheiniog. We rarely sense the presence of specific places in Traherne's writings. For Traherne, place has other parameters than local bounds. There is a sort of internal space-travel in Traherne, an enjoyment of voyaging in infinity, which contrasts markedly with Pascal's terror at the spaces between the stars. There is no spiritual vertigo in Traherne, as there is in George Herbert; instead, there is horror at emptiness, space which does not open to the infinite. For Traherne, 'the Infinity of God is . . . the Dwelling Place . . . of our Souls'.[24]

Traherne describes 'the Infinity of God' surrounding, filling and inspiring the soul: 'The Immensitie of God is an Eternal Tabernacle.'[25] This is the Church as the place of universal belonging. It may not be immediately apparent that Traherne's Church – thus understood – has a political significance; but his frequent use of imagery of the Kingdom should give us pause. We may think, too, of the 'Little church' in *Select Meditations*:

> When I see a Little church Environed with Trees, how many Things are there which mine Eye discerneth not. The Labor of them which in Ancient Ages Builded it; the conversion of a Kingdom to God from Paganism, its Protection by Laws, its subjection to Kings, its Relation to Bishops, usefulness and convenience for the Entertainment of christians, The Divine Service, office of the ministery, Solemn Assemblies Prayses and Thanksgivings, for the sake of which it was permitted, is Governed, Standeth and Flourisheth. Perhaps when I Look upon it, it is Desolate and Empty almost Like an heap of Stones: non of these things appearing to the Eye, which nevertheless are the Spirituall Beauties which adorn and clothe it. The uses Relations services and Ends being the Spiritual and Invisible Things: that make any material to be of worth.[26]

Here, the 'Invisible Things' brought to mind by the things he can see are, predominantly, historical and therefore have political significance. His sentiments are far from being those of a Puritan. Instead, the passage gives a movingly concrete embodiment to Traherne's 'passionate espousal of the concept of a national church'.[27] It is tempting to go beyond this and relate Traherne's idea of continuity to the *British* Church, as, according to M. Wynn Thomas, Vaughan espoused it and through which Vaughan affirmed his Welshness; but, again, we have no warrant for going so far. It is clear from this passage, however, that the breach in tradition during the Commonwealth that impelled Vaughan to become a sacred poet was the same breach that gave a special emotional resonance to Traherne's celebration of continuity, despite his service to the Puritans.

II

'Home' is a resonant word in the writings of Vaughan and Traherne, for whom it may be associated with Platonic anamnesis, but is certainly a fundamentally Christian concept of edenic vision. We may think Vaughan, in particular, a poet who expresses *hiraeth*;

but it is the moderns who bring their nostalgia to bear on the metaphysical poets, in whose work they find a more innocent, more integrated, more whole world. Of these, Edward Thomas is an especially poignant example.

Thomas's parents were Welsh, and, through visits, he came to know parts of Wales well. But he was brought up in the suburbs of London and spent his adult life in the south of England. He described the latter in the following terms: 'Yet is this country, though I am mainly Welsh, a kind of home, as I think it is more than any other to those modern people who belong nowhere.'[28] On vacation with relations at Pontardulais in August 1899 he had recorded in his notebook:

> Day by day grows my passion for Wales. It is like a homesickness, but stronger than any homesickness I ever felt – stronger than any passion. Wales indeed, is my soul's native land, if the soul can be said to have a *patria* – or rather, a *matria*, a home with the warm sweetness of a mother's love and with her influence, too.[29]

In Thomas's life and writing 'a kind of home' and homesickness for 'my soul's native land' complement one another. He consciously experienced a sense of divided identity – self and other – which related to a double sense of exile: from his ideal of Wales and from nature.

Significantly, Thomas discusses Traherne in a rural setting in *The South Country*. 'Such a day [in June in Hampshire], in the unblemished summer land,' he says, 'invariably calls up thoughts of the Golden Age. As mankind has looked back to a golden age, so the individual, repeating the history of the race, looks back and finds one in his own past.'[30] Thomas continues, 'few men can look back to their childhood like Traherne' and proceeds to discuss Traherne's expression of 'the spiritual glory of childhood'.[31] The discussion takes in childhood, nature, education and comparisons between Traherne and other writers. Significantly, it says little about theology, but describes Traherne's 'social mysticism'. Thomas relates Traherne to Walt Whitman, 'whom some have blamed for making the word "divine" of no value because he would apply it to all, whereas to do so is no more than to lay down the rule of veneration for men – and the other animals – which has produced and will produce the greatest revolutions'.[32]

It is clear from this, together with the context of a pagan concept, the mythic Golden Age, in which Thomas introduces his discussion of Traherne, that Thomas wants to leave God out of the equation. The result is an unfocused nostalgia, or a nostalgia that dwells upon nature. Thomas wrote three poems called 'Home'. The first shows the honesty for which he is justly celebrated:

> Not the end: but there's nothing more.
> Sweet Summer and Winter rude
> I have loved, and friendship and love,
> The crowd and solitude:
>
> But I know them: I weary not;
> But all that they mean I know.
> I would go back again home
> Now. Yet how should I go?
>
> This is my grief. That land,
> My home, I have never seen;
> No traveller tells of it,
> However far he has been.
>
> And could I discover it,
> I fear my happiness there,
> Or my pain, might be dreams of return
> Here, to these things that were.
>
> Remembering ills, though slight
> Yet irremediable,
> Brings a worse, an impurer pang
> Than remembering what was well.
>
> No: I cannot go back,
> And would not if I could.
> Until blindness come, I must wait
> And blink at what is not good.[33]

Like many of Thomas's poems, 'Home' is constructed round contraries and their interaction, for example, summer and winter, the crowd and solitude, there and here, happiness and pain. At its centre is the unobtainable 'land, / My home' for which he grieves. The sense of longing is palpable, as it is in Vaughan and Traherne, but Thomas treats it differently, because he is without the theological direction of their thinking and feeling.

> And could I discover it,
> I fear my happiness there,
> Or my pain, might be dreams of return
> Here, to these things that were.

The 'fear' is also a kind of acceptance: in returning to the past he might find out that the present is what he really wants. This, perhaps, is an inevitable conclusion for a poet who cannot really believe in 'that land / My home', as Vaughan and Traherne believed in theirs.

Thomas has the courage of his agnosticism:

> No: I cannot go back,
> And would not if I could.
> Until blindness come, I must wait
> And blink at what is not good.

It has been suggested in this chapter that the effectiveness of visionary seeing in Vaughan and Traherne depends upon their treatment of contraries. This could be taken further – seeing, with all its moral and metaphysical implications, is biblical and central to all religious literature. Thomas's poem is haunted by older meanings, but he is true to his agnostic experience. This includes diminished vision – blinking 'at what is not good' and death anticipated as 'blindness'.

Identity, as it relates to a sense of 'home' or belonging, is a central concern of Edward Thomas, and one he shares with Robert Frost. It may be surmised that personal struggle with a sense of identity was one of the things that united them during the time they spent together mainly in the March-lands, at intervals, during 1914.[34] Discussions of Thomas's debt to Frost for helping him to realize himself as a poet, and of their affinities, usually concentrate upon their ideas of the relation between poetry and speech. This is important; but their common preoccupation with identity and ideas of 'home' is equally important.

While it would be an exaggeration to describe either Thomas or Frost as a 'metaphysical' poet, both were poets who drew upon poetic tradition and showed a special attraction to the Metaphysicals. Richard Poirier remarks that 'some who persist in thinking that T. S. Eliot discovered Marvell, Donne and the seventeenth-century line for the twentieth century will wonder that Frost was already there in 1906–7'.[35] The influences upon Frost and Thomas can sometimes be seen in direct allusion. In Thomas's 'The Other', for example, 'moments of everlastingness' refers to 'Bright *shoots* of everlastingness' in 'The Retreat'. The context in Thomas's poem is the temporary achievement of oneness, in which the chronically divided speaker feels himself to be 'An old inhabitant of earth'.[36]

The presence of the Metaphysicals in the poetry of Thomas and Frost represents, like Thomas's treatment of Traherne in his prose, a partial secularization of religious vision applied to psychic experience and the realm of nature. Thomas's southern English landscapes are frequently presented in an imagery of 'hollowness' and 'darkness', which both intimates his sense of an 'other world' springing from his *hiraeth* for Wales and hints at a secular transformation of sacred landscapes, such as Vaughan's.[37] In reading and reviewing Frost's early volumes he would have found a 'strangeness' that mythologizes the familiar world.[38] This would have appealed to him because the search for a new mythology had been an early manifestation of Thomas's own inherently poetic imagination. The word itself occurs in 'After Apple-Picking':

> I cannot rub the strangeness from my sight
> I got from looking through a pane of glass
> I skimmed this morning from the drinking trough
> And held against the world of hoary grass.[39]

By seeing strangely Frost mythologizes the everyday world, intimating a deeper meaning – or the true meaning – in common things. Sometimes this is explicit, as in 'Mending Wall', where he sees his country neighbour 'like an old-stone savage armed' moving 'in darkness'.[40] More subtle is the poem in which the abandoned wood-pile prompts the thought

> ... that only
> Someone who lived in turning to fresh tasks
> Could so forget his handiwork on which

> He spent himself, the labor of his ax,
> And leave it there far from a useful fireplace
> To warm the frozen swamp as best it could
> With the slow smokeless burning of decay.[41]

Here, the thought modulates into a haunting image, which may provoke us to think about the 'use' of poetry, as well as that of an unused pile of wood, but certainly does not limit the reach of the thought.

In 'The Death of the Hired Man' the 'strangeness' of moonlight introduces a further difference between husband and wife:

> 'Home is the place where, when you have to go there,
> They have to take you in.'
>   'I should have called it
> Something you somehow haven't to deserve.'[42]

Long after the composition of the poem, Frost, in an interview, explicated the husband's view as 'the manly way' and the wife's as 'the New Deal, the feminine way of it, the mother way'.[43] The politicization of the poem may not be helpful; it does, however, emphasize how much the tension between contraries underlies Frost's thinking.

The most fitting poetic tribute to the friendship between Frost and Thomas is 'The Road Not Taken', in which Frost makes use of a recollection of Thomas's chronic hesitations. The scene is commonplace: two roads diverging 'in a yellow wood'; the uncertainty as to which to take is unremarkable. Yet Frost makes from an ordinary decision something extraordinary:

> Oh, I kept the first for another day!
> Yet knowing how way leads on to way,
> I doubted that I should ever come back.
>
> I shall be telling this with a sigh
> Somewhere ages and ages hence:
> Two roads diverged in a wood, and I –
> I took the one less travelled by,
> And that has made all the difference.[44]

Here, the transformation of experience through metaphor is the more haunting because of its intertextual connection to poems, such as 'The Path' and 'Lights Out', in which Thomas uses the setting of woods to suggest the border between life and death.

In their walks together in border country Thomas and Frost were on one occasion bound together by an extraordinary natural phenomenon, which resulted in something like an experience of the numinous. One evening, descending a slope in the Malverns, in mist and dampness, they found themselves surrounded by a moon-made rainbow. Writing of the experience to Eleanor Farjeon in the following year, Thomas described it in mythological terms. The rainbow 'seems like the first that ever was'. It was 'a new toy discovered by Apollo . . . It is more for a mythologist clad in skins'.[45]

Now, Thomas can joke about mythologists, because he has learnt, with Frost and independently of him, to express the strangeness inherent in life. Frost returned to the experience many years later in 'Iris By Night', which describes the two men 'gathered . . . together in a ring'.

> And we stood in it softly circled round
> From all division time or foe can bring
> In a relation of elected friends.[46]

The lines contain a distant but palpable echo of Henry Vaughan's 'I saw Eternity the other night / Like a great *Ring* of pure and endless light'.[47] The 'ring', in Frost's poem, excludes 'all division'. It is therefore an especially appropriate emblem for the friendship of two poets who cemented their relationship in border-country, and who shared a love of the metaphysical poets who were also, like them, 'borderers'.

Notes

[1] David Jones, *Epoch and Artist* (London: Faber, 1959), p. 86.
[2] The passages from Traherne considered in this chapter are from his prose, which constitutes some of his most highly poetic writing.
[3] Alan Rudrum (ed.), *Henry Vaughan: The Complete Poems* (Harmondsworth: Penguin, 1983), pp. 172–3.
[4] M. Wynn Thomas, *Corresponding Cultures: The Two Literatures of Wales* (Cardiff: University of Wales Press, 1999), pp. 22–4.

[5] Meic Stephens (ed.), *The Oxford Companion to the Literature of Wales* (Oxford: Oxford University Press, 1986), p. 258.
[6] Stevie Davies, *Henry Vaughan* (Bridgend: Seren, 1995), p. 28.
[7] Ibid., p. 53.
[8] Ibid., p. 46.
[9] Malcolm Chase and Christopher Shaw, 'The Dimensions of Nostalgia', *The Imagined Past: History and Nostalgia*, eds Malcolm Chase and Christopher Shaw (Manchester: Manchester University Press, 1989), pp. 1–17 (5).
[10] Svetlana Boym, *The Future of Nostalgia* (New York: Basic Books, 2001), p. xiv.
[11] Quoted from Georg Lukacs, *The Theory of the Novel*, in Boym, *The Future of Nostalgia*, p. 24.
[12] Ibid., p. 8.
[13] See Frank Kermode (ed.), *Selected Prose of T. S. Eliot* (London: Faber, 1975), pp. 59–67.
[14] Gladys I. Wade, *Thomas Traherne* (Princeton: Princeton University Press, 1944), p. 15.
[15] A. M. Allchin, 'The Sacrifice of Praise and Thanksgiving', *Profitable Wonders: Aspects of Thomas Traherne*, eds A. M. Allchin, Anne Ridler and Julia Smith (Oxford: The Amate Press, 1989), pp. 22–37 (24).
[16] Jones, *Epoch and Artist*, p. 202.
[17] Julia J. Smith, 'Traherne from his Unpublished Manuscripts', *Profitable Wonders*, pp. 38–51 (39).
[18] For example, Louis L. Martz placed Traherne in the tradition of Augustinian interior illumination and Christian Platonism; see Martz, *The Paradise Within* (New Haven and London: Yale University Press, 1964). Barbara Kiefer Lewalski, on the other hand, while acknowledging Traherne's originality, related him to 'the Protestant-Pauline paradigm of salvation'; see Lewalski, *Protestant Poetics and the Seventeenth-Century Religious Lyric* (Princeton: Princeton University Press, 1979).
[19] Ted Hughes, *Shakespeare and the Goddess of Complete Being* (London: Faber, 1992), p. 75.
[20] Anne Ridler (ed.), *Thomas Traherne: Poems, Centuries and Three Thanksgivings* (London: Oxford University Press, 1966), p. 264.
[21] Wade, *Thomas Traherne*, p. 207.
[22] Ridler (ed.), *Thomas Traherne*, p. 275.
[23] Edward Thomas, *The South Country* ([1909]; London: Dent, 1932), p. 140.
[24] Ridler (ed.), *Thomas Traherne*, p. 367.
[25] Ibid., pp. 367–8.
[26] Thomas Traherne, *Select Meditations*, ed. Julia Smith (Manchester: Carcanet, 1997), p. 100.
[27] Julia Smith, 'Introduction', *Select Meditations*, p. xix.
[28] Thomas, *The South Country*, p. 7.
[29] Quoted in R. George Thomas, *Edward Thomas: A Portrait* (Oxford: Clarendon Press, 1985), p. 80.
[30] Thomas, *The South Country*, p. 131.
[31] Ibid., p. 137.
[32] Ibid., p. 141.
[33] R. George Thomas (ed.), *The Collected Poems of Edward Thomas* (Oxford: Oxford University Press, 1981), p. 39.
[34] For a good description of the area in 'the north-west corner of Gloucestershire, pressing gently against Herefordshire and Worcestershire', in

which Thomas and Frost cemented their friendship, and of the friendship itself, see Sean Street, *The Dymock Poets* (Bridgend: Seren, 1994).

[35] Richard Poirier, *Robert Frost: The Work of Knowing* ([1977]; Stanford: Stanford University Press, 1990), p. 207. Poirier's major study contains a full treatment of the importance to Frost of his concept of 'home'.

[36] Thomas (ed.), *The Collected Poems of Edward Thomas*, pp. 10–13.

[37] For a fuller discussion of Edward Thomas's 'landscape of myth', see Jeremy Hooker, *Writers in a Landscape* (Cardiff: University of Wales Press, 1996), pp. 76–95.

[38] For Edward Thomas's reviews of Robert Frost's poetry, see *A Language Not to be Betrayed: Selected Prose of Edward Thomas*, ed. Edna Longley (Manchester: Carcanet, 1981), pp. 125–31.

[39] Edward Connery Lathem (ed.), *The Poetry of Robert Frost* (New York: Henry Holt, 1969), p. 68.

[40] Ibid., p. 34.

[41] Ibid., p. 102.

[42] Ibid., p. 38.

[43] Quoted in Poirier, *Robert Frost: The Work of Knowing*, p. 234.

[44] Lathem (ed.), *The Poetry of Robert Frost*, p. 105.

[45] Eleanor Farjeon, *Edward Thomas: The Last Four Years* (London: Oxford University Press, 1958), p. 141.

[46] Lathem (ed.), *The Poetry of Robert Frost*, p. 315.

[47] 'The World' (1), Rudrum (ed.), *Henry Vaughan: The Complete Poems*, p. 227.

19

'In a different place, / changed': Dannie Abse, Dylan Thomas, T. S. Eliot and Wales

JAMES A. DAVIES

After Every Green Thing (1949), Dannie Abse's first volume of poetry, rarely appears in his own lists of previous publications. Of that volume's poems only 'The Uninvited' has survived the cut for his three subsequent volumes titled *Collected Poems*.[1] One other poem, 'The Yellow Bird', has re-emerged, rewritten, in the 2003 *Collected Poems*. Abse has explained this calculated neglect: *After Every Green Thing* was 'immature. I was immature. I caught like an infection, the Neo-Romantic fashionable mode of the time'.[2] Dominating Neo-Romanticism, though never confined by it, was Dylan Thomas, then at the height of his fame.[3]

'Dylan Thomas's poems powerfully engaged me', Abse stated in his 1984 Gwyn Jones lecture, '– too much so, for a number of my own poems which can be discovered in my first volume, *After Every Green Thing*, are touched by his manner.' He offers two examples, which 'sound like Dylan's cast-offs: "harp of sabbaths", "choir of wounds"'.[4] There are many others, including 'vowelled birds', 'hands tick', 'fugue of birds on fire', plus a distant echo of 'After the Funeral' in 'Poem to a Younger Poet' ('how, when the spade rings, should my ghost protest') and, not so distant, of 'The force that through the green fuse' in 'Psychosis' ('and I am dumb to tell her angels and her visions'). Abse's language throughout this volume is lushly Thomasian, even to the use of the apostrophic or exclamatory 'O', sometimes, oddly, printed in lower-case. Ideas can also be derivative, one example being writing as shedding blood: 'you will expectorate a red star / of blood upon the white panic of a blank page' he informs that much-advised 'Younger Poet' who is also offered a hint of 'process' in 'the timeless flood of blood / that circles the street-ways beneath your flesh'. Elsewhere, with the poet still in sanguinary mode, 'the blood in the virgin's scream', in 'The Journey', in recalling 'The tombstone told when she died', suggests a Thomasian proclivity for sex and violence hardly typical of Abse's work.

After such knowledge there is an understandable drawing-down of blinds. Though Abse's second volume, *Walking Under Water* (1952), has similar moments – Ann Jones's 'fountain heart' in 'A Posy for Summer', for instance, and such Dylanesque flourishes as '[t]oday measure pain with a clock' and 'all the tall dead rise to break the crust of the imperative earth' – the influence is not so pervasive. The same can be said of *Ash on a Young Man's Sleeve* (1954), Abse's famous autobiographical novel. This has a general, perhaps unavoidable, affinity with *Portrait of the Artist as a Young Dog* (1940): less episodic, though a series of significant moments, but centred on home, park, seaside and so forth, to explore a journey into adolescence. There are echoes of 'Fern Hill': 'All day it was lovely' (42), for example, and, again more distantly, 'emperor of my eighteen years, king of the tall fading trees' (197). Here, however, most of such literary references are ironically deployed.

In *Tenants of the House* (1957) Abse finds a voice of his own. Almost two-thirds of its poems have always been collected; one other, 'Photograph and Yellow Tulips', omitted from the 'collecteds', re-emerges rewritten as 'Photograph and White Tulips', one of eight poems he chose to represent himself in *Twentieth Century Anglo-Welsh Poetry* (1997), his own anthology. In its 'yellow' version the poem is typically Abse's in uniting the conversational with the lyrical, the initially transparent with an ultimate opaqueness. It considers photography as reviving thoughts of a lost occasion and a sense of the past as dead, the camera as a 'little black coffin'. Dylan Thomas's influence has dwindled.

Indeed, the last three poems in *Tenants of the House* comprise a form of exorcism. The first is 'Elegy for Dylan Thomas', written in December 1953, shortly after Thomas's death. Abse writes of Thomas's fame during a life always close to death's 'essential kiss', of his posthumous fame and of his death as poetic loss: 'Suddenly others who sing seem older and lame.' 'Tenants of the House', the volume's penultimate poem, attacks the 'Movement', always hostile to Thomas's work and quick to offer his life and work as salutary examples of destructive excess. Yet, writes Abse, with Thomas dead, '[I]n bowler hats they sing with sharp, flat voices / but no-one dances, nobody rejoices'. The final poem continues this theme. 'Go Home the Act is Over', set in a circus and written in the first person, shows the poet as daring trapeze artist, flying above 'pedestrians who with iambics freeze'. He falls to his death, the circus leaves town, the field is empty. All three poems, as will be seen, though recognizing loss, offer distinct reservations about Thomas. All three poems imply closure: the field is clear for Abse's next volume, *Poems Golders Green 1956–61* (1962), which established him as a leading urban/suburban British poet.

Dylan Thomas is an important but not the only influence on Abse's early work. There are occasional borrowings from other poets, one example being 'the dazzled upturned faces' of 'Autumn', in *After Every Green Thing*, that recalls the 'upturned dreaming faces' of Alun Lewis's 'All Day it has Rained'. The second increasingly dominant influence is T. S. Eliot. From one perspective, that Eliot should replace Dylan Thomas is not surprising. The younger Abse so often looked outwards. He was first drawn to poetry through reading poems about the Spanish Civil War. He moved from Cardiff to London in 1943 to continue his medical studies at King's College and Westminster Hospital. Since then, apart from National Service as a doctor in the RAF, his main home has been in London: he and his wife brought up a family in Golders Green. Until his retirement in 1989 he worked as a doctor in a Soho chest clinic. During this time he has been a prominent figure in literary London. In the immediate post-war period he was part of Swiss Cottage café life, and has written engagingly about the aspiring writers – Bernice Rubens, Peter Vansittart and the Nobel prize-winner Elias Canetti amongst them – with whom he talked and drank coffee during his salad days. Viewed from the parochial Wales of that time, from which, of the serious writers, only Dylan Thomas had broken free into international stardom, this could seem (and perhaps was) like Hemingway's Paris, or Dorothy Parker's Algonquin. As John Tripp once wrote, not wholly tongue-in-cheek, there is 'a touch of glamour about Dannie Abse'.[5] His books, published in London, have sold well; *Ash on a Young Man's*

Sleeve (1954) has never been out of print. From 1978 to 1992 he was President of the Poetry Society; in 1983 he was elected a Fellow of the Royal Society of Literature. T. S. Eliot's international ambience and sophistication, the mandarin American thoroughly at home in Europe and a British subject since 1927, fitted nicely into the maturing Abse's sense of the Zeitgeist. His poetic tastes changed. T. S. Eliot apart, he wrote: 'I have grown to like Edward Thomas as much as, if not more than, Dylan Thomas. I have become as attached to the peculiarly modest "English" tradition as to the distinctive, aspiring "European" one.'[6] Immersion in metropolitan literary life took him far away from Anglo-Welsh writing with which, in any case, he had little sympathy. At times he tended to suggest there might be no such thing. Thus, in the Gwyn Jones Lecture he radiated well-mannered scepticism about such ideas as 'seepage' and of praise as being an uniquely Welsh characteristic.[7] In his introduction to *Twentieth Century Anglo-Welsh Poetry* he recalls stating in a 1960s broadcast that 'there is no such thing as a specific Anglo-Welsh style or tone, and the Welshness of an English poem simply depends on what the poem is about'.[8]

Eliot was a great poet, who forced contemporaries and successors to rethink notions of what poetry can do. His influence was inescapable, particularly in the 1940s and early 1950s. But lasting wholehearted enthusiasm for Eliot's writing would have been difficult for a young, Jewish, liberal-left-leaning poet like Abse. Eliot's anti-Semitism would surely have troubled him, even though he has noted, not unsympathetically, that after World War Two Eliot was profoundly contrite.[9] Further, the older poet represented the reactionary right. To quote Jonathan Raban, Eliot 'embodies very exactly a type of right-wing millennialism' that regards modern life as the remnants of 'a once great culture'. Despite his reputation as a modernist, he offers 'a doomed, elegiac celebration of an irretrievable (and nostalgically mythicized) past'. He is 'not . . . the first great modern poet, but . . . the last writer at the end of an era'.[10] Again, his essentially religious solutions to the modern world's deficiencies would hardly have appealed to secular Abse.

Yet Eliot's influence on Abse's early work is very strong. In *After Every Green Thing* the poems of *Prufrock and Other Observations* (1917), particularly 'The Love Song of J. Alfred Prufrock', 'Gerontion' (in *Poems, 1920*), *The Waste Land* (1922), *The Hollow Men* (1925) and *Four Quartets*, this last completed in 1942 when

Abse was in his formative late teens, affect the volume. Hence, for instance, 'the long unfocused street, / grinning like a greyhound', or 'walking through brown fog with blue hands / against the fractured lamp-posts', or '[f]or I have been here before, / many times and in different places' and 'In the bad yellow light of a yesterday lamp-post', or 'And after this Lord, what greater error, what / Wisdom known in the last experience of the last?' and even the insomnia of 'Poem at 4 a.m.'. He argues in verse, in the manner of *Four Quartets*:

> No less because of fear of the partial ecstasy,
> the intimate terrible sadness of knowing God, –
> I do not talk about possession, – but of the hint known,
> the stone deciphered under the water momentarily,
> and then lost again.

In *Walking Under Water*, the title itself suggesting the final lines of Prufrock's 'Love Song', Eliot takes over from Dylan Thomas as the dominant influence. Examples include a hint of *Burnt Norton*'s garden scene in 'The Welcome' ('Who will enter through the gate, who now will enter?'), and such Eliotic echoes as 'we die / with the dead' in 'A Posy for Summer', 'tuned in their own stillness' in 'Conversation', and 'space without sound . . . space without odour . . . space without image' in 'The Clock'. 'No lips that kiss whisper my name' in 'Ghost' links Abse's poem with *The Hollow Men*. 'Portrait of a Marriage' catches up both Prufrock's 'Love Song' and 'Portrait of a Lady':

> your artificial smile alone
> that floats between the ceiling and the floor
> like some quiet heartbreak, can almost condone
> what, after all, others too must slow endure[.]

The Prufrockian note is heard again in such poems of urban angst as 'Journeys and Faces' and 'The Descent'. 'Ordinary Heaven' even features a Prufrock lookalike: a 'plump man, now half bald' who might have 'dared, ah dared' to 'question: "Is it worth it, worth it . . .?" '

Abse's next two books, *Ash on a Young Man's Sleeve* and *Tenants of the House*, have, of course, titles drawn from Eliot's writing. In the former, Abse quotes as epigraph the relevant lines from *Little Gidding*, as follows:

> Ash on an old man's sleeve
> Is all the ash burnt roses leave.
> Dust in the air suspended
> Marks the place where a story ended.
> Dust inbreathed was a house —[11]

The famous first line, here eponymously rewritten, opens section two of *Little Gidding*, the first three stanzas of which describe death as the absolute end, without any sense of spiritual hope. They are followed by the bleak Dantean encounter in Blitzed London of the narrator and the 'familiar compound ghost' who contrasts despairingly secular old age with necessary restoration by 'refining fire'. Abse's title associates such bleakness with youth. Yet the novel is one of hope and essential joy: the ending, the narrator as medical student sitting in the park some years after his friend Keith's death from a German bomb, has its autumnal mood and late-adolescent angst redeemed, as so often in Abse's work, by the narrator's humour and ironic self-awareness.

The line from 'Gerontion' that forms the title of *Tenants of the House* (1957) makes a similar unexpected association. The conclusion of Eliot's poem – 'Tenants of the house, / Thoughts of a dry brain in a dry season' – is all too appropriate for Eliot's deeply pessimistic study of an anti-Semitic old man lamenting both his age and the deficiencies of his past life, but a surprising source of inspiration for a young Jewish writer. We may be further surprised by Eliot's continuing influence elsewhere in the volume. For example, 'The Trial' and 'Duality' can be read as meditations on the Prufrock line, 'prepare a face to meet the faces that you meet'; stanza four of 'Photograph and Yellow Tulips' –

> we shall hold it, this most sad witness,
> and smile please and come a little nearer
> to a time that was never twice, to a place
> that could never be thanked enough . . .

– suggests both Prufrock and *Four Quartets*. 'The Field' opens with a recollection of 'Little Gidding': 'Should you stroll this way'.

Yet, to repeat, in this volume Abse finds his own poetic voice. The title requires reinterpretation in terms of Abse's work: the 'tenants' are the poems and the 'house' is his poetic sensibility. The poems include a section entitled 'The Identity of Love'; we begin to understand such poems as 'Poem and Message', 'Anniversary' and 'The Moment' – and the volume titles – as, now, effecting a dialogue with Eliot's sombre influence. These passionately tender explorations of newly married love are absolutely Abse's own. T. S. Eliot, for all his towering poetic gifts, could never write 'blind in the pandemonium / of the kiss', as Abse does in 'Anniversary'.

This is not to say that the mature Abse discards Eliot. Rather, he uses him in a consciously strategic way. Two poems make the point. The first is 'Funland', regarded by some as 'Abse's masterpiece'.[12] Certainly it is one of his finest achievements. The poem is a surrealistic treatment of life in a mental hospital, used here as a metaphor for human society.[13] It explores Abse's abiding concern with the nature and exercise of authority, in particular, its readiness to suppress minorities and to repress and control all variations – poetry, imagination, magic – from a totalitarian ideal. Behind such concern is the fact of the Holocaust, a substantial presence in much of his work, and his secularity: a related theme is the failure of religion. 'Funland' dramatizes and universalizes such themes, in part through the use of intertextual references, mainly to T. S. Eliot's poetry. Thus the narrator offers a version of a line in 'Ash Wednesday', asking of a reborn magician, 'Why should the agèd peacock / stretch his wings?' The hospital's poet is reduced to an *East Coker* lumpen peasant as 'he lifts up and down in slow motion / up and down his heavy feet', before being silenced. The hospital superintendent is 'sullen as a ruined millionaire'. The poem's final line – 'Do not wake us. We may die' – increases even the pessimism of Prufrock lingering 'in the chambers of the sea . . . / Till human voices wake us, and we drown'. But the main thrust of the poem is to set against Eliot's bleak view of modern social collapse aided by religious sterility, supported by such echoes and the poems they evoke, an insistence that, no matter how cruel and despairing life can be, there are always other possibilities. In particular, man's capacity to love, sustained against so much totalitarian pressure, guarantees human worth.

The second poem is 'Prufrock at the Seaside', a product of Abse's late seventies. An elderly Prufrock is at the seaside. A proposal of marriage having failed long ago, he has lived a bachelor's masturbatory life, full of regrets. He has become a voyeur. Here is a humorous poem concerned to satirize Eliot's angst-laden construct, partly by opposing his romantic generalities with realist detail, whilst never being indifferent to Prufrock's aching unhappiness. The final couplet reads: 'The waves lash on but the sea's in its chains. / The beach becomes desolate. The dog remains.'[14] Enter, or re-enter, Dylan Thomas through the echo of the famous ending of 'Fern Hill' and Thomas's 'young dog'.

The mature Abse's dialectical relationship with T. S. Eliot exists in parallel with his developing engagement with Thomas. This last is evident in the publishing and textual history of those three poems, already mentioned, that close *Tenants of the House*: 'Elegy for Dylan Thomas', 'Tenants of the House', 'Go Home the Act is Over'.

'Elegy for Dylan Thomas', extensively revised, is included in all three 'collecteds'. In 1977, when the first 'collected' appeared, much more was known about Thomas's life and death than in December 1953. Brinnin and Fitzgibbon had published their biographies, with detailed accounts of the careless living that hastened death, the perhaps apocryphal whisky drinking during his last days and the death itself. The scandalous life attracted enormous posthumous interest. Many voyeuristic tourists, often wholly ignorant of literature, let alone Thomas's writing, were drawn to Laugharne, where he was buried not in a tomb but in a simple grave. The new version reflects all this.

Thus, 'tomorrow the unconscious kids will cry in the dandelion fields / and tall tourists inspect his tomb' in the earlier version, becomes 'wrong-again Emily will come to the dandelion yard / and, with rum tourists, inspect his grave'.[15] There is a new realization that 'Death was his voluntary marriage' ('involuntary' in the *Tenants of the House* version) and that Thomas died because, the poem suggests, 'he rode / the whiskey-meadows of [Death's] breath' ('water-meadows' in the first version). In the revised version Abse is honest and even more compassionate about Thomas's life, hints at neglect (perhaps familial) of the grave and is contemptuous of the ghoulish tourism. And when he rewrites 'without a shadow his free ghost flies' as 'no fat ghost but a quotation cries' he emphasizes the penetrating power of Thomas's writing.

'Tenants of the House', in which Dylan Thomas is the unnamed 'famous tenant', was omitted from *Collected Poems 1948–1976* but restored in 1989 and 2003, in more explicit form. The new title is 'Enter the Movement'. The 'strange house' of stanza one is changed to 'the Boat-house'. Thomas's poetry – of which Abse may have never been less than a fan – is now described with a fresh enthusiasm: for 'every light put out' in stanza one, we now have 'half the lights put out'; 'his brute songs' becomes 'his gorgeous music'. The final line of stanza two, 'well, he sang the great passion others lacked', becomes 'well, he sang the Welsh passion others lacked'. The original fourth stanza is as follows:

> Then winter came when whistling beggars freeze.
> He, from inner fires, sang catastrophes
> While neighbours jigged with roaring joy outside
> Until laughing that tragic singer died.

The new one is:

> Then winter came when whistling beggars freeze.
> He, to quench inner fires, drank catastrophes
> while corybants, roaring, jigged with joy outside
> till, delirious, that lyric singer died.

'Quench' stresses Thomas's compulsive necessity to write poetry out of personal tension and trouble, his wild living as escape, while the appearance of 'corybants', and so the shift into mythology – corybants were the fertility goddess Cybele's wild dancers – suggests the universal appeal of Thomas's poetry. In the stanza's final line, for apparent carelessness about life is substituted explanation: Thomas was caught up in and destroyed by wild public acclaim. In the poem's penultimate line, already quoted, '[I]n bowler hats they sing with sharp, flat voices', becomes '[p]roudly English, they sing with sharp, flat voices'. The new poem thinks more of his poetry and is more understanding of his tragic predicament. It trumpets Thomas's poetic virtues in terms of a contrast between Welsh writing in English and *English* writing, as demonstrated by the 'Movement'. In publicly highlighting the difference we mark a sea-change in Abse's attitude to literary Wales.

'Go Home the Act is Over' was omitted from *Collected Poems 1948–1976*, only to reappear, revised, in *White Coat, Purple Coat*

(1989). The first-person case is replaced by the third person singular. The poet is now 'Dionysian'. The earlier line, '[a]gainst the roof my two shadows dance' becomes '[t]all against the roof his two shadows dance'. The result is the same: the daring, performing poet falls from his high poetic wire to a death the audience seems to expect, and the circus leaves town. The revisions treat Thomas more favourably, but the two versions of the poem make the same central points: he tended to play to his audience and was destroyed by money's lure ('but seeing gold, trips and loses balance'). Significantly, this poem is omitted from *New and Collected Poems* (2003).

Abse has always made frequent visits to Wales: to see his ageing parents, for instance, or to see Cardiff City play soccer. But, as he put it in 'Return to Cardiff', each visit was 'less a return than a raid / on mislaid identities'. The turning point – the small beginning – in his relationship with Welsh writing could well be dated to 1972, with his purchase of Green Hollows cottage in Ogmore-on-Sea where, as a child, he spent idyllic family holidays. During the three decades since he has strengthened his literary and academic ties with Wales. He was elected a Fellow of the Welsh Academy in 1992 and became its President in 1995. An Honorary Doctorate from the University of Wales in 1989 was followed by one from the University of Glamorgan in 1997 and by an Honorary Fellowship of the University of Wales College of Medicine in 1999. For over twenty years he has given great support to Poetry Wales Press, whose Seren imprint has made it an important poetry publisher. Abse is a director of the firm. In 1997 he published *Welsh Retrospective* and *Twentieth Century Anglo-Welsh Poetry*. The former collects all his poems about Wales. They dramatize a shift from, to use a line from 'Sons', 'the hesitant sense of not belonging quite'. This poem of the 1970s is one that demonstrates how much of an exile Abse has been:

> Strange a London door should slam
> and I think thus, of Cardiff evenings
> trying to rain, of quick dark where raw brick could hide.

His Wales is mainly the past, that country from which all are exiled. He looks into family history, insisting affectionately that 'if this be not true, I never lived'; he recalls his childhood, remembering a piano teacher, a cricketer, footballers, cinema-going and family holidays. Later romantic adventures, racial tension, incidents from his medical career, familial deaths and entrances, the observations of age, are all described with a deceptive, because slightly distancing precision, all too aware of the problems of remembering.

Pressing through these poems is Abse's Jewishness: sometimes overt – his dying father 'thin as Auschwitz' – more often implicit in familial explorations and his sense of history. Pressing with equal strength is a British literary tradition, evident in echoes of Shakespeare, Wordsworth, Tennyson, Arnold, Larkin and others, as well as of T. S. Eliot and Dylan Thomas.

Welsh Retrospective makes three important points about Abse and Wales. Firstly, the greater engagement with place and landscape in some of the later poems – 'At Ogmore-by-Sea this August Evening' and 'A Wall' for instance – succeeds the slightly distanced narration of earlier writing, such as 'Down the M4' and 'Return to Cardiff'. Secondly, Abse includes three versions of medieval Welsh poems – 'Meurig Dafydd to his Mistress', 'The Boasts of Hywel ab Owain Gwynedd' and 'Lament of Heledd' – published in his earlier volumes, and places them immediately before 'Elegy for Dylan Thomas' and 'A Sea-shell for Vernon Watkins', thus suggesting a tradition of Welsh writing that, suitably modified, includes Abse himself. This, plus the actual publishing of this book, the third point, stresses Abse's nationality with a new overtness. Ultimately his work floats free of national or racial limitations – 'I hail / the world within a word', he writes in 'A Letter from Ogmore-by-Sea' – but he is now much concerned to exhibit his Welshness. In a volume published in Wales he demonstrates an increasing sense of national identity.

What he makes of this identity, of Welshness generally, can be gauged from *Twentieth Century Anglo-Welsh Poetry*, the anthology he edited, also for Seren, in 1997. 'Anglo-Welsh' in the title is immediately problematic: two writers as different as Jan Morris and Donald Davie, for example, have used it to describe a person with one Welsh and one English parent. In not using the now usually preferred 'Welsh writing in English' Abse betrays some cultural uncertainty. His editorial principles of selection cause further problems: poets are no longer adjudged Anglo-Welsh because of their subject-matter but on the basis of 'Welsh affiliation', which means ancestry, residence or birth-and-breeding.

This leads to inconsistencies: Kingsley Amis out, Jean Earle in, is only one of many examples. And though such eclecticism may reflect a suitably postmodern sense of Welshness as an ever-changing construct, it also creates further problems of definition. These are not solved by the volume's 'Prologue', a stimulating and controversial collection of statements about Welsh poetry in English. Examples include an insistence on the dependence of Welsh poetry in English on the Welsh language, and on what Jeremy Hooker calls positional 'responsibilities' – Anglo-Welsh poets sited between 'Welsh language and culture and the Anglicizing influences of their medium' – and R. S. Thomas's belief that truly Welsh poetry has compulsory links with 'the true Wales', meaning an oddly timeless rurality. Roland Mathias asserts that 'a Biblical tone is a Welsh quality'. He offers Dylan Thomas as an example but, biblically speaking, could equally well link him to an English tradition that includes Jeremy Taylor, John Donne's *Devotions* and Milton. Abse's own contribution to the 'Prologue' debate is an extract from *A Strong Dose of Myself* (1983), which cites an awareness of the past as an aspect of Welshness and suggests difference from the English does not depend on the Welsh language. This, so far as it goes, is not a great help. Neither is the Prologue: its various quotations merely confuse. All is further complicated by two generalizations in Abse's introduction: that Welsh poets 'side with the losers of history and of life's procession – the underdogs, the outsiders, the downtrodden' and that Welsh poems, in the main, 'aim at the tropopause of feeling'.

His selection of poems makes further points. One is an egalitarian stance, perhaps typically Welsh. The maximum number of poems by any one author is eight; thirteen poets have the full complement. They are Edward Thomas, Wilfred Owen, Jean Earle, R. S. Thomas, Dylan Thomas, Alun Lewis, Leslie Norris, John Ormond, Dannie Abse, Gillian Clarke, Tony Curtis, Sheenagh Pugh and Robert Minhinnick. This is an impressive list. But it is also a list in which some are far more equal than others. Secondly, with few exceptions, the choice of poems reflects the principle of accessibility, the poet speaking to his or her community, a point emphasized in Abse's introduction. Dylan Thomas, for instance, is represented only by immediately accessible poems, in his case the most famous ones. But one welcome consequence of applying the accessibility principle is the inclusion of a substantial amount of humorous verse: A. G. Prys-Jones, Harri Webb, Mercer Simpson, Douglas Houston, John Davies, Christopher Meredith and Abse himself, with 'Welsh Valley Cinema 1930s' and 'Thankyou Note'. They help tweak the introduction's stereotype.

David Jones apart, the token High Modernist, there's not much engagement with the last century's more extreme poetic approaches. Ironically, given Abse's one-time hostility, the main basic influence here is the 'Movement', though there is much that escapes. So many of the poets are uneasy with realism per se, and reach readily for symbolism, historical allegory, rhetorical transformations; from which it could be said that, wherever possible, Abse chooses poets like himself. Further, he is unable to offer a precise, or even a convincingly inclusive, notion of Welshness. He has long recognized the problem: 'Not for one second, I know / can I be the same man twice' he wrote in 'Leaving Cardiff'. The older man who acknowledges the existence of 'Welsh writing in English' is not the same person as the younger self who once rejected its validity. The country where he has a second home is very different from the one he left in 1943. His anthology seeks to make sense of these changes. The result is both stereotyped and blurred, which may be appropriate for the inhabitants of a fractured country.

It is surely significant that 'The Uninvited' is the single surviving poem from *After Every Green Thing*, for it ends with lines that can describe some permanent effects of exile:

> and we are here, in a different place,
> changed and incredibly alone,
> and we did not know, we do not know ever.

Via escape from the Dylan Thomas effect, the establishing of difference from T. S. Eliot, and a renewed appreciation of Dylan Thomas, Abse has come to embrace literary and geographical Welshness. For Wales this is not all gain: its maverick outlook, its cosmopolitan outpost, both lose force and definition. Abse is no longer as much the salutary Other which a small literary world probably needs. His anthology's uncertain stereotyping – perhaps, paradoxically, its most valuable, thought-provoking characteristic – echoes our own confusion. Dylan Thomas also puzzled over Welshness: on the one hand he sought to foster 'the development of Anglo-Welsh poetry',[16] on the other he stated that 'Anglo-Welsh poetry . . . is an ambiguous compromise'. He ended: 'It's the poetry that counts . . . not his continent, country, island.'[17] In Dannie Abse's case it counts a lot as an achievement of the first importance, whatever we might think of his thoughts about Wales.

Notes

[1] *Collected Poems 1948–1976* (London: Hutchinson, 1977), p. 1; *White Coat, Purple Coat: Collected Poems 1948–1988* (London: Hutchinson, 1989), p. 3; *New and Collected Poems* (London: Hutchinson, 2003), pp. 3–4.

[2] Joseph Cohen, 'Conversations with Dannie Abse', *The Poetry of Dannie Abse*, ed. Joseph Cohen (London: Robson Books, 1983), p. 151.

[3] The starting point for all discussions of Abse, Thomas and Eliot is Tony Curtis, *Dannie Abse*, Writers of Wales (Cardiff: University of Wales Press, 1985). The present writer seeks to build on Curtis's useful pages.

[4] *Journals from the Ant-Heap* (London: Hutchinson, 1986), p. 151.

[5] 'Dannie Abse Revisited', *Poetry Wales*, 13, 2 (Autumn 1977), 19.

[6] *A Poet in the Family* (London: Robson Books, 1974), p. 156.

[7] *Journals from the Ant-Heap*, pp. 145ff.

[8] Dannie Abse (ed.), *Twentieth Century Anglo-Welsh Poetry* (Bridgend: Seren, 1997), p. 13.

[9] *Intermittent Journals* (Bridgend: Seren, 1994), pp. 180–1.

[10] Jonathan Raban, *The Society of the Poem* (London: Harrap, 1971), pp. 11, 15.

[11] The second line is often misquoted in editions of *Ash on a Young Man's Sleeve*. It should read 'Is all the ash the burnt roses leave.' The omission of the article makes the line more lyrical but more general, seemingly an unconscious minor mitigation of the older poet's pessimism.

[12] Gigliolá Sacerdoti Mariani, 'From Funland to Funland: An Ellipse', *The Poetry of Dannie Abse*, ed. Joseph Cohen, p. 74. The poem is the title poem of *Funland and Other Poems* (London: Hutchinson, 1973).

[13] My comments on 'Funland' are, in part, drawn from my article 'Dramatizing "Funland" ', *New Welsh Review*, 15 (Winter 1991–2), 38–41.

[14] *New and Collected Poems* (2003), pp. 414–15.

[15] In the revised version (*Collected Poems 1948–1976*, pp. 32–3) these lines, rewritten, are all that survive from the *Tenants of the House* stanza two and replace the last two lines of stanza one. 'Dylan Thomas told the story of how a certain American lady said how much she admired his Hornblower series. When Dylan remarked that C. S. Forester was the author, the lady's husband shouted out "Wrong again, Emily" ': Cary Archard, notes on the poems in Dannie Abse, *Welsh Retrospective* (Bridgend: Seren, 1997), p. 65.

[16] Dylan Thomas, *The Collected Letters*, new edn, ed. Paul Ferris (London: J. M. Dent, 2000), p. 385.

[17] Dylan Thomas, *The Broadcasts*, ed. Ralph Maud (London: J. M. Dent & Sons, 1991), pp. 31–2.

20

'Extravagant and wheeling stranger[s]': Dylan Thomas, Derek Walcott and the House of English Literature

KATIE GRAMICH

When Othello is called an 'extravagant and wheeling stranger' by the jealous Roderigo in the first scene of Shakespeare's play, it is meant as an insult – Othello is an outsider who has wandered out of bounds (the literal meaning of 'extravagant'): he is exotic, unpredictable, un-Venetian. Yet Othello knows that he has 'done the state some service'; in fact he is indispensable, as the Venetians reluctantly admit. Drawing, then, on a canonical English text, I see Othello's anomalous position in Venetian society as an image of the status of both Derek Walcott and Dylan Thomas in the realm of English literature.

Like Shakespeare's Venice, 'English literature' was for many years a flourishing, self-contained bastion created to exalt its inhabitants and to repulse outsiders. Yet English literature may be seen as an invention, a flight of the elite's collective imagination, just as surely as Shakespeare's Venice was. From the turn of the nineteenth century, the prestige of English in the universities and its stature as the humanist discipline above all others began to grow. By 1921, the Newbolt Report concluded that '[English] is one of the greatest subjects to which a University can call its students'.[1] The Newbolt Report, like the English Association, established fifteen years earlier, championed along with the English language a cultural nationalism which was to be propagated to all parts of the British Empire, including Wales and the Caribbean, during the first half of the twentieth century. The Newbolt Report, moreover, displays its Arnoldian credentials in discussing the various 'tributaries' which flow into the great stream of English literature, which had been successfully incorporated (and thus erased) for the greater good:

> If we explore the course of English literature, if we consider from what source its stream has sprung, by what tributaries it has been fed, and with how rich and full a current it has come down to us, we shall see that it has other advantages not to be found elsewhere. There are mingled in it, as only in the greatest of rivers could be mingled, the fertilising influences flowing down from many countries and from many ages in history. Yet all these have been subdued to form a stream native to our own soil.[2]

Forty years later, so-called 'Commonwealth' literature was frequently discussed in very similar terms, as providing a quaint tributary to the English mainstream. Derek Walcott has said that, as a young poet he could not hope to be accepted as a poet in his own right; his work could be regarded only as a minor 'contribution': 'There was folk-poetry, colonial poetry, Commonwealth verse, etc., and their function, so far as their mother country was concerned, was filial and tributary.'[3] Thus, his work could be regarded only as a 'tributary' and indeed a 'tribute' to that great flood of English poetry with which the colonies of the Empire had been blessed.

What distinguishes Othello from the Venetians, apart from his emblematic blackness, is the extravagant, metaphorical beauty of his speech. Although he claims to be a plain, rough soldier, he is in fact nothing of the sort. Shakespeare makes both Othello's exoticism and his nobility evident in his language: far from being a barbarian, he is a poet, whose words seduce Desdemona – and the audience. The similarity between Othello and our poets, then, is not limited to their status as cultural outsiders, but is continued in their 'extravagant' language. If metaphor is Othello's medium, so too is it Walcott's and Thomas's. And this compounded their otherness because it set them apart from their English contemporaries.

Walcott was not only an outsider to the edifice of English literature, since he was born and raised on the Caribbean island of St Lucia, which he himself has called a 'colonial backwater'; he was also, to an extent, a stranger in his own land. He was brought up as a Methodist in a predominantly Catholic country and he writes mostly in standard English, although the main language of 'Ste Lucie' is a French patois. He is also divided racially, which has proved to be an important theme in his poetry, but has caused problems with critics; for the English literary establishment he started out as what he calls a 'prodigy of the wrong colour', but for a number of West Indian critics he is still not 'black' enough. Similarly, Dylan Thomas suffered from divisions and contradictions: he lived in Wales, but could not speak Welsh (although both his parents could); he was estranged in this way from his own history and culture, like Walcott, who has described West Indian consciousness of history as a 'voluntary amnesia'. Wales, like St Lucia, has also been something of a colonial backwater, and exile to London has been a continuing temptation for generations of the Welsh and West Indians. The temptation of escape is there, too, for both poets, who wanted to get beyond the confines of their islands; unsurprisingly, both eventually gravitated towards the United States, where their talent was more readily acknowledged than in England.

Walcott has described his childhood as 'schizophrenic' because he led two lives: the inner one of English poetry and the outer one of street life and patois. As Ned Thomas has pointed out, this division is reminiscent of Dylan Thomas growing up in the Uplands, Swansea, that 'ugly, lovely town', brawling with the sailors in the pubs and going home to read Marlowe and Yeats. In 'Reminiscences of Childhood', Thomas says of Swansea: 'This sea town was my world', and a similar nostalgic yet unsentimental affection is shown for the town of Castries in Walcott's work. In fact, one of Walcott's best early achievements is a sonnet about the destruction of Castries by fire, which occurred when the poet was eighteen years old. The episode is also brilliantly described in his later autobiographical poem, *Another Life*, but this early sonnet shows clearly the young Walcott's precocious, exuberant skill with words and the powerful influence of Dylan Thomas. The poem is entitled 'A City's Death By Fire' and begins:

After that hot gospeller had levelled all but the churched sky,
I wrote the tale by tallow of a city's death by fire;
Under a candle's eye, that smoked in tears,
Wanted to tell, in more than wax, of faiths that were snapped like wire.[4]

The language is immediately reminiscent of Dylan Thomas: its energy and inventiveness, its metaphorical nature, its revelling in sound effects, its religious reverberations, its self-conscious, bardic narrator. It calls to mind particularly the poem 'When I Woke' from *Deaths and Entrances* (1946), which begins and ends:

> When I woke, the town spoke.
> Birds and clocks and cross bells
> Dinned aside the coiling crowd,
> The reptile profligates in a flame,
> Spoilers and pokers of sleep
> . . .
> I heard this morning, waking,
> Crossly out of the town noises
> A voice in the erected air,
> No prophet-progeny of mine,
> Cry my sea town was breaking.
> No Time, spoke the clocks, no God, rang the bells,
> I drew the white sheet over the islands
> And the coins on my eyelids sang like shells.[5]

Although the tone of both poems is elegiac, mourning the death of a sea town, both end on a positive, energetic note. Walcott's poem, particularly, sounds a note of reconciliation and even celebration, which was to become characteristic of his later work and which, arguably, he initially borrows from Thomas:

> In town, leaves were paper, but the hills were a flock of faiths;
> To a boy who walked all day, each leaf was a green breath
> Rebuilding a love I thought was as dead as nails,
> Blessing the death and the baptism by fire.[6]

Another early poem, 'As John to Patmos', ends in a similarly celebratory vein, with a blast of Thomasian oratory:

> As John to Patmos, in each love-leaping air,
> O slave, soldier, worker under red trees sleeping, hear
> What I swear now, as John did:
> To praise lovelong, the living and the brown dead.[7]

Walcott acknowledges the fact that much of his early work is imitative: 'The whole course of imitations and adaptations was simply a method of apprenticeship . . . I knew I had to absorb everything in order to be able to discover what I was eventually trying to sound like.'[8] Although Dylan Thomas was certainly the strongest influence on the young Walcott, imitations of other poets, such as Eliot, Auden, Yeats and Marvell, are also present in the early oeuvre. For Walcott, his mature style constituted 'the assimilation of the features of every ancestor'.[9] Despite the fear of and distaste for provincialism which haunted both Thomas and Walcott, both were remarkably confident in their own poetic powers from a very early age. In 'The Muse of History' Walcott writes:

> Fear of imitation obsesses minor poets . . . but the great poets have no wish to be different, no time to be original . . . their originality emerges only when they have absorbed all the poetry which they have read, entire, [and] their first work appears to be the accumulation of other people's trash but . . . they become bonfires.[10]

'English literature' by the 1930s, when Thomas began to publish his work, had become a hallowed academic realm, presided over by messianic figures such as the Cambridge critic F. R. Leavis, who identified clearly which writers were great and which were not; who was in the house of English literature and who was – and ever would remain – outside it. Both Walcott and Thomas received good grammar-school educations, which would have included the canon of English literature as it was conceived of at the time. Thomas's father was himself a gifted grammar-school English teacher, who ensured that his son would be well aware of the golden treasury of English verse from an early age. Meanwhile, Walcott has written that: 'Like any colonial child I was taught English Literature as my natural inheritance . . . the snow and the daffodils . . . were real, more real than the heat and the oleander, perhaps, because they lived on the page, in imagination, and therefore in memory.'[11] Walcott's attitude towards this imposed canon is not one of resentment, although he is acutely aware of the ironies, but one of acceptance and excitement. In *Another Life*, he talks again about the colonial literary inheritance which was his:

> I saw, as through the glass of some provincial gallery
> the hieratic objects which my father loved:
> the stuffed dark nightingale of Keats,

> bead-eyed, snow-headed eagles,
> all that romantic taxidermy,
> and each one was a fragment of the True Cross,
> each one upheld, as if it were The Host;
> those venerated, venerable objects
> borne by black hands (reflecting like mahogany)
> of reverential teachers, shone the more
> they were repolished by our use.[12]

Works of literature are figured in terms of actual objects, like exhibits in a museum, in the devoted care of fathers and teachers. These were the keepers of the colonial patrimony, upholding the values and perpetuating the reverence.

Again, the image of the provincial museum withholding its hieratic objects suggests the notion of being inside a formidable edifice, which might be identified as the house of English literature itself. Henry James was, according to Leavis, an inhabitant of this hallowed house, despite his American birth, and it is James who has elaborated the best known image of what he calls the 'house of fiction':

> The house of fiction has in short not one window, but a million – a number of possible windows not to be reckoned, rather; every one of which has been pierced, or is still pierceable, in its vast front, by the need of the individual vision and by the pressure of the individual will.[13]

James's vision is vibrant and democratic; what he does not explain is how the artist enters this great house in the first place.

Derek Walcott has drawn productively upon this image of the house of English literature in his poetry, merging the Jamesian image of the house of a myriad artists with the historical fact of the West Indian Great House, emblem of Empire and of the exploitative plantation system. He nods, too, in the direction of the traditional English 'country house' poem and at the same time undermines that genre's certainties. In his autobiographical poem, *Another Life*, Walcott describes his entry into the Great House of English literature like this:

> I had entered the house of literature as a houseboy,
> filched as the slum child stole,

> as the young slave appropriated
> those heirlooms temptingly left
> with the Victorian homilies of *Noli tangere*.[14]

The speaker represents himself as a subordinate, 'houseboy', and *persona non grata*, 'slum child', 'slave', who transgresses the written rules imposingly couched in the original language of empire, Latin. And yet, Walcott acknowledges equally '[t]he midsummer sea, the hot pitch road, this grass, these shacks that made me'[15] – not only the great house of English literature but also the slum shacks of the Morne create what he describes in *Another Life* as 'the divided child'. As in the earlier extract from *Another Life*, literary works in the great house are seen as actual objects, 'heirlooms', to be lovingly touched, handled and ultimately 'filched' by the picaresque intruder, escaped from 'the shacks that made [him]'. Similarly, in the poem 'Ruins of a Great House', the speaker:

> ... climbed a wall with the grille ironwork
> Of exiled craftsmen protecting that great house
> From guilt perhaps, but not from the worm's rent
> Nor from the padded cavalry of the mouse.
> And when a wind shook in the limes I heard
> What Kipling heard, the death of a great empire, the abuse
> Of ignorance by Bible and by sword.[16]

Even in this slightly later poem the echoes of Thomas's poetic diction are still perceptible: neither 'the worm's rent' nor 'the padded cavalry of the mouse' would be out of place in any of Thomas's works. The concern with death and decay is also consonant with the characteristic mood of early Thomas, who wrote in a letter of 1933:

> For the time at least, I believe in the writing of poetry from the flesh and, generally, from the dead flesh. So many modern poets take the living flesh as their object, and, by their clever dissecting, turn it into a carcase. I prefer to take the dead flesh, and, by any positivity of faith and belief that is in me, build up a living flesh from it.[17]

Such 'positivity' is certainly present in Walcott's poem, which ends on a note of reconciliation and compassion.

If Walcott entered the house of literature surreptitiously, the same could also be said of Dylan Thomas, though perhaps the image of a boisterous gatecrasher at a Bloomsbury party would be more appropriate in Thomas's case. For, as James A. Davies has pointed out, the acclaim which greeted the publication of Dylan Thomas's *Collected Poems* in 1952 was almost entirely that of 'lay' readers of poetry, while the English academic establishment rejected Thomas with a virulence which was often compounded by an explicit animosity towards the Welsh.[18]

Dylan Thomas uses the image of the impregnable house quite differently from Walcott, however. In the early poem 'Ears in the Turrets Hear', the speaker is not locked out but locked in. The 'white house' described in the poem appears to be commensurate with the speaker's own body; as in James's house of fiction, here the artist looks out of his various windows upon the world but he is utterly alone:

> Ears in the turrets hear
> Hands grumble on the door,
> Eyes in the gables see
> The fingers at the locks.
> Shall I unbolt or stay
> Alone till the day I die
> Unseen by stranger-eyes
> In this white house?[19]

Interestingly, Thomas goes on to elaborate this conceit by figuring the body as a solitary island 'bound / By a thin sea of flesh / And a bone coast' in a poetic strategy reminiscent of Walcott's in his collections, *The Castaway* and *The Gulf*. Clearly, both poets are drawing upon feelings of isolation and difference as self-conscious artists living on small islands. Both poets also seem to project a feeling of deracination and strangeness, even though 'this island' is actually home. In a letter of 1933, to Pamela Hansford Johnson, Thomas explains his use of this image thus: 'Every idea, intuitive or intellectual, can be imaged and translated in terms of the body, its flesh, skin, blood, sinews, veins, glands, organs, cells and senses ... Through my small, bonebound island I have learnt all I know, experienced all, and sensed all. All I write is inseparable from the island.'[20] The sense of displacement and dispossession is underlined in Thomas's poem by the fragmented nature of the body, whose members are strangely unattached, not appearing to belong to the speaker, who consistently eschews the possessive pronoun: not '*my* ears . . . hear' but 'ears . . . hear', not '*my* eyes . . . see' but 'eyes . . . see'. Thomas's speaker, like Walcott's, is a castaway on the island, perhaps destined never to make contact with the 'ships [which] anchor off the bay'. The topography of Thomas's island is a strange mixture of the exotic and the familiarly Welsh ('sand and slates') while the questions repeated throughout the poem about the possibility of escape and human contact remain finally unanswered. Similarly, in Walcott's 'The Castaway', the speaker remains marooned and possibly going mad ('the ripe brain rotting') as the flotsam and jetsam are washed ashore, offering tantalizing mirages of redemption:

> That green wine bottle's gospel choked with sand,
> Labelled, a wrecked ship,
> Clenched sea-wood nailed and white as a man's hand.[21]

In later poems, though, Thomas uses the house image in a more positive and celebratory fashion. The farm which is 'home' in 'Fern Hill', for instance, is a 'lilting house' with a 'happy yard'; it returns every morning like 'a wanderer white / with the dew'.[22] In 'Poem on His Birthday' he sits content in 'his house on stilts high among beaks / And palavers of birds'.[23] Thomas's speaker makes no assault on the Great House; he remains in his remote, peripheral place, which is unassailably home.

Although the overt influence of Dylan Thomas soon diminished in Walcott's work, arguably the underlying affinity, which we might term post-colonial, still remains. Moreover, as mentioned above, Walcott proudly calls himself a 'mongrel', an assimilator, and, as Edward Baugh has observed, he is the kind of poet who does not shed influences, but digests and transforms them into his own individual style. Walcott progresses far beyond the tribute of the colonial imitator, and imagines a new Adamic vision for the poet of the New World: 'What would deliver him [the West Indian poet] from servitude was the forging of a language that went beyond mimicry, a dialect which had the force of a revelation as it invented names for things.'[24] Dylan Thomas is a similar kind of poet: his revelatory dialect is quite distinctive, and he, too, is taken with the prototypical figure of Adam; as Aneirin Talfan Davies has remarked, the biblical Adam had a fast hold upon Thomas's imagination, as 'the ribbed original of love'.[25] Like Adam, Walcott felt that he was confronted with an unnamed, if tainted, Eden: 'if there was nothing, there was everything to be made'.[26] Both Walcott and Thomas are capable of making disparaging remarks about the constricting provincialism of their colonial backwater homes and yet both appear to devote themselves to chronicling that neglected landscape. As Walcott puts it in *Another Life*:

> ... drunkenly, or secretly, we swore,
> disciples of that astigmatic saint,
> that we would never leave the island
> until we had put down, in paint, in words,
> as palmists learn the network of a hand,
> all of its sunken, leaf-choked ravines,
> every neglected, self-pitying inlet
> muttering in brackish dialect ...[27]

Dylan Thomas's attitude to Wales is similarly contradictory. In the Prologue to the *Collected Poems*, Wales is glorified: 'Hark: I trumpet the place, / From fish to jumping hill!' while in a letter he rants about Wales's ugliness:

> little colliers, diseased in mind and body as only the Welsh can be, standing in groups outside the Welfare Hall ... All Wales is like this ... It's impossible for me to tell you how much I want to get out of it all, out of narrowness and dirtiness, out of the eternal ugliness of Welsh people, and all that belongs to them.[28]

The savagery of the self-loathing is quite startling but it has occasional parallels in Walcott when he is in satirical mode. One also suspects that Thomas is writing deliberately to shock and impress his English correspondent.

Dylan Thomas's sudden appearance on the English literary scene of the 1930s was certainly a nasty shock for his English peers, who were on the whole following in the restrained footsteps of T. S. Eliot. It was an era of pared-down language, of reticence and irony, of political commitment, and Dylan Thomas's approach to poetry shocked, not only because of the extravagance of his language, but also because of the earthiness and overt sexuality of his themes. Stephen Spender's review of Dylan Thomas's *Collected Poems* perfectly expresses this difference; he says:

> Dylan Thomas represents a romantic revolt against the classicist tendency which has crystallized around the theological views of Eliot and Auden. It is a revolt against more than this, against the Oxford, Cambridge, and Harvard intellectualism of much modern poetry in the English language; against the King's English of London and the South, which has become a correct idiom capable of refinements of beauty, but incapable of harsh effects, coarse texture, and violent colours.[29]

Although Spender is championing Thomas against the establishment, his choice of adjectives, 'harsh', 'coarse' and 'violent', suggest that he nevertheless regarded Thomas as something of an 'extravagant and wheeling stranger'. Dylan Thomas himself was very pleased with the review and called it 'the truest I have ever seen of my writing'.

Both poets were precocious: Dylan Thomas's *18 Poems* appeared when he was twenty years old, Walcott's *Twenty-five Poems* when he was only eighteen years old, and this title itself is a tacit acknowledgement of Dylan Thomas's influence, for it is the same as that of Thomas's second collection, which appeared in 1936. Several critics have noted that Walcott's poetry grows plainer as he matures; the poet himself has said that his poetry is getting so plain that it frightens him. After the intoxicated exuberance of the early work, there is indeed a tendency towards the laconic, a rejection of melodrama. As he says in the early collection, *In A Green Night* (1962):

> I seek
> As climate seeks its style, to write
> Verse crisp as sand, clear as sunlight.
> Cold as the curled wave, ordinary
> As a tumbler of island water.[30]

Yet this repeated claim that he desires plainness is misleading, for Walcott in later work returns to his difficult, allusive style. There is nothing plain about his poetic autobiography, *Another Life* (1978), or his Caribbean epic, *Omeros* (1990). Walcott tends to use autobiography to chronicle West Indian history as well as to explore the role of the poet, a subject which continually fascinated Dylan Thomas. *Another Life* has frequently been compared with Wordsworth's *The Prelude*, his unfinished poem chronicling the 'growth of a poet's mind', but it is also reminiscent of Dylan Thomas's prose autobiography, *Portrait of the Artist as a Young Dog*, as well as of his radio play, *Under Milk Wood*. Both *Another Life* and *Under Milk Wood* provide us with a gallery of humorous characters, a mock epic, a controlling artist's consciousness and presence. The sea and the sailor figure are important throughout both poets' work; both Shabine in Walcott's 'The Schooner *Flight*' and Captain Cat in Thomas's *Under Milk Wood* are alter egos for the poets, questing, wheeling strangers like themselves.

Figures such as the sailor, the castaway and the new Adam recur in Walcott's poetry as images of the poet, the solitary outsider who seeks something indefinable. In Thomas's work, this solitary figure is often a child or even an embryo, cut off from the world, yet contemplating it. Both poets are fundamentally concerned with individual identity, with basic human questions. Their status as outsiders has afforded them the freedom to experiment and transform the 'given' language as few members of the establishment have dared. As Ned Thomas observes in his book on Walcott, *Poet of the Islands*: 'Those in Wales who write in English, no less than Derek Walcott, write a *new* literature. West Indians can say with R. S. Thomas: "Despite our speech, we are not English".'[31]

The great edifice of English literature would be far less imposing without the work of its 'outsiders', beginning with the Irish, Welsh and Scottish and, more recently, African, Australian and West Indian, to give only a few examples. The contribution of our two poets, though in many ways different, has been to recharge the language, to shock with the sensual delight of their imagery, to challenge a literary establishment which has become too self-satisfied.

More than thirty years after his early apprenticeship imitating the poems of Dylan Thomas, Walcott published a poem entitled 'Wales', in the wake of his visit to this country. It is a poem which shows the Caribbean poet's sympathetic understanding of Welsh history and suggests his empathy with a landscape, language and people which, though far removed from the colonized island of his birth, he clearly sees as echoing something deeply familiar in his own cultural memory.

For Walcott, the landscape of Wales *is* the landscape of poetry:

> Those white flecks cropping the ridges of Snowdon
> will thicken their fleece and come wintering down
> through the gap between alliterative hills,
> through the caesura that let in the Legions,
> past the dark disfigured mouths of the chapels,
> till a white silence comes to green-throated Wales.[32]

Both lush and succinct, Walcott's lines capture the colonial, religious, linguistic and agricultural history of Wales, as well as its poetic underpinning. The 'gap', 'caesura', 'flecks' and 'silence' also suggest absences and dispossession, at the same time as the abandonment of the mountainsides calls to mind the other Thomas's, R. S.'s, 'depopulation of the Welsh hill country'. The alliteration and rhyme which are at the heart of the Welsh metrical tradition are echoed in the English words of the Caribbean poet. Though this Wales is far from Dylan Thomas's Swansea, it is not so far from 'Fern Hill' and very close to the aural exuberance which Thomas restored to poetry in English in the 1930s. In the second part of the poem, we move down the valleys and the centuries to see the Welsh houses which the speaker contemplates with compassion and tenderness:

> Down rusty gorges, cold rustling gorse,
> over rocks hard as consonants, and rain-vowelled shales
> sang the shallow-buried axe, helmet and baldric
> before the wet asphalt sibilance of tires.
> A plump raven, Plantagenet, unfurls its heraldic
> caw over walls that held the cult of the horse.
> In blackened cottages with their stony hatred
> of industrial fires, a language is shared
> like bread to the mouth, white flocks to dark byres.[33]

The symmetrical alliteration of 'rusty gorges' and 'rustling gorse' echoes the intricate patterning of *cynghanedd groes*, while the land continues to reveal its poetic language and its colonial history. The British monarch's victory is figured appropriately in aural, as well as visual, terms – the harsh 'caw' of the predatory raven silences the soft speech of its prey. Yet the poem is not despairing, for the language secretly survives and is shared in a sacramental way within the modest walls of the cottages. The contrastive imagery of black and white that patterns the whole poem culminates in the last memorable phrase, 'white flocks to dark byres'. The image suggests a homecoming, a return to comfort and safety. It is a concern which punctuates Walcott's Caribbean work, too. In 'Homecoming: Anse La Raye', for example, the speaker finds that 'there are homecomings without home' in a post-colonial island, for a poet brought up with 'the shades / of borrowed ancestors'.[34]

Both Dylan Thomas and Derek Walcott continue to occupy an ambivalent position with regard to the great house of English literature. Each was, in poetic terms, both a transgressive outsider and an enthusiastic inheritor of the literary tradition. Long before postcolonial critics such as Homi Bhabha began to publish work pinpointing the liberating power of 'hybridity' and extolling the value of 'interstitial' texts,[35] Thomas and Walcott were embodying poetic hybridity and producing interstitial works which refused to be swallowed comfortably by the literary mainstream. Roderigo's speech in the first scene of *Othello* goes on to call the Moor 'an extravagant and wheeling stranger / Of here and everywhere'.[36] Despite their outsider status, both Dylan Thomas and Derek Walcott have acquired worldwide poetic reputations while still remaining imaginatively rooted in their homelands, a Janus-like position which might justify their description as 'of here and everywhere'.

Notes

[1] *The Teaching of English in England* (London: HMSO, 1921), p. 200.

[2] *The Teaching of English in England*, p. 13.

[3] Derek Walcott, 'What the Twilight Says: An Overture', *Dream on Monkey Mountain and Other Plays* (London: Cape, 1972), pp. 3–40 (31).

[4] Derek Walcott, 'A City's Death By Fire', *Collected Poems 1948–1984* (New York: Farrar, Straus & Giroux, 1986), p. 6.

[5] Dylan Thomas, 'When I Woke', *Collected Poems 1934–53*, ed. Walford Davies and Ralph Maud (London: Dent, 1988), p. 112.

[6] Walcott, 'A City's Death By Fire', *Collected Poems*, p. 6.

[7] Walcott, 'As John to Patmos', *Collected Poems*, p. 5.

[8] Edward Hirsch, 'An Interview with Derek Walcott', *Contemporary Literature*, 20, 3 (Summer 1979), 279–83 (282).

[9] Derek Walcott, 'The Muse of History', *Is Massa Day Dead? Black Moods in the Caribbean*, ed. Orde Coombs (New York: Anchor/Doubleday, 1974), pp. 1–28 (1).

¹⁰ Ibid., p. 25.
¹¹ Ibid., p. 7.
¹² Walcott, *Another Life*, Book 1, Chapter 7, I, *Collected Poems*, pp. 183–4.
¹³ Henry James, Preface to *The Portrait of a Lady* ([1881]; Oxford: Oxford University Press, 1998), pp. 3–18 (8).
¹⁴ Walcott, *Another Life*, Book 2, Chapter 12, II, *Collected Poems*, p. 219.
¹⁵ Walcott, 'Midsummer', LIV, *Collected Poems*, p. 510.
¹⁶ Walcott, 'Ruins of a Great House', *Collected Poems*, p. 20.
¹⁷ Dylan Thomas, *Collected Letters*, ed. Paul Ferris (London: Dent, 1985), pp. 72–3.
¹⁸ James A. Davies, 'Questions of Identity: The Movement and "Fern Hill" ', *Dylan Thomas: New Casebook*, eds John Goodby and Chris Wigginton (Basingstoke: Palgrave, 2001), pp. 158–171.
¹⁹ Dylan Thomas, 'Ears in the Turrets Hear', *Collected Poems*, p. 48.
²⁰ Thomas, *Collected Letters*, p. 39.
²¹ Walcott, 'The Castaway', *Collected Poems*, p. 58.
²² Thomas, 'Fern Hill', *Collected Poems*, p. 134.
²³ Thomas, 'Poem on His Birthday', *Collected Poems*, p. 146.
²⁴ Walcott, 'What the Twilight Says: An Overture', *Dream on Monkey Mountain and Other Plays*, p. 17.
²⁵ Aneirin Talfan Davies, *Dylan: Druid of the Broken Body* (London: Dent, 1964), p. 13.
²⁶ Walcott, 'What the Twilight Says: An Overture', *Dream on Monkey Mountain and Other Plays*, p. 4.
²⁷ Walcott, *Another Life*, Chapter 8, *Collected Poems*, p. 194.
²⁸ Thomas, *Collected Letters*, p. 30.
²⁹ Stephen Spender, 'A Romantic in Revolt', review of *Collected Poems* by Dylan Thomas, *The Spectator* (5 December 1952), 780–1 (781).
³⁰ Walcott, 'Islands', *Collected Poems*, p. 52.
³¹ Ned Thomas, *Poet of the Islands/Bardd yr Ynysoedd* (Cardiff: Welsh Arts Council, 1980), p. 2.
³² Walcott, 'Wales', *Collected Poems*, p. 455.
³³ Ibid.
³⁴ Walcott, 'Homecoming: Anse La Raye', *Collected Poems*, p. 127.
³⁵ Homi K. Bhabha, *The Location of Culture* (London: Routledge, 1994), p. 113.
³⁶ William Shakespeare, *Othello*, I. i. 137–8.

VI
EPILOGUE

21

SEAMUS HEANEY

Brothers
for Wynn Thomas

from the Irish of Laoisioch Mac an Bhaird (sixteenth/seventeenth century)

You who opt for English ways
And crop your curls, your crowning glory,
You, my handsome specimen,
Are no true son of Donncha's.

If you were, you would not switch
To modes in favour with the English;
You, the flower of Fola's land,
Would never end up barbered.

A full head of long, fair hair
Is not for you; it is your brother
Who scorns the foreigners' close cut.
The pair of you are opposites.

Eoghan Ban won't ape their ways,
Eoghan beloved of noble ladies
Is enemy to English fads
And lives beyond the pale of fashion.

Eoghan Ban is not like you.
Breeches aren't a thing he values.
A clout will do him for a cloak.
Leggings he won't wear, nor greatcoat.

He hates the thought of jewelled spurs
Flashing on his feet and footwear,
And stockings of the English sort,
And being all prinked up and whiskered.

He's Donncha's true son, for sure.
He won't be seen with a rapier
Angled like an awl, out arseways,
As he swanks it to the meeting place.

Sashes worked with threads of gold
And high stiff collars out of Holland
Are not for him, nor satin scarves
That sweep the ground, nor gold rings even.

He has no conceit in feather beds,
Would rather stretch himself on rushes,
Dwell in a bothy than a bawn,
And make the branch his battlement.

Horsemen in the mouth of a glen,
A savage clash, kernes skirmishing –
This man is in his element
Taking on the foreigner.

But you are not like Eoghan Ban.
You're a laughing stock on stepping stones
With your dainty foot: a sad disgrace,
You who opt for English ways.

VII
BIBLIOGRAPHY

22
Bibliography of M. Wynn Thomas
(1970–2003)

RHIAN REYNOLDS

Critical Studies

Morgan Llwyd (Cardiff: University of Wales Press, 1984).
The Lunar Light of Whitman's Poetry (Cambridge, MA; London: Harvard University Press, 1987).
Emyr Humphreys (Caernarfon: Gwasg Pantycelyn, 1989).
Morgan Llwyd, Ei Gyfeillion a'i Gyfnod (Cardiff: University of Wales Press, 1991).
Internal Difference: Twentieth-century Writing in Wales (Cardiff: University of Wales Press, 1992).
John Ormond (Cardiff: University of Wales Press, 1997).
Corresponding Cultures: The Two Literatures of Wales (Cardiff: University of Wales Press, 1999).
James Kitchener Davies (Cardiff: University of Wales Press, 2002).

Editions

Llyfr y Tri Aderyn, Morgan Llwyd (Cardiff: University of Wales Press, 1988).
A Toy Epic, Emyr Humphreys (Bridgend: Seren Books, 1989).

Edited Collections

R. S. Thomas: Y Cawr Awenydd (Llandysul: Gomer Press, 1990).
The Page's Drift: R. S. Thomas at Eighty (Bridgend: Seren Books, 1993).
DiFfinio Dwy Lenyddiaeth Cymru (Cardiff: University of Wales Press, 1995).
Gweld Sêr: Cymru a Chanrif America (Cardiff: University of Wales Press, 2001).

James Kitchener Davies: Detholiad o'i Waith, joint ed. with Manon Rhys (Cardiff: University of Wales Press, 2002).
Emyr Humphreys: Conversations and Reflections (Cardiff: University of Wales Press, 2002).
R. S. Thomas, *Residues* (Tarset: Bloodaxe, 2002).
Welsh Writing in English (Cardiff: University of Wales Press, 2003).

Special Edition

Walt Whitman, *Wrenching Times: Poems from Drum-taps*, poems selected by M. Wynn Thomas, wood engravings by Gaylord Shanilec (Newtown: Gregynog Press, 1991).

Pamphlet

R. S. Thomas: Bardd Rhyfel/R. S. Thomas: War Poet (Cardiff: Welsh Arts Council, 1996).

Contributions to Books

'Cotton Mather's Wonders of the Invisible World: Some Metamorphoses of Salem Witchcraft', *The Damned Art*, ed. Sidney Anglo (London: Routledge & Kegan Paul, 1977), pp. 202–26.
'Literature in English', *Glamorgan County History*, vol. 6, ed. Prys Morgan (Glamorgan History Trust Limited, 1988), pp. 353–66.
'Morgan Llwyd y Piwritan', *Cof Cenedl: Ysgrifau ar Hanes Cymru*, 3, ed. Geraint H. Jenkins (Llandysul: Gomer Press, 1988), pp. 59–88.
Introduction, *R. S. Thomas: Y Cawr Awenydd*, pp. xiii–xxiv.
'Agweddau ar Farddoniaeth y Chwedegau', *R. S. Thomas: Y Cawr Awenydd*, pp. 23–41.
'Y Duw Cudd'. *R. S. Thomas: Y Cawr Awenydd*, pp. 77–95.
'Pwys Llên a Phwysau Hanes', *Sglefrio ar Eiriau* (Llandysul: Gwasg Gomer, 1992), pp. 1–21.
'Disgybl a'i Athro: Morgan Llwyd a Walter Cradoc', *Agweddau ar Dwf Piwritaniaeth yng Nghymru yn yr Ail Ganrif ar Bymtheg*, ed. J. Gwynfor Jones (Lampeter, New York: Edwin Mellen Press, 1992), pp. 111–26.
'Keeping his Pen Clean: R. S. Thomas and Wales', *Miraculous Simplicity: Essays on R. S. Thomas*, ed. William V. Davis (Fayetteville: University of Arkansas Press, 1993), pp. 61–79.
Introduction, *The Page's Drift*, pp. 9–21.

'Whitman and the Dreams of Labor', *Walt Whitman: the Centennial Essays*, ed. Ed Folsom (Iowa City: University of Iowa Press, 1994), pp. 133–52.

'Fratricide and Brotherly Love', *The Cambridge Companion to Walt Whitman*, ed. Ezra Greenspan (Cambridge: Cambridge University Press, 1995), pp. 27–44.

'Whitman and the British Isles', *Walt Whitman and the World*, eds Gay Wilson Allen and Ed Folsom (Iowa City: University of Iowa Press, 1995), pp. 11–70.

'Shaman of Shifting Form: Tony Conran and the Welsh Poetic Tradition', *Thirteen Ways of Looking at Tony Conran*, ed. Nigel Jenkins (Cardiff: Welsh Union of Writers, 1995), pp. 78–102.

'Prints of Wales: Contemporary Welsh Poetry in English', *Poetry in the British Isles: Non-Metropolitan Perspectives*, eds Hans-Werner Ludwig and Lothar Fietz (Cardiff: University of Wales Press, 1995), pp. 97–114.

Bilingual Introduction, *Ysbrydoliaeth R. S. Thomas Inspiration* (Cyfeillion Oriel Plas Glyn-y-Weddw, 1995), pp. 2–3.

Emyr Humphreys, *Outside the House of Baal*, textual notes by M. Wynn Thomas (Bridgend: Seren, 1996).

Introduction, *DiFfinio Dwy Lenyddiaeth Cymru*, pp. 1–6.

'Symbyliad y Symbol: Euros Bowen a Vernon Watkins', *DiFfinio Dwy Lenyddiaeth Cymru*, pp. 170–89.

'Seventeenth-century Puritan Writers: Morgan Llwyd and Charles Edwards', *A Guide to Welsh Literature: c.1530–1700*, ed. R. Geraint Gruffydd (Cardiff: University of Wales Press, 1997), pp. 190–209.

'Gillian Clarke: Staying to Mind Things', *Trying the Line*, ed. Menna Elfyn (Llandysul: Gwasg Gomer, 1997), pp. 44–68.

'Yr Efrydd a'r Almonwydden: Pennar Davies, y Llenor o Lyn Cynon', *Cwm Cynon*, ed. Hywel Teifi Edwards (Llandysul: Gwasg Gomer, 1997), pp. 309–28.

'Place, Race and Gender in the Poetry of Gillian Clarke', *Dangerous Diversity: The Changing Faces of Wales*, eds Katie Gramich and Andrew Hiscock (Cardiff: University of Wales Press, 1998), pp. 3–19.

'Outside the House of Baal: The Evolution of a Major Novel', *Seeing Wales Whole: Essays on the Literature of Wales*, ed. Sam Adams (Cardiff: University of Wales Press, 1998), pp. 121–43.

'Emyr Humphreys: Regional Novelist?', *The Regional Novel in Britain and Ireland: 1800–1900*, ed. K. D. M. Snell (Cambridge: Cambridge University Press, 1998), pp. 201–20.

'Tir Neb: M. Wynn Thomas yn Holi Emyr Humphreys am ei Nofelau a'i Straeon Byrion', *Dal Pen Rheswm: Cyfweliadau gyda Emyr Humphreys*, ed. R. Arwel Jones (Cardiff: University of Wales Press, 1999), pp. 55–99.

'Sisial Ganu: M. Wynn Thomas yn Holi Emyr Humphreys am ei Gerddi', *Dal Pen Rheswm: Cyfweliadau gydag Emyr Humphreys*, pp. 163–90.

'M. Wynn Thomas, Adolygiad ar *Y Pla*', *Rhyddid y Nofel*, ed. Gerwyn Wiliams (Cardiff: University of Wales Press, 1999), pp. 278–80.

'M. Wynn Thomas, Adolygiad ar *Dirgel Ddyn*', *Rhyddid y Nofel*, pp. 305–7.

Introduction, *Nations and Relations: Writing across the British Isles*, eds Tony Brown and Russell Stephens (Cardiff: New Welsh Review, 2000), pp. i–iv.

With Tony Brown, 'Colonial Wales and Fractured Language', *Nations and Relations: Writing across the British Isles*, pp. 71–88.

'America: Cân fy Hunan', *Gweld Sêr: Cymru a Chanrif America*, pp. 1–29.

'Caethiwed Branwen: Agweddau ar Farddoniaeth Alun Llywelyn-Williams', *Merthyr a Thaf* (Llandysul: Gwasg Gomer, 2001), pp. 393–414.

'Representatives and Revolutionaries: The New Urban Politics Revisited', *Whitman East and West: New Contexts for Reading Whitman*, ed. Ed Folsom (Iowa: University of Iowa Press, 2002), pp. 145–58.

'Ynghylch Llenydda a Beirniadaeth', *Alan*, ed. Huw Meirion Edwards (Caernarfon: Cyhoeddiadau Barddas, 2003), pp. 122–58.

Introduction, *Welsh Writing in English*, pp. 1–6.

With Tony Brown, 'The Problems of Belonging', *Welsh Writing in English*, pp. 165–202.

With Jane Aaron, ' "Pulling you Through Changes": Welsh Writing in English Before, Between and After Two Referenda', *Welsh Writing in English*, pp. 278–309.

' "Time's Changeling": Autobiography in *The Echoes Return Slow*', *Echoes to the Amen: Essays after R. S. Thomas*, ed. Damian Walford Davies (Cardiff: University of Wales Press, 2003), pp. 183–205.

'The Valleys', *Yn Gymysg Oll i Gyd*, ed. Hywel Teifi Edwards (Llandysul: Gwasg Gomer, 2003), pp. ix–xv.

'Postscript: Reliving the Life', *A Welsh Countryside Revisited: A New Social Study of Llanfihangel yng Ngwynfa* (Welshpool: Powysland Club, 2003), pp. 165–70.

With Daniel Williams, ' "A Sweet Union?": Dylan Thomas and Post-War American Poetry', *I Sang in My Chains: A Tribute to Dylan Thomas*, eds G. Bennett, E. Jenkins and E. Price (Swansea: The Dylan Thomas Society of Great Britain, 2003), pp. 68–79.

Contributions to Works of Reference

Editor of Welsh Studies section, Annotated Bibliography of English Studies European Society for the Study of English, 1997 [on CD-ROM].

Entries on Emyr Humphreys, R. S. Thomas and Glyn Jones, the latter two co-authored with Dr Tony Brown, for ABES.

Entries on D. T. Davies, J. A. Davies, Barbara Hardy, Emyr Humphreys, Gwyneth Lewis, John Pikoulis, *New Welsh Review*, *A Toy Epic*, R. S. Thomas in *Cydymaith i Lenyddiaeth Cymru* and *The New Companion to the Literature of Wales*, ed. Meic Stephens (Cardiff: University of Wales Press, 1998).

Entries on 'New York', the 'British Isles', and 'Labor', for *Walt Whitman: An Encyclopedia*, eds J. R. LeMaster and Donald R. Kummings (New York, London: Garland Publishing, 1998).

Section on modern Wales in *The Oxford Guide to Literature in English Translation*, ed. Peter France (Oxford: Oxford University Press, 2000), pp. 187–9.

Entry on Welsh Writing in English, *Encarta Encyclopaedia Plus 2003*, 2003 [on CD-ROM].

Conference Proceedings

'Emyr Humphreys: Mythic Realist', *Proceedings of the 1990 International Literature of Region and Nation Conference*, eds J. J. Simon and Alain Sinner (Centre Universitaire de Luxembourg, 1991), pp. 264–81.

'Anglo-Welsh Poets and the Welsh Language during the 1980s', *Writing Region and Nation, Proceedings of the 4th International Conference of the Literature of Region and Nation*, eds James A. Davies and Glyn Pursglove (Swansea: special number of *The Swansea Review*, 1994), 511–21.

'Whitman in Translation', transcript of a two-day seminar held at the University of Iowa, March 1992, *Walt Whitman Quarterly Review*, 12, 1 and 2 (Summer/Fall 1996), 1–58.

'Walt Whitman and Risorgimento Nationalism', *Literature of Region and Nation, Proceedings of the 6th International Conference of the Literature of Region and Nation*, vol. I, ed. Winnifred M. Bogaards (Saint John, Canada: University of New Brunswick in Saint John, 1998), pp. 345–67.

'Being Ecumenical with the Truth: Literature and the Politics of Identity in Twentieth-century Wales', *Literature and Politics in the Celtic World: Papers from the Third Australian Conference of Celtic Studies*, University of Sydney, July 1998, eds Pamela O'Neill and Jonathan M. Wooding (Sydney: Foundation for Celtic Studies, University of Sydney, 2000), pp. 94–114.

'Ewtopia: Cyfandir Dychymyg y Cymry', *Cymru a'r Cymry 2000 Wales and the Welsh 2000: Proceedings of the Millennium Conference of the University of Wales Centre for Advanced Welsh and Celtic Studies*, ed. Geraint H. Jenkins (Aberystwyth: Centre for Advanced Welsh and Celtic Studies, 2001), pp. 99–118.

Translations

Books

Dail Glaswellt, tr. from Walt Whitman, *Leaves of Grass*, includes introduction and notes (Cardiff: Academi Gymreig/Welsh Academy, 1995).

Individual translations

'Cymodi', tr. from Walt Whitman, 'Reconciliation', *Golwg* (26 March 1992), 18.
'Cân fy Hunan', tr. from Walt Whitman, 'Song of Myself', *Taliesin*, 78–9 (Winter 1992), 81–6.
'Yr Oedd Plentyn a Âi Allan', tr. from Walt Whitman, 'There Was a Child Went Forth', *Barddas*, 18 (6 October 1992), 14.
'Gwersyll Agored ar Lechwedd Mynydd'; 'Wrth Fflam Wamal y Gwersyll Agored'; 'Corryn Hir Ymarhous, Di-stŵr', tr. from Walt Whitman, 'Bivouac on a Mountain Side'; 'By the Bivouac'; 'A Noiseless, Patient Spider', *Barn*, 369 (October 1993), 20.

Articles

'Y Nofel a Duw ar Drai ar Orwel Pell', *Diwinyddiaeth*, 21 (1970), 3–15.
'"Strangers in a Strange Land": Katherine Anne Porter's *Noon Wine*', *American Literature* (May 1975), 230–46; reprinted in *Contemporary Literary Criticism in the United States*, 10 (1979).
'Rhannu Problem Dwy Iaith', *Y Faner* (5 December 1980), 10–11.
'A Study of Whitman's Late Poetry', *Walt Whitman Review*, 27, 1 (March 1981), 1–14.
'Whitman and the American Democratic Identity, Before and During the Civil War', *Journal of American Studies* (April 1981), 73–93.
'"A New World of Thought": Whitman's Early Reception in England', *Walt Whitman Review*, 27 (2 June 1981), 744–8.
'Agweddau Pellach ar Gymreigrwydd Morgan Llwyd', *Y Traethodydd*, 137 (1982), 141–53.
'Sisial y Sarff: Ymryson oddi mewn i Forgan Llwyd', *Y Traethodydd*, 138 (1983), 173–83.
'Whitman and the Obligations of Memory', *Walt Whitman Quarterly Review*, 28, 24 (September 1982), 43–54.
'Walt Whitman and Mannhatta-New York', *American Quarterly*, 34, 4 (Fall 1982), 362–78.
'Song of Myself and Possessive Individualism', *Delta: revue du centre d'étude et de recherches sur les écrivains du Sud aux États-Unis*, 16 (May 1983), 3–17.
'Ann Griffiths and Morgan Llwyd: A Comparative Study of Two Welsh Mystics', *Studies in Mystical Literature*, 5, 3 (June 1983), 23–39.
'Whitman's Achievements in the Personal Style of *Calamus*', *Walt Whitman Quarterly Review*, 1, 3 (December 1983), 36–47.
'Whitman's *Calamus* and Emerson's *Friendship*', *American Transcendental Quarterly*, 55 (January 1985), 49–61.

'Ceisio a Chael: Perthynas Morgan Llwyd a William Erbery', *Y Traethodydd*, 142 (1987), 38–49.
'Walt Whitman's Welsh Connection: Ernest Rhys', *Anglo-Welsh Review*, 82 (1986), 77–85.
'Airs on a Shoe String', *Planet*, 63 (June/July 1987), 3–8.
'Mosaic', *Taliesin*, 60 (Christmas 1987), 102–4.
'English Budgerigars & Welsh Publishers: Public Funding in Wales', *Book News from Wales* (Autumn 1987), 5–6.
'*Llyfr y Tri Aderyn* a Beibl Morgan Llwyd', *Y Traethodydd*, 143 (1988), 147–58.
'*My People* and the Revenge of the Novel', *New Welsh Review*, 1 (Summer 1988), 17–22.
'Cymru: Gwlad Dychymyg y Sais', *Taliesin*, 61 (March 1988), 94–100.
'Y Ddau Alun: Alun Lewis ac Alun Llywelyn Williams', *Taliesin*, 64 (October 1988), 25–35.
'Raymond Williams's Medium', *Book News from Wales* (Autumn 1988), 5–6.
'Hanes Dwy Chwaer: Olrhain Hanes y Tri Llais I', *Barn*, 312 (January 1989), 23–5.
'Hanes Dwy Chwaer: Olrhain Hanes y Tri Llais II', *Barn*, 313 (February 1989), 23–5.
'Yma o Hyd: Delwedd o Gymru', *Taliesin*, 67 (August 1989), 94–8.
'Raymond Williams a Llên Cymru', *Efrydiau Athronyddol*, 52 (1989), 32–47.
'The Poetry of Emyr Humphreys', *Poetry Wales*, 25, 2 (September 1989), 10–12.
'Tu Hwnt i'r Llen', *Taliesin*, 70 (July 1990), 54–61.
'Flintshire and the Regional Weather Forecast', *New Welsh Review*, 8 (Summer 1990), 10–15.
'The Relentlessness of Emyr Humphreys', *New Welsh Review*, 13 (Summer 1991), 37–40.
'Iaith Newid y Byd: Yr Angen am Chwyldroadwyr', *Golwg*, 12 (March 1992), 19–21.
'Morgan Llwyd a Hanes y Presennol yn y Gorffennol', *Y Cofiadur*, 57 (May 1992), 4–15.
'From Walt to Waldo: Whitman's Welsh Admirers', *Walt Whitman Quarterly Review*, 10, 2 (Fall 1992), 61–73.
' "Unfamiliar Affections": Dylan Thomas and the Novelists', *Swansea Review*, 10 (Autumn 1992), 45–53.
'Reviewing R. S.', *Books in Wales* (Summer 1993), 5–7.
'Barddonia[i]th Saesneg yn y Gymru Gyfoes', *Taliesin*, 83 (Winter 1993), 102–7.
'Peter Pan a'r Pentecost: Golwg ar Gerddi Rhyfel Diweddar', *Barddas*, 195–6 (July/August 1993), 28–33.
'R. S. Thomas: Bardd Enbydrwydd Bywyd', *Barn* (May 1993), 40–1.

'Dadeni Gwefreiddiol a Chwarae Bach', *Golwg*, 26 (August 1993), 20–1.
'Llenyddiaeth a'r Famiaith', *Golwg*, 9 (September 1993), 20–1.
'Revisiting Welsh Castles: The Recent Poetry of Tony Conran', *Swansea Review*, 12 (1994), 21–6.
'Whitman's Tale of Two Cities', *American Literary History*, 6, 4 (Winter 1994), 633–57.
'Hidden Attachments: Aspects of the Two Literatures of Modern Wales', *Welsh Writing in English: A Yearbook of Critical Essays*, 1 (1995), pp. 145–63.
'Glyn Jones: 1905–95: Teyrnged', *Barn*, 388 (May 1995), 11.
'Amgylchu'r Cylchgronau', *Llais Llyfrau*, 2, 95 (Summer 1995), 8–9.
'On Translating Whitman's Poetry into Welsh', *Modern Poetry in Translation*, New Series, 7 (Spring 1995), 202–3.
'O na bai Walt yn Gymro!', *Barn*, 393 (October 1995), 24–5.
'No Englishman: Wales's Henry Vaughan', *Swansea Review*, 15 (1995), 1–19.
'R. S. Thomas: War Poet', *Welsh Writing in English: A Yearbook of Critical Essays*, 2 (1996), pp. 82–97.
'Wales and Postcolonialism', responses to questionnaire, *S.P.A.N., Journal of the South Pacific Association for Commonwealth Literature and Language Studies*, 41 (October 1995), 56–60.
'Pennar Davies y Llenor', *Y Traethodydd*, 152 (1997), 83–8.
'"All Lenient Muscles Tensed": The Poetry of Roland Mathias', *Poetry Wales*, 33, 3 (January 1998), 21–6.
'"Never Seek to Tell thy Love": Rhys Davies's Fiction', *Welsh Writing in English: A Yearbook of Critical Essays*, 4 (1998), pp. 1–21.
'"*In Occidentem & Tenebras*": Putting Henry Vaughan on the Map of Wales', *Scintilla*, 2 (1998), 7–24.
'Weathering the Storm: Whitman and the Civil War', *Walt Whitman Quarterly Review*, 15, 2/3 (Autumn 1998), 87–109.
'Irony in the Soul: The Religious Poetry of R. Socrates Thomas', *Agenda*, 36, 2 (Winter 1998), 49–69.
'"Keeping the Rhondda for Wales": The Case of James Kitchener Davies', *Transactions of the Honourable Society of Cymmrodorion*, New Series, 6 (2000), 119–34.
'"He Belongs to the English": Welsh Dylan and Welsh-language Culture', *Swansea Review*, 20 (2000), 122–34.
'Wales', 'Translation and Nation', *New Comparison*, 29 (Spring 2000), 108–14.
'Remembering R. S. Thomas: A Great Religious Poet of the Calvinistic Sublime', *New Welsh Review*, 51 (2000–1), 12–13.
'R. S.: Teyrnged', *Barddas*, 260 (2000–1), 18–19.
'R. S. Thomas, 1913–2000', *A470*, 11 (Autumn 2000), 2–3.
'R. S. Thomas: A Tribute', *Transactions of the Honourable Society of Cymmrodorion*, New Series, 6 (2000), 7–8.

'Dylanwadau: Dylan Thomas a Llenorion Cymraeg', *Taliesin*, 112 (Summer 2001), 13–29.
'Menna Elfyn: Flying by the Seat of her Panties', *New Welsh Review*, 53 (Summer 2001), 4–7.
'Gwlad o Bosibiliadau: Golwg ar Lên Cymru ac America', *Y Traethodydd*, 157 (2002), 38–52.
'Gwenallt: The Welsh Anti-capitalist', *New Welsh Review*, 57 (Summer 2002), 83–8.
'Saethu'r BWLET', *Taliesin*, 116 (Eisteddfod 2002), 124–6.
'In Memoriam: Roger Asselineau, 1915–2002', *Walt Whitman Quarterly Review*, 20, 2 (Fall 2002), 97–8.
'Cyfiethu: Cynnyrch Cyffindir Iaith', *Taliesin*, 118 (Spring 2003), 109–13.
'Between Here and Now: The Recent Work of Christine Kinsey', *The David Jones Journal*, 4, 1–2 (Winter 2002/Spring 2003), 130–3.

Reviews

Alun Lewis: A Miscellany, ed. John Pikoulis, *Anglo-Welsh Review*, 74 (1983), 92–6.
Jeremy Hooker, *A View from the Source*, *Anglo-Welsh Review*, 75 (1983), 90–2.
Twentieth Century Welsh Poems, ed. and tr. Joseph P. Clancy, *Anglo-Welsh Review*, 75 (1984), 88–95.
Pennar Davies, *E. Tegla Davies*, *Anglo-Welsh Review*, 77 (1984), 114–16.
J. Kimberley Roberts, *Ernest Rhys*, *Welsh History Review*, 12 (1984), 453–4.
Jan Morris, *The Matter of Wales*, *Book News from Wales* (Spring 1985), 10–11.
Emyr Humphreys, *Salt of the Earth*, *Book News from Wales* (Summer 1985), 7–8.
R. S. Thomas, *Growing Thoughts*, *Book News from Wales* (Autumn 1985), 8–9.
Common Ground, ed. Susan Butler, *Book News from Wales* (Winter 1985), 8–9.
John Pikoulis, *Alun Lewis: A Life*, *Anglo-Welsh Review*, 78 (1985), 90–4.
John Davies, *The Visitor's Book*, *Anglo-Welsh Review*, 81 (1985), 114–17.
The Plays of Saunders Lewis, vol. I, ed. and tr. Joseph P. Clancy, *Planet*, 52 (August/September 1985), 116–18.
The Oxford Companion to the Literatures of Wales, ed. Meic Stephens, *Book News from Wales* (Spring 1986), 3–5.
Emyr Humphreys, *An Absolute Hero*, *Planet*, 55 (February/March 1986), 105–6.
Roland Mathias, *A Ride Through the Wood*, *Book News from Wales* (Summer 1986), 8.

Gareth Alban Davies, *Trigain*, *Barddas*, 13 (September 1986), 15.
Kingsley Amis, *The Old Devils*, *Book News from Wales* (Summer 1987), 7–8.
The Welsh Connection, ed. W. Tydeman, *Book News from Wales* (Summer 1987), 11.
Jeremy Hooker, *The Presence of the Past*, *Book News from Wales* (Autumn 1987), 10–11.
Wiliam Owen Roberts, *Y Pla*; Geraint Lewis, *Y Malwod a Storïau Eraill*, *Llais Llyfrau* (Winter 1987), 14–15.
Douglas Houston, *With the Offal Eaters*, *Anglo-Welsh Review*, 87 (1987), 117–18.
Vernon Watkins, *The Collected Poems*, *Poetry Wales*, 22, 2 (1987), 87–9.
Welsh Verse, ed. and tr. Tony Conran, *Poetry Wales*, 22, 4 (1987), 79–81.
Morgan Llwyd, ed. P. J. Donavan, *Welsh History Review*, 13 (1987), 501–2.
Robert Shulman, *Social Criticism and Nineteenth-Century American Fiction*; Donald E. Pease, *Visionary Compacts: American Renaissance Writings in Cultural Context*, *Walt Whitman Quarterly Review*, 6, 2 (1988), 97–101.
Emyr Humphreys, *Open Secrets*, *Book News from Wales* (Summer 1988), 5–6.
Malcolm Kelsall, *Byron's Politics*, *Swansea Review*, 5 (November 1988), 51–5.
Caradoc Evans, *Nothing to Pay*, *New Welsh Review*, 5 (Summer 1989), 81–5.
The Gregynog Poets Series, *Poetry Wales*, 25, 2 (September 1989), 62–3.
Betsy Erkkila, *Walt Whitman: The Political Poet*, *Walt Whitman Quarterly Review*, 7, 1 (Summer 1989), 28–32.
Helen Fulton, *Dafydd ap Gwilym in the European Context*, *Wales on Sunday* (17 December 1989), 14.
'Karl's Darl: A Biography of Faulkner', *London Review of Books* (11 January 1990), 12–13.
Ioan Williams, *Capel a Chomin*, *Planet*, 80 (April/May 1990), 105–6.
R. S. Thomas, *Counterpoint*, *Golwg*, 23 (November 1990), 22–3.
Poetry Wales: 25 Years, ed. Cary Archard, *Book News from Wales* (Spring 1991), 10.
Wiliam Owen Roberts, *Pestilence*, *New Welsh Review*, 13 (Summer 1991), 46–7.
Graham Clarke, *Walt Whitman: The Poem as Private History*, *Walt Whitman Quarterly Review*, 9, 1 (Summer 1991), 30–2.
Christopher Meredith, *Griffri*, *Golwg*, 27 (February 1992), 18.
Whitman in His Time, ed. Joel Myerson, *Walt Whitman Quarterly Review*, 9, 1 (Summer 1991), 30–2.
Robin Llywelyn, *Seren Wen ar Gefndir Gwyn*, *Barn*, 357 (Autumn 1992), 41.
John Rowlands, *Ysgrifau ar y Nofel*, *Llais Llyfrau* (Winter 1992), 16–17.
Nigel Jenkins, *John Tripp*, *Llên Cymru*, 17 (1993), 339–40.
R. S. Thomas, *Mass for Hard Times*, *Golwg*, 21 (January 1993), 18.
Critical Essays on R. S. Thomas, ed. Sandra Anstey, *Planet*, 99 (June/July 1993), 99.

Derec Llwyd Morgan, *Ni Cheir Byth Wir Lle bo Llawer o Feirdd*, *Taliesin*, 81 (Summer 1993), 91–5.

Dana Gioia, *Can Poetry Matter?*, *Acumen*, 18 (October 1993), 90–2.

Saunders Lewis: Selected Poems, ed. and tr. Joseph P. Clancy; *Euros Bowen: Priest-Poet*, ed. and tr. Cynthia Davies, *New Welsh Review*, 21 (Summer 1993), 105–7.

James Dougherty, *Walt Whitman and the Citizen's Eye*, *Nineteenth-century American Literature*, 48, 3 (December 1993), 373–6.

'"When Hollywood Comes to Holyhead", Hedd Wyn, Armageddon Poet', *Times Literary Supplement* (25 March 1994), 18.

M. J. Van Buren, *Waiting: The Religious Poetry of Ronald Stuart Thomas: Welsh Priest and Poet*, *Planet*, 106 (1994), 108.

Six from Sinclair Stevens, *Acumen*, 20 (1994), 84–6.

Don Coles, *Someone has Stayed in Stockholm*; Peter Porter, *Millennial Fables*, *Acumen*, 21 (1995), 93–5.

Gweithiau Morgan Llwyd o Wynedd, III, J. Graham Jones, Goronwy Wyn Owen, *Taliesin*, 89 (Spring 1995), 117–20.

Ed Folsom, *Whitman's Native Representations*, *American Literature*, 67, 1 (March 1995), 151–2.

Douglas Houston, *Hunters in the Snow*; Carole Satyamurti, *Striking Distance*, *Acumen*, 22 (May 1995), 82–4.

Fire Green as Grass, ed. Belinda Humfrey, *New Welsh Review*, 29 (Summer 1995), 92–4.

Charles Simic, *Frightening Toys*, *Acumen*, 23 (September 1995), 85–8.

Ralph Maud, *Wales in His Arms: Dylan Thomas's Choice of Welsh Poetry*, *Planet*, 110 (April/May 1995), 96–8.

Menna Elfyn, *Eucalyptus*; Gwyneth Lewis, *Parables and Faxes*, *Barddas*, 223 (November 1995), 22–4.

R. S. Thomas, *No Truce with the Furies*, *Poetry Wales*, 31, 3 (January 1996), 60–1.

Harri Webb, *Collected Poems*, *New Welsh Review*, 32 (April 1996), 103–4.

W. S. Merwin, *The Vixen*, *Acumen*, 25 (May 1996), 83–5.

Sam Adams, *Roland Mathias*, *Planet*, 117 (June/July 1996), 105–6.

Nicholas Murray, *A Life of Matthew Arnold*, *Planet*, 120 (December 1996/January 1997), 104–6.

Catherine Merriman, *State of Desire*, *New Welsh Review*, 35 (Winter 1996/97), 90–1.

Kate Clancy, *Slattern*; Ifgenija Simonovic, *Striking Root*, *Acumen*, 27 (June 1997), 90–2.

Walt Whitman: The Contemporary Reviews, ed. Kenneth M. Price, *Journal of American Studies*, 3 (December 1997), 440–1.

Justin Wintle, *Furious Interiors: Wales, R. S. Thomas and God*; Elaine Shepherd, *R. S. Thomas: Conceding an Absence*, *New Welsh Review*, 36 (Spring 1997), 82–4.

Gregory Eiselein, *Literature and Humanitarian Reform in the Civil War Era*, Whitman Quarterly Review, 14, 4 (Spring 1997), 186–9.

Denise Levertov, *Tesserae*; Jenny Joseph, *Extended Similes*, Acumen, 29 (September 1997), 89–92.

Collected Stories of Rhys Davies, ed. Meic Stephens, Planet, 126 (December 1997/January 1998), 101–3.

R. S. Thomas, *Autobiographies*, tr. Jason Walford Davies, Taliesin, 99 (October 1997), 116–18.

Tony Conran, *Frontiers in Anglo-Welsh Poetry*, New Welsh Review, 38 (Autumn 1997), 86–8.

Gerwyn Wiliams, *Tir Neb*, Welsh History Review, 19, 2 (December 1998), 367–8.

Gillian Clarke, *Collected Poems*, Books in Wales (Summer 1998), 12–13.

Jim Perrin, *Spirits of Place and Visions of Snowdonia*, New Welsh Review, 42 (Summer 1998), 20–3.

Emyr Humphreys, *Collected Poems*, New Welsh Review, 44 (Spring 1999), 82–4.

Sheri Ceniza, *Walt Whitman and Nineteenth-Century Women Reformers*, Walt Whitman Quarterly Review, 16, 2 (Fall 1998), 96–9.

Glyn Jones, *Collected Short Stories*, ed. Tony Brown, Taliesin, 107 (Autumn 1999), 117–18.

J. Loving, *Walt Whitman: The Song of Himself*, Journal of American Studies, 34 (2000), 179–80.

A Nation and its Books: A History of the Book in Wales, eds P. H. Jones and E. Rees, The Papers of the Bibliographical Society of America, 94, 2 (2000), 299–301.

Y Sêr yn eu Graddau, ed. John Rowlands, Taliesin, 111 (Spring 2001), 143–5.

Menna Elfyn, *Cusan Dyn Dall: Blind Man's Kiss*, New Welsh Review, 53 (Summer 2001), 4–7.

Angharad Price, *Robin Llywelyn*, www.gwales.com, Welsh Books Council website (Summer 2001).

Gwenallt, *Cerddi Cyflawn*, New Welsh Review, 56 (Spring 2002), 83–8.

Goronwy Wyn Owen, *Rhwng Calfin a Böhme: Golwg ar Syniadaeth Morgan Llwyd*, Taliesin, 119 (Summer 2003), 161–4.

Mark Maslan, *Whitman Possessed: Poetry, Sexuality and Popular Authority*, Walt Whitman Quarterly Review, 20, 3–4 (Winter/Spring 2003), 177–9.

Published Interviews

'An Interview with Rita Dove by M. W. Thomas', *Modern American Poetry* (12 August 1995); reprinted as 'Rita Dove talks to M. Wynn Thomas', *Swansea Review*, 19 (2000), 158–63. Also published at: www.english.uiuc.edu/maps/poets/a-f/dove/mwthomas.htm.

Conversations 1: Interview with Helen Vendler, Swansea Review, 16 (1996), 1–8.

Conversations 2: Interview with Jorie Graham, Swansea Review, 16 (1996), 8–15.

Conversations 1: Interview with Les Murray, Swansea Review, 17 (1997), 1–10.

Conversations 2: Interview with Denise Levertov, Swansea Review, 17 (1997), 11–15.

Index

Aaron, Jane 38, 42
Abercanaid 118, 119
Abercynon 87
Aberfan 119
Abergavenny Eisteddfod (1842) 162
Abergwesyn 91
Abse, Dannie 38, 42, 43–6, 50–1, 223–36
  After Every Green Thing 223, 226–7, 235
  'Anniversary' 229
  Ash on a Young Man's Sleeve 44, 224, 225–6, 227–8
  'At Ogmore-by-Sea this August Evening' 233
  'Autumn' 225
  'Boasts of Hywel ab Owain Gwynedd, The' 233
  'Clock, The' 227
  Collected Poems 223, 230
  'Descent, The' 227
  'Down the M4' 233
  'Duality' 228
  'Elegy for Dylan Thomas' 224–5, 230, 233
  'Enter the Movement' 231
  'Field, The' 228
  'Funland' 229
  'Ghost' 227
  'Go Home the Act is Over' 225, 230, 231–2
  Goodbye 20th Century 43–4
  'Journey, The' 224
  'Journeys and Faces' 227
  'Lament of Heledd' 233
  'Leaving Cardiff' 235
  'Letter from Ogmore-by-Sea, A' 233
  'Meurig Dafydd to his Mistress' 233
  'Moment, The' 229
  New and Collected Poems 232
  'Ordinary Heaven' 227
  'Photograph and Yellow Tulips' ('Photograph and White Tulips') 224, 228
  'Poem and Message' 229
  'Poem at 4 a.m.' 227
  'Poem to a Younger Poet' 223
  Poems Golders Green 1956–61 225
  'Portrait of a Marriage' 227
  'Posy for Summer, A' 224, 227
  'Prufrock at the Seaside' 229–30
  'Psychosis' 223
  'Quench' 231
  'Return to Cardiff' 232, 233
  'Sea-shell for Vernon Watkins, A' 233
  'Sons' 232
  Strong Dose of Myself, A 234
  Tenants of the House 224, 227–9, 230
  'Tenants of the House' 225, 230–1
  'Thankyou Note' 235
  'Trial, The' 228
  Twentieth Century Anglo-Welsh Poetry (ed.) 224, 232, 233–5
  'Uninvited, The' 223, 235
  Walking Under Water 224, 227
  'Wall, A' 233
  'Welcome, The' 227
  Welsh Retrospective 232, 233
  'Welsh Valley Cinema 1930s' 235
  White Coat, Purple Coat 231–2
  'Yellow Bird, The' 223
Act of Union 60
Aelwyd Angharad 12, 16
Alexandria 194
Allchin, A. M. 210

Allingham, Helen 13
American Communist Party (CPUSA) 142
American Literature 100
American Wales 10, 133
Améry, Jean 44–5, 46
Amis, Kingsley 234
Amserau, Yr (newspaper) 179
Anderson, Benedict 195
Anglesey 168
Anglican Church 118, 159, 161, 207, 208, 211
Anglo-Welsh writing / literature / poetry 17, 226, 233–4, 235–6
Anthropos *see* Rowland, Robert David
anti-colonialism 57, 58
anti-semitism 39, 40, 41, 42, 43, 44, 45–6, 47, 50, 190, 226, 228
Applebee, Elaine 76
Aristippus 187
Armstrong, Louis 134
Arnold, Matthew 188–9, 233, 238
Athens 194
Auden, W. H. 241, 247
Auschwitz 44

Baker, Houston A. 136, 138, 140–1
Baker, John 12–13
Bala 11
Balkans, the 188
Barber, Benjamin
    'Jihad vs. McWorld' 191
Barddoniaeth Dafydd ab Gwilym see Myfyr, Owen
Barrie, J. M. 12
    Auld Licht Idylls 12
    Little Minister, The 12
    Margaret Ogilvy 12
    Peter Pan 12
    Window in Thrums, A 12, 13
Barrymore, Ethel 133
Bates, H. E. 21, 22, 24
Bateson, F. W. 138
Bateson, Gregory 190
Baugh, Edward 245
Beckett, Samuel 198
Beddoe, Deirdre
    Out of the Shadows 86

Benhall 23, 35
Bethesda 18
Bhabha, Homi 250
Bidgood, Ruth 90–3
    'Heol y Mwyn' 91–2
    'Slate-Quarry, Penceulan' 91, 92–3
Blake, William 110
Blue Books controversy (1847) 10, 58, 73–4
border / borders 24, 35, 206–20
Bosse-Griffiths, Kate 46–7, 48, 50, 51
    Mae'r Galon wrth y Llyw 47
Boston 101, 102
Bowdler, Thomas 165
Boym, Svetlana
    Future of Nostalgia, The 210
Brennan, Timothy
    At Home in the World: Cosmopolitanism Now 193
Brinnin, J. M. 230
Britain 60, 142, 161, 177, 188, 198, 210
Brittan, Arthur 72
Brittany 189
Bromwich, Rachel 163
Brycheiniog 213
Budapest 128
Burns, Robert 169–70
Bute, Lady 59
Bwlch-y-gwynt 18

Caernarfonshire 24, 25, 29, 31, 33
Callahan, John F. 142
Calvinism 62, 67
Cambrian, The 159
Cambrian Quarterly Magazine, The 159, 160
Canetti, Elias 225
Cardiff 22, 42, 59, 74, 225, 232
Cardiganshire 1, 15, 18
Caribbean, the 237, 238
Carnhuanawc (Thomas Price) 160
Cassell, John 174, 177, 179
Castells, Manuel 191, 194
Castle Rackrent (Maria Edgeworth) 24
Castries 239–40
Cathleen ní Houlihan 64
Ceiriog (John Ceiriog Hughes) 9, 15, 62, 67, 138

Index

'Alun Mabon' 15
Cenhadwr Americanaidd, Y
  (periodical) 178, 179
Ceredigion 49
Chagall, Marc 127
Chaucer, Geoffrey 162
Chechnya 190
cities 194–6
Clarke, Gillian 234
Coffey, Brian 198
Coleridge, S. T. 125
Collier, Catrin (Karen Watkin) 94, 96
  Past Remembering 94
colonialism 58, 135, 241–2, 246
colonized 57, 58, 60
colonizer 58
colony / colonies 188
'Commonwealth' literature 238
Communism 75, 78
Connell, R. W. 72, 81
Constantinople 117, 124, 194
Cornwall 189
Corwen 12, 13
cosmopolitanism 187–8, 190, 191, 193–4, 195, 196, 197
  see also macrocosmopolitanism, microcosmopolitanism
Coulmas, Peter 187–8, 189
  Weltbürger: Geschichte einer Menschheitssehnsucht 187–8
country 8–9, 11–19, 22, 23, 35, 194–6
Cowen, Laurence
  Joneses, The 16
Creunant 88
Cronin, Michael
  Across the Lines 192
Crosland, T. W. H.
  Taffy was a Welshman 16
Cruikshank, George 174
Crwys (W. Crwys Williams) 16
  'Gwerin Cymru' 16
Curtis, Tony 48, 234
Cyfaill, Y (periodical) 177–8, 179, 180–1, 182
Cylch Cadwgan 47
Cylchgrawn, Y (periodical) 177, 178
Cymmrodorion Society 159

Cymru (periodical) 11, 14, 17
Cymru Fydd 65
Cymru Fydd: Cylchgrawn y Blaid Genedlaethol Gymreig
  (periodical) 60, 61
Cymru'r Plant (periodical) 11, 15

Dafydd ap Gwilym 62, 67, 158–70
  'Echo Rock, The' 167–8
  'Morvyth's Pilgrimage' 168
  'Offeren y Llwyn' ('The Woodland Mass') 162–4
  'Peat Pool, The' 167
  'To an Echo in Snowdon' 168
  'Trafferth mewn Tafarn' ('Trouble in a Tavern') 164, 166
  'Wylan, Yr' ('The Seagull') 166
Dafydd Nanmor 62
Dame Wales 59–60
Davies, Aneirin Talfan 246
Davies, Arthur Llewelyn 12
Davies, Idris 84
Davies, James A. 244
Davies, John 235
Davies, Rhys 84
Davies, Stevie 208–9
Davies, Walford 103, 106, 108, 109
Delanty, Gerard 194, 197
  Citizenship in a Global Age 197
Denbigh 21, 24
Denmark 117
Devlin, Denis 198
diaspora 42, 46, 65, 182, 197, 198–9
Dickens, Charles 176, 177
Diogenes 187
disestablishment 61, 62
dissent *see* Nonconformity
Donne, John 210, 218
  Devotions 234
Douglass, Frederick 178
Dublin 194
Dyffryn Nantlle 22

Earle, Jean 234
Edelman, Maurice 39
Edwards, Hywel Teifi 59
Edwards, J. M. 8, 14
  'Aradr, Yr' 8

'Pentref, Y' 8
'Pentrefi Cymru' 8
Edwards, O. M. 9–12, 14–15, 16, 17, 18
  Clych Atgof 12
Ehrenberg, Ilya 45
Eliot, T. S. 225, 226–30, 233, 235, 241, 246, 247
  'Ash Wednesday' 229
  Burnt Norton 227
  East Coker 229
  Four Quartets 226–7, 228
  'Gerontion' 226, 228
  Hollow Men, The 226, 227
  Little Gidding 228
  'Love Song of Alfred J. Prufrock, The' 226, 227, 228, 229
  'Metaphysical Poets, The' 210
  'Portrait of a Lady' 227
  Prufrock and Other Observations 226
  Waste Land, The 226
Ellison, Ralph 133–5, 136, 138–9, 140, 142, 143–4
  'In a Strange Country' 139, 140, 141–4
  Invisible Man 133, 134, 135, 136, 138–40, 142
  'Red Cross at Morriston, Swansea, S.W., The' 133–4
Emerson, Ralph Waldo 174
Emrys ap Iwan (Robert Ambrose Jones) 3
England 8–9, 18, 39, 41, 58, 102, 118, 176–7, 189, 198, 213, 239
English Association 237
English language 14–15, 22, 158, 159, 160, 161, 174, 182, 196, 199, 208, 237, 239
English literature 9, 100, 237–50
Englishness 9
Erasmus, Desiderius 187
Eriugena, Johannes Scotus 198
Eryri (Snowdon) 121
European Union 191
Evans, Caradoc 14, 15–18, 19, 71
  My People 14, 15, 16–17
Evans, D. Gareth 73
Evans, Evan Eynon 77

Cold Coal 72, 76, 77, 79–81
Evans, Margiad (Peggy Whistler) 21–9, 30, 31, 32, 33, 34–6
  Autobiography 29
  'Boy Who Called For a Light, The' 26, 34
  Country Dance 23, 24
  'Lost Fisherman, The' 28, 29, 34–5
  'Mrs Pike's Eldorado' 26
  Old and the Young, The 26–9, 33, 34–5
  'Old and the Young, The' 33, 34
  'Old Woman and the Wind, The' 25
  'People of his Pasture' 27
  'Ruin, The' 27–8
  'Solomon' 33
  'Thomas Griffiths and Parson Cope' 26
Everett, Robert 178–80, 183

F. S. 159
Farjeon, Eleanor 220
feminism 57–8, 65
feminist 57–8, 63, 64
feminization 58
Finkielkraut, Alain
  Défaite de la pensée, La 191
First World War 9, 12, 35, 42
Fisher, Philip 175–6
Fitzgibbon, Constantine 230
Fogg Museum (Harvard) 101, 102
Foley, Barbara 142, 143
Ford, John 133
fractal differentialism 192–3
France 188, 189
Francis, J. O. (John Oswald Francis) 17, 71, 75
  Change 71–6, 77
French Revolution 57
Friedman, Jonathan 191
Frost, Robert 206, 217–20
  'After Apple-Picking' 218
  'Death of the Hired Man, The' 219
  'Iris By Night' 220
  'Mending Wall' 218
  'Road Not Taken, The' 219–20

Gallie, Menna 88

The Small Mine 88–9
Garthmyl 159
gender 1, 57, 72, 81, 86, 175
Germany 41, 46, 47, 117, 126, 188
ghetto 39, 50
Glamorgan 59, 77, 167
Glieck, James 192
globalization 191, 193, 194, 197
Gower 101
Grand, Sarah 63
Grimm's Fairy Tales 24
Gruffudd, Heini 46
Gruffudd, Robat 46–7
Guedalla, Philip 138
Gwallter Mechain (Walter Davies) 160
'Gwarth Y Cymro Sydd Yn Gwadu Iaith ei Wlad' 180–1
Gwenallt (David James Jones) 159
gwerin 10, 15, 16, 17, 18, 73–4, 76, 79, 81
Gwynedd 167

Habad Hasidism 123
Hall, Lady Augusta (Llanover) 160
Hardy, Sir Alister 85
Hardy, Barbara 39
Hardy, Thomas 32–3
Harper, Michael S. 119
    'Visit to Abercanaid: for Denise Levertov' 119
Harries, Howel 67
Harris, J. P. 183
Heaney, Seamus 115
Hebrew 48
Hemingway, Ernest 225
Henry VII (Harry Tudor) 60
Henry VIII 60
Herbert, George 213
Herefordshire 23, 210
Herman, Josef 47–8, 50, 51
    'Strange Son of the Valley, A' 48
Herman, Nini 48
Herring, Robert 23–4
hiraeth 208, 211, 214, 218
history of translation 197–9
Hobsbawm, Eric 195
Hofer, Johannes 209–10
Holocaust 42, 43, 44, 45, 46, 47, 229

Holywell 117, 118, 119–20
home 29, 35, 42, 43, 49, 65, 119, 122, 214–15, 216–17, 219, 224
Hooker, Jeremy 234
Hopkins, Gerard Manley 101
Houston, Douglas 235
Hughes, T. Rowland 18
    Chwalfa 18
Hughes, Ted 211
Huntington, Samuel 191

Iconoclasts, the 124
Ifor Hael 166
Ilford (Essex) 117, 118
Independent, The (periodical) 178, 183
Industrial Revolution 9
Inismore 192
Innes, C. L. 59
International Monetary Fund 191
Iolo Morganwg (Edward Williams) 10, 50, 159, 166–7, 168, 170
    'Dream, The' 167
    Poems, Lyric and Pastoral 158
    'Summer, The' (orig. attributed to Dafydd ap Gwilym) 160, 167
Ireland 64, 186–7, 189, 191, 192–3, 194–5, 196, 197–9
Irish language 186, 196, 197–8, 199
Israel 46, 48–9

Jackson, Lawrence 139
James, Henry 242, 244
Jameson, Storm 22, 30, 32
Jenkins, David 15–16
Jewish emancipation 39
Jewishness 38, 41, 42, 43–4, 45–7, 50, 51, 233
Johnes, Arthur James (Maelog) 159–70
    Essay on the Causes which have produced Dissent from the Established Church in the Principality of Wales 159, 161–2
    Philological Proofs of the Original Unity and Recent Origin of the Human Race. Derived from a Comparison of the Languages of Asia, Europe, Africa, and America 160–1

Translations into English Verse from the Poems of Davyth ap Gwilym 159, 160, 162–70
Johnson, Arthur Tyssilio
  Perfidious Welshman, The 16
Johnson, Pamela Hansford 244
Jones, Angel 123
Jones, David 206, 211, 235
Jones, Edward (Bardd y Brenin)
  Bardic Museum 159
Jones, Glyn 84
Jones, Gwyn 22, 23–4, 84, 223, 226
Jones, Jack 77–8
  Bidden to the Feast 78
  Land of My Fathers 72, 76, 77–9, 81
  Rhondda Roundabout 78
Jones, LeRoi
  Blues People 144
Jones, Lewis 84
Jones, Maggie Pryce 88
  Kingfisher of Hope 88
Jones, Marian Henry 159
Jones, Sonia Birch 39
Joyce, James 198
Judaism 40, 41, 47

Kant, Immanuel 125
Karachi 194
Keats, John 10, 241
Kipling, Rudyard 243
Kossuth, Lajos 159
Krayer, Stevie 49–50, 51
  'Displaced Person' 49, 50
  'Teifi Pools' 49–50
  'Voices from a Burning Boat' 50

labour movement 74, 75, 86
Ladurie, Emmanuel Leroy
  Montaillou 192
'Lady Gwen, or the days that are to be' 60–8
Landore 87
Larkin, Philip 233
Laugharne 101, 102, 230
Leavis, F. R. 241, 242
Levertoff, Beatrice 116, 117, 118–22, 124, 127, 128, 129, 130
Levertoff, Olga 116, 117, 123

Levertoff, Paul 117–18, 124, 125–6, 129–30
Levertov, Denise 116–30
  '90th Year, The' 122
  'Arrival (North Wales 1897), An' 119–20
  'Day the Audience Walked Out on Me and Why, The' 129
  'From a Notebook, October '68 – May '69' 122
  'Illustrious Ancestors' 122
  'Instant, The' 120–1
  'Link' 120–1, 127–8
  'Nightingale Road' 119
  Tesserae 116, 117, 122, 123–6, 127, 128
  'Vron Woods (North Wales), The' 120
  'Web' 126–7
Levi, Primo 44
Levy, Mervyn 39
Lewis, Alun 234
  'All Day it has Rained' 225
Liberal Party 15, 74, 75
Liberalism 75
liberalism 197
Lincoln, Abraham 173
Llangarron 23, 26, 29
Llangrannog 15
Llanuwchllyn 9, 11, 14
Llewellyn, Richard 133
  How Green Was My Valley 133
Lloyd-Morgan, Ceridwen 29
Llwyd, Angharad 160
Llwynypia 90
Llŷn 141
Llyn Tegid 9, 18
Lockwood Library (University of Buffalo) 101
London 39, 75, 77, 87, 125, 137, 138, 177, 194, 215, 225, 239
Lord, Peter 47
Louvain 198
Lukacs, Georg 210

Mabinogion 23
McCray, Florine Thayer 174–5, 182
McFarland, Thomas

Romanticism and the Forms of Ruin 125
McGreevy, Thomas 198
Mac Grianna, Seosamh 186
 Bhreatain Bheag, An 186
McIntosh, Alastair 199
Mackenzie, Compton 138
macrocosmopolitanism 188–90, 191, 196, 200
Maelog *see* Johnes, Arthur James
Magner, Eugene 101–2
Mandelbrot, Benoît 192
Marches of Wales 206
margin /margins 35
Marlowe, Christopher 239
Maro, Judith 49, 50, 51
 Hen Wlad Newydd 48–9
Martinus Hiberniensis 198
Marvell, Andrew 218, 241
masculinism 71–81
masculinity / masculinities 58, 72, 73, 74–5, 76, 77, 80, 81
Masson, Ursula 68
Mathias, Roland 234
Maud, Ralph 103
Melmoth, Sidney 160
memory 12, 13–14, 33–5, 118, 196, 209
Menai, Huw 84
Meredith, Christopher 235
Merioneth 12, 14
Merthyr Tydfil 84, 117
metaphysicals / metaphysical poetry 206–14, 215, 217–18
Mexico City 194
microcosmopolitanism 189–96, 197, 199, 200
Miller, Jill
 You Can't Kill the Spirit 93–4
Millward, E. G. 175, 179
Milton, John 234
Miners' Strike (1984–5) 93
Minhinnick, Robert 234
Monmouthshire 59, 136, 137
Monreale 124
Montreal 194
Moore, George 195
Morgan, Clare 23
Morgan, Derec Llwyd 35

Morgan, Elaine 85–6, 87–8, 90, 93
 Descent of Woman, The 85–6
 Struggle or Starve 87–8, 95, 96
Morgan, Olive 88, 90
Morgan, Prys 161
Morris, Desmond 85
Morton, H. V.
 In Search of England 9
Mother Ireland 59
Mountain Ash 87
Mumford, Lewis 194
Myfyr, Owen and William Owen Pughe (eds)
 Barddoniaeth Dafydd ab Gwilym 158, 159, 161, 163, 164, 166–7

Napoleon, Emperor 128
nation, the 57–8, 59, 61, 64, 66, 68
National Eisteddfod
 (1911) 16
 (1913) 16
 (1937) 8
 (1944) 8
 (2003) 38
National Era, The 173
nationalism 43, 57, 58, 59–60, 62, 141, 143, 159–60, 187, 188–9, 190, 191, 193, 195, 199, 237–8
Nazism 9, 44, 45, 47, 50
Neoplatonism 198
Neo-Romanticism 23, 223
New Woman 63, 65
New York 133, 194
Newbolt Report 237–8
Nonconformity 10, 29, 73, 74–5, 79, 88, 89–90, 133, 159, 161, 162, 239
Norris, Leslie 234
Northern Ireland 188
nostalgia 161, 188, 208, 209–10, 215, 216

Observer (newspaper) 87
Ogmore-by-Sea 50, 232
O'Grady, Standish 195
Ormond, John 234
Owen, Daniel 17
Owen, Wilfred 234
Oxford 137, 138

Palestine 39, 42
Paris 194, 225
Parker, Dorothy 225
Parry, Thomas
   Gwaith Dafydd ap Gwilym 158, 163
Pascal, Blaise 188, 213
pastoral 12
pastoralism 9
Penmark Press 22
Pennant, Lisa
   Tai Mas a Thai Bach 18
Penrhyn strike (1900–3) 18
Penyberth 141
Petrarch 169, 170
Plaid Cymru 47
Planet (periodical) 49
Platonism 208, 214
Plumwood, Val 199, 200
Poetry Wales Press 232
Poitier, Richard 218
Pontardulais 215
Pontllyfni 22
Pontypridd 85, 94
post(-)colonial 58, 65, 245, 250
Prague 198
Prichard, Caradog 18–19
   Un Nos Ola Leuad 18–19
Prichard, T. J. Llywelyn
   Cambrian Wreath, The 159
Protestantism 162
Proud Valley (film) 143
Prys-Jones, A. G. 235
Pugh, Sheenagh 234
Pughe, William Owen 159, 160, 161, 166
   Cambrian Register (ed.) 159, 161
   see also Myfyr, Owen and William Owen Pughe (eds), *Barddoniaeth Dafydd ab Gwilym*
Puritans 207, 208, 211, 214

Quakers 49–50

Raban, Jonathan 226
race 173, 175, 176, 239
Raglan, Lord 136–7, 138–9, 140
   Hero: A Study in Tradition, Myth and Drama, The 138–9

'I Take My Stand' 137
Raine, Allen 15
   Welsh Witch, A 15
Ransom, John Crow 137
Ravensbrück 46
Rees, William (Gwilym Hiraethog) 175, 177, 178, 179
Rhiwbina 43
Rhondda 95
Rhosgadfan 22
Rhydlewis 15
Rhydychenwr 159
Riverdance 195
Roberts, Kate 21–3, 24–5, 26, 29–36
   'Condemned, The' 31–2, 33
   Ffair Gaeaf 22
   'Folded Hands' 29–30, 31, 33
   Gobaith 24
   Hyn o Fyd 24
   'Last Payment, The' 33
   'Loss, The' 29, 31, 33–4
   O Gors y Bryniau 22
   'Old Age' 30, 34
   Prynu Dol 24
   'Quilt, The' 32, 33
   Rhigolau Bywyd 22
   'Sisters' 32
   Summer Day, A 21, 22, 24–5, 29–34, 35–6
   'Summer Day, A' 33
   'Two Storms' 30
   'Wind, The' 31
Roberts, Rhian 87
   'Pattern, The' 87
Robertson, Roland 191
Robeson, Paul 142–3
Robinson, Tim 192–3
   Stones of Aran: Labyrinth 192–3
Roman Catholic Church 161–2, 198, 199, 239
Romantics 9, 10, 125, 164, 167, 195
Rome 194, 198
Ross-on-Wye 23, 28
Rowe, Dilys 87
   'View across the Valley, A' 87
Rowland, Robert David (Anthropos) 11–14, 16, 17–18, 19
   Pentre Gwyn, Y 11–13, 14, 17, 18, 19

Index

Pentre'r Plant. Atgofion Bore Bywyd 13–14
Rubens, Bernice 38, 42, 43, 44, 45, 46, 50, 51, 225
  Brothers 39–42, 44, 45–6
Ruskin, John 9
Russia 125–6, 127, 130, 143

St Anthony's College (Louvain) 198
St David's 168
St Lucia 238, 239
Salamanca 198
Saõ Paolo 194
Sarnicol (Thomas Jacob Thomas) 16
  'Aelwyd y Cymro' 16
Sassen, Saskia 194
Scarpetta, Guy
  Éloge du cosmopolitanisme 191
Scotland 187, 191, 196, 198
Scruton, Roger 18
Second World War 9, 12, 18, 25, 94, 226
Sedulius Scotus 198
Senghennydd 41, 45
Seven Sisters 91
Shakespeare, William 165, 233, 238
  Othello 237, 238, 250
Shoreditch 118
shtetl 39, 50
Simon, Sherry 194
Simpson, Mercer 235
slavery 173, 174, 175, 176, 178, 180, 182
Smith, Dai 142
Smith, Julia 211
socialism 43, 75, 85, 90
South Wales Miners' Federation 75
Spanish Civil War 225
Spender, Stephen 247
Staniforth, J. M. 58–9
Stephens, Russell 140
Stowe, Calvin 182
Stowe, Harriet Beecher 136, 173–83
  Uncle Tom's Cabin; Or, Life Among the Lowly 136, 173–83
  translations:
    'Bwthyn F'Ewythr Tom; Neu Fywyd yn Mhlith yr Iselradd' 179

Caban F'Ewythr Twm (trans. Robert Everett) 179–80, 183
'Caban 'N Ewythr Twm; Neu, Fywyd Negroaidd yn Nhalaethau Caethwasawl America' (trans. 'Y Lefiad' (Thomas Levi)) 179
Susser, Bernard
  'Jewish Ideology of Affliction, The' 38, 39, 40, 41–2, 44, 45, 46
Swansea 101, 116, 133, 239, 240, 249
Swansea Jewish Debating Society 48
Swansea Review (periodical) 116
Synge, John Millington 193, 195

Tate, Allen 137
Taylor, Jeremy 234
Tennyson, Alfred 233
Theroux, Paul 192
Thomas, Alfred
  In the Land of the Harp and Feathers 15
Thomas, Dylan 101–15, 223–5, 226, 227, 230, 233, 234, 235–6, 237, 238, 239–41, 243, 244–50
  18 Poems 247
  'After the Funeral' 223
  Child's Christmas in Wales, A 102
  Collected Poems 244, 246, 247
  Deaths and Entrances 240
  'Ears in the Turrets Hear' 244
  'Fern Hill' 224, 230, 245, 249
  'Poem on His Birthday' 245
  Portrait of the Artist as a Young Dog 224, 248
  'Reminiscences of Childhood' 239
  Under Milk Wood 101, 102, 103–15, 248
  'When I Woke' 240
Thomas, Ed 93
Thomas, Edward 206, 213, 215–18, 219–20, 226, 234
  'Home' 216–17
  'Lights Out' 220
  'Other, The' 218
  'Path, The' 220
  South Country, The 215
Thomas, Gwyn 84
Thomas, H. Elwyn

Where Eden's Tongue is Spoken Still 15
Thomas, M. Wynn 17, 44, 71, 76, 100–1, 116, 118, 121, 132–3, 135, 136, 186–7, 193, 197, 199, 200, 208, 214
'All Change: The New Welsh Drama before the Great War' 71
Corresponding Cultures 1
Thomas, Ned 49, 239
Poet of the Islands 248
Thomas, R. S. 101, 234, 248, 249
Thomas, William
'Cân Mewn Cystudd' 106
Tibet 189
Tobias, Lily 39, 42–3, 50, 51
My Mother's House 42
'Nationalists, The' 42
Tokyo 194
Töpffer, Rodolphe 189
trade unions 74, 85
Traherne, Thomas 206, 208, 209, 210–14, 215–16, 217, 218
Centuries of Meditations 211–13
'Felicity' 213
Select Meditations 211, 214
translation 158–70, 174–83, 197–9
Tredegar riots (1911) 41
Treharris 88
Trelewis 88
Tresaith 15
Trezise, Rachel 95
In and Out of the Goldfish Bowl 95–6
Tripp, John 226
Tryfan, Dic (Richard Hughes Williams) 30
Trysorfa'r Plant (periodical) 11
tylwyth teg (fairies) 60
Tŷ'n-y-cefn (Merioneth) 12–13

unemployment 76, 77, 78, 79, 80, 95–6
United Nations 191
United States of America 1, 100, 117, 122, 142, 173, 175, 176, 179, 180, 183, 191, 198, 239
University College, London 159
University of Glamorgan 232
University of Wales 232
University of Wales College of Medicine 232
Uxbridge 23

Valleys, the 40, 44, 84–96
Vansittart, Peter 225
Vaughan, Henry 206–9, 212, 213, 214, 216, 217, 220
'Retreat, The' 206–8, 209, 218
Silex Scintillans 208
'World, The' 220
Vienna 194
villages 8–9, 11–19, 22, 24, 33, 89
Vitepsk 127
Vogel, Julius
Anno Domini 2000; or, Woman's Destiny 66

Wade, Gladys I. 210, 212
Walcott, Derek 237, 238–43, 244, 245–50
Another Life 239, 241–3, 246, 247–8
'As John to Patmos' 240
Castaway, The 244, 245
'City's Death By Fire, A' 239–40
Gulf, The 244
'Homecoming: Anse La Raye' 250
In a Green Night 247
'Muse of History, The' 241
Omeros 247
'Ruins of a Great House' 243
'Schooner *Flight,* The' 248
Twenty-five Poems 247
'Wales' 248–50
Wales 9–11, 12, 14, 16, 23, 24, 40, 59, 81, 101, 186, 189, 190, 191, 196, 198, 199, 200, 211, 215, 218, 231, 232–3, 235–6, 237, 239, 246, 249
Wales (periodical) 14–15, 137
Walters, Evan 47
Ward, Margaret 64
Warner, Marina 64
Warren, C. H.
England is a Village 9
Washington 100
Waterloo 127, 128
Webb, Harri 235

Welsh Academy 232
Welsh language 2, 10, 16, 17, 21, 22–3, 24, 42–3, 47, 48, 49, 50, 64, 65, 73, 84, 122, 132, 135, 137, 138, 140, 159, 160, 161, 175, 176, 177, 178, 179–83, 196, 210, 234, 239
Welsh literature 9, 10, 11, 17, 23, 100
Welsh Mam 88–90, 94–6
Welsh National Pageant (1909) 59–60, 68
'Welsh Nationalist, A' 60–1
Welsh Review (periodical) 22
Welsh writing in English 71, 76, 78, 231, 232, 233, 234, 235, 248
Welshness 9, 24–5, 47, 50, 51, 117, 211, 213, 214, 226, 233, 234, 235
West Indies 239, 242, 248
Western Mail (newspaper) 58
Whitman, Walt 100, 215
  Leaves of Grass 2
Williams, Emlyn 133, 135, 136–8, 140–1, 143, 144
  'A Dyma Fi, Druan o Gymro, Yn Sefyll' 137–8
  Corn is Green, The 132–3, 134–7, 138, 140, 141
Williams, Gwyn A. 73
Williams, Hugh 174, 179–80
Williams, Ifor 16, 23
Williams, Mallt ('Un o'r ddau Wynne')
  'Patriotism and the Women of Cymru' 65

Williams, Michael 26, 27
Williams, Morris T. 25
Williams, Raymond 3
  Culture 188
Williams, Rhydwen 84
Wood, Nancy 44–5
Woolf, Virginia 28
Wordsworth, William 110, 233
  'Lines Composed a Few Miles above Tintern Abbey' 164
  Prelude, The 248
Workers' Educational Asssociation 75
World Bank 191
World Health Organization 191
Wuthering Heights (Emily Brontë) 24

Yeats, W. B. 195, 239, 241
Yiddish 48
Young Wales (periodical) 65
Ystalyfera 43
Ystradgynlais 47, 48, 88

Zimmern, Alfred 133
Zionism 42, 43
Zolo, Danilo
  Cosmopolis: Prospects for World Government 193
Zulman, Schneour 123
Zwingli, Huldrych 187

List of Subscribers

The following have associated themselves with the publication of this volume through subscription.

Dannie and Joan Abse, London
Linda Adams, Y Bontfaen
Sam and Muriel Adams, Caerleon
Rosamund Allen, University of London
Sandra Anstey and Robert Harding, Llantrisant
Mari Arthur, Caerdydd
John Barnie, Comins Coch
Ruth Bidgood, Beulah
Pauline and Roy Birch, Lampeter
Martyn Branford, Bridgend College
Rachel Bromwich, Llangorwen
T. Robin Chapman, Aberystwyth
Alun Creunant Davies, Aberystwyth
Cennard Davies, Treorci
Ceri a Michelle Davies, Abertawe
Damian Walford Davies and Francesca Rhydderch, Aberystwyth
Derek and Jayne Davies, Newtown
James A. Davies, Swansea
Jason Walford Davies, Prifysgol Cymru, Bangor
Stevie Davies, University of Wales Swansea
Walford a Hazel Davies, Aberystwyth
Moira Dearnley, Llandogo
Marion Eames, Dolgellau
Siân Edwards, Caerdydd
Tom Ellis, Rhiwabon
Geraint Evans and Helen Fulton, University of Sydney
Meredydd Evans, Cwmystwyth
Peter Freeman, Swansea
Beti George, Caerdydd
David Gidwell, Cardiff

Ifor ap Glyn, Caernarfon
Katie Gramich, Bristol
Sarah Eluned Griffiths, Llangynidr
Geraint a Luned Gruffydd, Aberystwyth
J. T. Grugeon, Cheltenham
Teulu Haines, Penyrheol
Rosalind Harries, Rickmansworth
John Harris, Aberystwyth
Ann Heilmann and Mark Llewellyn, Swansea
Mererid Hopwood, Caerfyrddin
Cyril M. Howells, Billericay
Glyn Tegai Hughes, Tregynon
H. G. A. Hughes, Cerrigydrudion
Iestyn and Marian Hughes, Bow St, Aberystwyth
Elinor ac Emyr Humphreys, Llanfairpwll
Jerry Hunter, Prifysgol Cymru, Bangor
G. E. Jenkins, Porth Tywyn
Nigel Jenkins, University of Wales Swansea
Bill Jones, Cardiff
Bobi Jones, Aberystwyth
Elwyn Jones, Aberystwyth
Glenson T. Jones, Ottawa, Canada
Gwerfyl Pierce Jones, Aberystwyth
Lenna a Harri Pritchard Jones, Caerdydd
Louise Marie Jones, Llandaff
R. Arwel Jones, Aberystwyth
R. Brinley Jones, Porthyrhyd
Sally R. Jones, Port Talbot
Stephen Knight, Cardiff University
Catrin Gwawr Ladd, Ysgol Tregib, Llandeilo
Joy Leman, London
Meirick Lloyd a Nesta Davies, Cefn Meiriadog
Rheinallt Llwyd, Aberystwyth
Katharine T. Loesch, Chicago, Illinois
Stephen Logan, Magdalene College, Cambridge
J. Lionel Madden, Aberystwyth
Susan Manning, University of Edinburgh
Owen Martell, Llandeilo
Roland Mathias, Brecon
Patrick McGuinness ac Angharad Price, Caerdydd

J. G. Miller, Wrecsam
J. Lawrence Mitchell, Texas A & M University
Clare Morgan, University of Oxford
Derec Llwyd Morgan, Tregaian
Prys Morgan, Swansea
Anne L. Morris, Swansea
John Trefor Morris, Cwmbrân
Mary a Philip Nicholas, Caerdydd
Meurig Owen, Lewisham
Richard Owen, Cyngor Llyfrau Cymru
Ieuan Parri, Penrhyndeudraeth
Alexandra J. Perry, London
Claire Powell, Swansea
Shahed Power, Manchester
Anne Price-Owen, The David Jones Society
Sheenagh Pugh, University of Glamorgan
Glyn and Parvin Pursglove, Swansea
N. H. Reeve, University of Wales Swansea
Manon Rhys a T. James Jones, Caerdydd
Gareth Roberts, Prifysgol Cymru, Bangor
John Stuart Roberts, Cardiff
Elizabeth Rokkan, Llandaf
John Rowlands, Y Groeslon
Johan Schimanski, University of Tromsø
Gerald E. Seager, Bridgend
Mercer Simpson, Cardiff
Meic Stephens, Cardiff
Catrin Stevens, Casllwchwr
Brynmor Thomas, Aberystwyth
Ned Thomas and Ceridwen Lloyd-Morgan, Aberystwyth
Donald a Nesta Treharne, Pontarddulais
A. Treloar, University of New England
Andrew and Moya Varney, Port Eynon and Bordeaux
John Powell Ward, University of Wales Swansea
Julia Ward, Alsace, France
Warren E. Watkins, National Welsh-American Foundation, USA
Josephine Way, Swansea
Dafydd Wigley, Caernarfon
Gerwyn Wiliams, Prifysgol Cymru, Bangor
Anne Williams, Seven Sisters

Glanmor Williams, Swansea
Jeni Williams, Trinity College, Carmarthen
Merryn Williams, Oxford
Mike Elfed Williams, Deganwy
Rhys Williams, Cwmann, Llanbedr Pont Steffan
Robert Coleman Williams, Bruree, County Limerick
William Williams-Wynne, Llanegryn
Justin Wintle, London
Nicholas Wroe, London

Community of the Sisters of the Love of God, Oxford
Hugh Owen Library, University of Wales, Aberystwyth
Llyfrgell Genedlaethol Cymru, Aberystwyth
Llyfrgell Prifysgol Cymru, Bangor
National Museums and Galleries of Wales, Library
St Deiniol's Library, Hawarden
Yr Academi Gymreig